A Guide to Employment Statutes

About the author

Erich Suter, BA, LLM, FCIPD, barrister of the Middle Temple was for many years the CIPD's Employment Law Adviser

The Chartered Institute of Personnel and Development is the leading publisher of books and reports for personnel and training professionals, students, and all those concerned with the effective management and development of people at work. For details of all our titles, please contact the Publishing Department:

tel: 020-8612-6204
e-mail: publish@cipd.co.uk
The catalogue of all CIPD titles can be viewed on the CIPD website:
www.cipd.co.uk/bookstore

A Guide to
Employment Statutes

(*Employment Law Checklist*, 8th edition)

Erich Suter

Chartered Institute of Personnel and Development

Published by the Chartered Institute of Personnel and Development,
151 The Broadway, London, SW19 1JQ

This edition published 2005
First published 1981 as *Legislation for Personnel Managers: A checklist*
by the Institute of Personnel Management
Reprinted 1982; 2nd edition 1982; 3rd edition 1985;
4th edition 1990; 5th edition 1992;
6th edition published as *Employment Law Checklist* 1997; 7th edition 2000

The right of Erich Suter to be identified as author of this work
has been asserted by him in accordance with
sections 77 and 78 of the Copyright, Designs and Patents Act 1988.

Typeset by Fakenham Photosetting Ltd, Fakenham, Norfolk
Printed in Great Britain by The Cromwell Press, Trowbridge, Wiltshire

British Library Cataloguing in Publication Data
A catalogue record for this book is available from the British Library

ISBN 1–84398–137–8

Throughout this book the pronoun 'he' should be taken to
include 'she' where appropriate.

The views expressed in this publication are the author's own and may
not necessarily reflect those of the CIPD.

The CIPD has made every effort to trace and acknowledge copyright-holders. If any source
has been overlooked, CIPD Enterprises would be pleased to redress this for future editions.

Chartered Institute of Personnel and Development,
151 The Broadway, London, SW19 1JQ
Tel: 020-8612-6200
E-mail: cipd@cipd.co.uk   Website: www.cipd.co.uk
Incorporated by Royal Charter.   Registered Charity No. 1079797

CONTENTS

INTRODUCTION

This edition of *A Guide to Employment Statutes* (formerly *The Employment Law Checklist*) revises and updates previous editions, the last of which was published in 2000. There have, again, been significant changes in the law, with an even greater emphasis on law made by statutory regulations rather than by statutes. Of the 90 or so new items that have been taken into account in this edition only a handful are Acts of Parliament and many of these are only of marginal significance in employment terms. It should be borne in mind that this book is, and is intended to be, no more than a 'thumbnail' guide to employment legislation. Much of the statutory material covering employment matters – eg health and safety at work – is contained in statutory instruments and other delegated legislation, supported by codes of practice. Even with the continuing increase in coverage of statutory instruments in this edition, much of the material that is dealt with in Regulations is of more restricted application or is relevant to only a small part of industry and has therefore not been included. Apart from delegated legislation, a considerable part of the law surrounding employment has not been codified into Acts of Parliament and many fundamental parts of the law (eg contract, negligence, etc) remain the province of the common law (or 'judge-made law'). For the above reasons, readers should rely on this guide merely as a starting-point to ensure that they are aware of the more basic requirements of the law relating to employment, and to update their knowledge of those requirements. Those with specific legal problems are recommended to take professional legal advice.*

The 'new' format for the List of Legislation (first adopted for the 4th edition in 1990) has been maintained with slight modifications. An Appendix of law due to take effect in October 2005 has been added. The overall layout is as follows:

- Part 1: Chronological list of legislation – lists in date order all the legislation detailed in Part 2.

- Part 2: Alphabetical list of legislation – gives a brief outline of the contents, scope and effect of each Act, Order, or set of Regulations or Rules.

- Appendix – details new legislation due to take effect in October 2005.

- The index – designed to help readers follow particular topics through the various bits of legislation relating to them.

* The author's practice at Park Chambers, Park Drive, Weybridge, Surrey can be contacted for professional advice and assistance with employment tribunal cases, appeals to the EAT, drawing up contracts of employment and handbooks etc, on 01932–820082 (email: ES@TheEmploymentLawyer.co.uk).

As always, the CIPD library will be keeping up to date with new publications and the library staff will be pleased to help members with any queries.

Acknowledgements

The extracts from the *IPM Digest/PM Plus* are reproduced by kind permission of the Chartered Institute of Personnel and Development.

Dedication

This book is dedicated to the memory of Deirdre Gill, who was IPM Assistant Director, Information and Advisory Services, a friend and mentor.

1 CHRONOLOGICAL LIST OF LEGISLATION

1870	Apportionment Act
1919	Sex Disqualification (Removal) Act
1920	Employment of Women, Young Persons and Children Act
1933 to 1969	Children and Young Persons Acts
1936	Public Health Act
1938	Young Persons (Employment) Act (repealed)
1950 to 1965	Shop Acts
1961	Factories Act
1963	Offices, Shops and Railway Premises Act
1969	Employers' Liability (Compulsory Insurance) Act
	Employers' Liability (Defective Equipment) Act
	Family Law Reform Act
1970	Equal Pay Act
1971	Attachment of Earnings Act
	Banking and Financial Dealings Act
	Fire Precautions Act
	Immigration Act
1972	Children Act
	Employment Medical Advisory Services Act
	European Communities Act – the Treaty of Rome
1973	Employment Agencies Act
1974	Health and Safety at Work etc Act
	Rehabilitation of Offenders Act
1975	Sex Discrimination Act
1976	Race Relations Act
1977	Job Release Act
	Patents Act
	Safety Representatives and Safety Committees Regulations 1977 (SI 1977 No 500)
	Unfair Contract Terms Act
1978	Employment (Continental Shelf) Act

Social Security (Incapacity for Work) Act

Statutory Sick Pay Act

1995   Collective Redundancies and Transfer of Undertakings (Protection of Employment)
        (Amendment) Regulations (SI 1995 No 2587)

Disability Discrimination Act

Jobseekers Act

Pensions Act

1996   Armed Forces Act 1996

Asylum and Immigration Act

Education Act 1996

Employment Protection (Continuity of Employment) Regulations 1996 (SI 1996 No
    3147)

Employment Rights Act

Employment Tribunals Act

Health and Safety (Consultation with Employees) Regulations 1996 (SI 1996 No 1513)

Reserve Forces Act

1997   Education Act 1997

Fire Precautions (Workplace) Regulations 1997

Health and Safety (Young Persons) Regulations 1997 (SI 1997 No 135)

Police Act

Police (Health and Safety) Act 1997

Protection from Harassment Act 1997

1998   Children (Protection at Work) Regulations 1998 (SI 1998 No 276)

Data Protection Act 1998

Deregulation (Deduction from Pay of Union Subscriptions) Order 1998 (SI 1998 No 1529)

Disability Discrimination (Exemption for Small Employers) Order 1998 (SI 1998 No
    2618)

Employment Rights (Dispute Resolution) Act 1998

Human Rights Act 1998

Lifting Operation and Lifting Equipment Regulations 1998 (SI 1998 No 2307)

Provision of Work Equipment Regulations 1998 (SI 1998 No 2306)

Public Interest Disclosure Act 1998

Social Security (Welfare to Work) Regulations 1998 (SI 1998 No 2231)

Teaching and Higher Education Act 1998

Working Time Regulations 1998 (SI 1998 No 1833)

1999   Collective Redundancies and Transfer of Undertakings (Protection of Employment)
        (Amendment Regulations) 1999 (SI 1999 No 1925)

Contracts (Rights of Third Parties) Act 1999

Disability Rights Commission Act 1999

Employment Relations Act 1999

Equal Opportunities (Employment Legislation) (Territorial Limits) Regulations 1999
    (SI 1999 No 3163)

Immigration and Asylum Act 1999

Management of Health and Safety at Work Regulations 1999 (SI 1999 No 3242)

Maternity and Parental Leave etc Regulations 1999 (SI 1999 No 3312)

National Minimum Wage Act 1998 and National Minimum Wage Regulations 1999 (SI 1999 No 584)

Redundancy Payments (Continuity of Employment in Local Government, etc) (Modification) Order 1999

Sex Discrimination (Gender Reassignment) Regulations 1999 (SI 1999 No 1102)

Tax Credits Act 1999

Unfair Dismissal and Statement of Reasons for Dismissal (Variation of Qualifying Period) Order 1999 (SI 1999 No 1436)

Welfare Reform and Pensions Act 1999

2000   Children (Protection at Work) Regulations 2000 (SI 2000 No 1333)

Children (Protection at Work) (No 2) Regulations 2000 (SI 2000 No 2548)

Education (Restriction of Employment) Regulations 2000 (SI 2000 No 2419)

Education (Restriction of Employment) (Wales) Regulations 2000 (SI 2000 No 2906)

Part-Time Workers (Prevention of Less Favourable Treatment) Regulations 2000 (SI 2000 No 1551)

Race Relations Amendment Act 2000

Regulation of Investigatory Powers Act 2000

Statutory Maternity Pay (General) (Modification and Amendment) Regulations 2000 (SI 2000 No 2883)

Telecommunications (Lawful Business Practice) (Interception of Communications) Regulations 2000 (SI 2000 No 2699)

2001   Employment Protection (Continuity of Employment) (Amendment) Regulations 2001 (SI 2001 No 1188)

Maternity and Parental Leave (Amendment) Regulations 2001 (SI 2001 No 4010)

Part-time Workers (Prevention of Less Favourable Treatment) Regulations 2001 (SI 2001 No 1107)

Sex Discrimination (Indirect Discrimination and Burden of Proof) Regulations 2001 (SI 2001 No 2660)

Working Time (Amendment) Regulations 2001 (SI 2001 No 3256)

2002   Control of Asbestos at Work Regulations 2002 (SI 2002 No 2675)

Control of Lead at Work Regulations 2002 (SI 2002 No 2676)

Control of Substances Hazardous to Health Regulations 2002 (S1 2002 No 2675)

Employment Act 2002

Fixed-term Employees (Prevention of Less Favourable Treatment) Regulations 2002 (SI 2002 No 2034)

Flexible Working (Eligibility, Complaints and Remedies) Regulations 2002 (SI 2002 No 3236)

Flexible Working (Procedural Requirements) Regulations 2002 (SI 2002 No 3207)

Maternity and Parental Leave (Amendment) Regulations 2002 (SI 2002 No 2789)

Part-time Workers (Prevention of Less Favourable Treatment) Regulations 2000 (Amendment) Regulations 2002 (SI 2002 No 2035)

Paternity and Adoption Leave Regulations 2002 (SI 2002 No 2788)

Statutory Maternity Pay and Statutory Sick Pay (Miscellaneous Amendments) Regulations 2002 (SI 2002 No 2690)

Statutory Paternity Pay and Statutory Adoption Pay (General) Regulations 2002 (SI 2002 No 2822)

Tax Credits Act 2002

Working Time (Amendment) Regulations 2002 (SI 2002 No 3128)

2003   Conduct of Employment Agencies and Employment Businesses Regulations 2003 (SI 2003 No 3319)

Disability Discrimination Act 1995 (Amendment) Regulations 2003 (SI 2003 No 1673)

Disability Discrimination Act 1995 (Pensions) Regulations 2003 (SI 2003 No 2770)

Disability Discrimination (Blind and Partially Sighted Persons) Regulations 2003 (SI 2003 No 712)

Employment Equality (Religion or Belief) Regulations 2003 (SI 2003 No 1660)

Employment Equality (Sexual Orientation) Regulations 2003 (SI 2003 No 1661)

Equal Pay Act 1970 (Amendment) Regulations 2003 (SI 2003 No 1656)

Equal Pay (Questions and Replies) Order 2003 (SI 2003 No 722)

Income Tax (Earnings and Pensions) Act 2003

Management of Health and Safety at Work and Fire Precautions (Workplace) (Amendment) Regulations 2003 (SI 2003 No 2457)

Paternity and Adoption Leave (Adoption from Overseas) Regulations 2003 (SI 2003 No 921)

Race Relations Act 1976 (Amendment) Regulations 2003 (SI 2003 No 1626)

Road Vehicles (Construction and Use) (Amendment) (No 4) Regulations 2003 (SI 2003 No 2695)

Sex Discrimination Act 1975 (Amendment) Regulations 2003 (SI 2003 No 1657)

Sunday Working (Scotland) Act 2003

Working Time (Amendment) Regulations 2003 (SI 2003 No 1684)

2004   ACAS Arbitration Scheme (Great Britain) Order 2004 (SI 2004 No 753)

ACAS (Flexible Working) Arbitration Scheme (Great Britain) Order 2004 (SI 2004 No 2333)

Employment Act 2002 (Disputes Resolution) Regulations 2004 (SI 2004 No 752)

Employment Appeal Tribunal (Amendment) Rules 2004 (SI 2004 No 2526)

Employment Relations Act 2004

Employment Tribunals (Constitution and Rules of Procedure) Regulations 2004 (SI 2004 No 1861)

Employment Tribunals (Constitution and Rules of Procedure) (Amendment) Regulations 2004 (SI 2004 No 2351)

Equal Pay Act 1970 (Amendment) Regulations 2003 (SI 2004 No 2352)

Gender Recognition Act 2004

Information and Consultation of Employees Regulations 2004 (SI 2004 No 3426)

National Minimum Wage Regulations 1999 (Amendment) Regulations 2004 (SI 2004 No 1161)

National Minimum Wage Regulations 1999 (Amendment) (No 2) Regulations 2004 (SI 2004 No 1930)

Patents Act 2004

Paternity and Adoption Leave (Amendment) Regulations 2004 (SI 2004 No 923)

Pensions Act 2004

Statute Law (Repeal) Act 2004

Statutory Paternity Pay and Statutory Adoption Pay (Amendment) Regulations 2004 (SI 2004 No 488)

2005   Disability Discrimination Act 2005

Employment Tribunals (Constitution and Rules of Procedure) Amendment Regulations 2005 (SI 2005 No 435)

Statutory Maternity Pay (General)(Amendment) Regulations 2005

Transfer of Employment (Pension Protection) Regulations 2005 (SI 2005 No 649)

LIST OF ABBREVIATIONS

DDA	Disability Discrimination Act 1995
EPCA	Employment Protection (Consolidation) Act 1989
ERA	Employment Rights Act 1996
ERelA	Employment Relations Act (1999 or 2004)
HASWA	Health and Safety at Work etc Act 1974
RRA	Race Relations Act 1976
SDA	Sex Discrimination Act 1975
TULRA	Trade Union and Labour Relations (Consolidation) Act 1992
TUPE	Transfer of Undertakings (Protection of Employment) Regulations 1981
TURERA	Trade Union Reform and Employment Rights Act 1993
ACAS	Advisory, Conciliation and Arbitration Service
CAC	Central Arbitration Committee
CRE	Commission for Racial Equality
EAT	Employment Appeals Tribunal
ECJ	European Court of Justice
EOC	Equal Opportunities Commission
HSE	Health and Safety Executive
NI	National Insurance
SI	Statutory Instrument
AML	additional maternity leave
DSE	display screen equipment
EWC	expected week of childbirth/confinement
GOQ	genuine occupational qualification
IC	information and consultation (of workers)
OML	ordinary maternity leave
PPE	personal protective equipment
s	section
Sch	Schedule
SMP	statutory maternity pay
SSP	statutory sick pay

2 ALPHABETICAL LIST OF LEGISLATION

1 ACAS Arbitration Scheme (Great Britain) Order (SI 2004 No 753)

Amends and replaces the ACAS Arbitration Scheme (England and Wales) Order 2001 SI 2001 No 1185.

The 2001 ACAS Scheme took effect in England and Wales. From 6 April 2004 it was extended, with revisions, to Scotland. It applies only to unfair dismissal claims which are not complicated by legalities. (There is another ACAS scheme which applies to flexible working disputes.) The level of take-up under the 2001 scheme was low and is expected to remain low under the 2004 scheme.

1.1 The arbitration agreement

- The scheme the employer and employee must enter into a binding, written arbitration agreement.
- Once the arbitration agreement is entered into, the employer cannot unilaterally withdraw from arbitration.
- If the employee withdraws, his claim is dismissed.
- The case can be settled before it reaches the arbitration hearing.

1.2 General duty

- The parties are under a duty to do everything necessary for the proper and expeditious conduct of the arbitral proceedings.
- This includes complying without delay with any decision of the arbitrator in relation to procedural or evidential matters and co-operating in the arrangement of the hearing.

1.3 The arbitration hearing

a) Before the hearing

- A written statement of case must be provided by each party 14 days prior to the hearing.
- The statement of case must be accompanied by any supporting documentation and the party's list of witnesses.
- The statement of case is a brief statement of the matters which led to the dismissal, including details of any relevant meetings, discussions or interviews.

b) The hearing

The hearing is informal.

- The arbitrator has no power to compel witnesses to attend the hearing, although the arbitrator may draw adverse inferences if an employer does not allow current employees time off to attend.

- Witnesses who have not been included on the list of witnesses may only be heard with the arbitrator's permission.

- Evidence is not on oath and there is no cross-examination.

- The parties must be prepared to deal with the practicability of the employee's re-engagement or reinstatement at the hearing if that is what the employee is seeking.

c) The decision

- The arbitrator's decision on fairness is based on general concepts of good employee relations practice.

- Like the employment tribunals the arbitrator must not substitute his own view for that of the employer. He must test what the employer has done against good employee relations practice.

- The arbitrator can award reinstatement, re-engagement or compensation.

- Enforcement of an award is via the employment tribunal system.

1.4 Challenging the arbitrator's award

There is no appeal from an arbitrator's award – other than on very limited grounds. These include challenges:

- under the arbitration agreement itself – on the basis that what the arbitrator did was outside what had been agreed between the parties;

- for serious irregularities – eg where the proceedings have been improperly conducted or where there has been another irregularity affecting the arbitrator or the proceedings;

- on questions of EC law or under the Human Rights Act 1998.

2 Access to Medical Reports Act 1988

Amended by the Data Protection Act 1998.

This Act came into force on 1 January 1989. It relates to medical reports obtained for employment purposes.

2.1 Definitions

The Act defines a medical report as a report

- relating to the physical or mental health of the individual;

- which is prepared by a medical practitioner who is or who has been responsible for the clinical care of the individual. 'Care' is defined by the Act as including examination, investigation or diagnosis for the purposes of or in connection with any form of medical treatment.

Where a one-off medical report is sought from doctor who has not been involved in the employee's clinical care the Act will not apply.

2.2 Notification to employee

Section 3 of the Act provides that no employer/prospective employer may ask a medical practitioner for a medical report, covered by the Act, unless the employee to whom it relates gives his consent.

The notification given by an employer must inform the employee of the various rights provided for by the Act, ie:

a) *the employee's right to withhold his consent*

b) *the employee's right to be given access to the medical practitioner's report before it is supplied to the employer*

> If the employee consents to the report being sought and asks that he be given access to it, under this provision, then the medical practitioner must be informed by the employer of the employee's wish to have access to the report before it is given to the employer.
>
> Under the terms of the Act, however, it appears to be for the employee to make his own arrangements with the medical practitioner to obtain access to the report.
>
> The employee asking for and obtaining inspection of the report is significant, since a number of the rights in relation to the report only arise if he has had access to it.
>
> If the employee asks for access to the report, the medical practitioner may not give the report to the employer unless: the employee has either been given access to it (and certain other requirements have been met – see below); or 21 days have passed and he has not made arrangements to obtain access to the report.

c) *the employee's right to notify the medical practitioner directly that he wishes to have access to the report*

> If the employee consents to the report being applied for, but does not say at that time that he wants to have access to it before it is passed to his employer, he can ask the medical practitioner directly to give him access to the report. In such cases, again, the medical practitioner may not give the report to the employer unless the employee has either been given access to it (and certain other requirements have been met – see below) or 21 days have passed and the employee has not made arrangements to obtain access to the report.

d) *the employee's right to be given access to earlier reports*

> If the employee has consented to any report being given, he may ask the medical practitioner to give him access to any reports he has supplied in the previous six months.

e) *the employee's right to refuse his consent to the report's being given to his employer*

> If the employee has had access to the report, the report can be passed on to his employer only with his consent.
>
> Once the employee has consented to the report's being sought, the individual generally only has further rights under the Act if he has had access to the report. There are two exceptions to this limitation:

- where the employee retains the right to access a report made within the previous six months; or

- where the report is one to which he has not been allowed access, despite asking for it, because the medical practitioner has refused access on specified grounds (see below). If the whole of the report is covered by these grounds, so that the employee is not entitled to access to any of it, the report may still be passed on to his employer only with his express consent.

f) *the employee's right to request the medical practitioner to amend the report*

The employee may ask the medical practitioner to amend any part/s of a report he considers to be incorrect or misleading. The medical practitioner may amend the report to the extent that he is prepared so to do. If he is not prepared to amend, or to amend as much as the individual wants, the individual may ask that a statement of his views be attached to the report. Any such request must also be made in writing.

2.3 Grounds on which a medical practitioner may refuse an individual access to a medical report

A medical practitioner may refuse an individual access to all or parts of a medical report where he considers that disclosure of the report, or of those parts:

- would be likely to 'cause serious harm to the physical or mental health of the individual or others'; or

- would indicate the intentions of the medical practitioner in relation to that individual; or

- would be likely to reveal information about another person without that person's consent; or

- would be likely to reveal the identity of another person (ie a non-health professional) who has given information to the practitioner about the individual – again, unless that person consents to the disclosure.

In any such case the medical practitioner must inform the individual that he considers that the above criteria apply either to all or to parts of the report. The individual is then entitled to have access only to the parts of the report, if any, that are not covered by the above grounds. But the report may still only be passed to the individual's employer with his express consent.

2.4 Enforcement of the Act

Enforcement of the Act is through the county court (sheriff's court in Scotland). If it appears to the court that any person has failed or is likely to fail to comply with any part of the Act, the court may order their compliance. Failure to comply with such an order would amount to contempt of court and be punishable as such.

3 Agricultural Training Board Act 1982

Amended by Employment Act 1989.

Consolidates the law relating to the Agricultural Training Board.

4 Apportionment Act 1870

The effect of ss 2 and 5 is that 'salaries … shall be considered as accruing from day to day, and shall be apportioned in respect of time accordingly'.

5 Armed Forces Act 1996

Amends Equal Pay Act 1970, Rehabilitation of Offenders Act 1974, SDA and Race Discrimination Act 1976.

Makes various provisions extending the protection of the equal pay and the sex and race discrimination legislation to complaints arising from service in the armed forces, subject to a requirement that the complaint must be taken up under the internal machinery before a complaint is made to an employment tribunal. The provisions of the Rehabilitation of Offenders Act 1974 are also extended to encompass certain sentences imposed by Courts Martial.

6 Asylum and Immigration Act 1996

Amends the Immigration Act 1971. Amended by Immigration and Asylum Act 1999 and by the Code of Practice for employers on the avoidance of race discrimination in recruitment practice while seeking to prevent illegal working. The Code was made by the Secretary of State under the 1995 Act (**see 6.4 Race discrimination, below**).

For employment purposes, the most important effect of the Asylum and Immigration Act is that it makes it an offence for an employer to employ someone who is not entitled to be in and to work in the UK.

6.1 The offence

a) An employer commits an offence if:

  (i) he employs a person of 16 or over (the 'employee'); and

  (ii) the employee is subject to immigration control; and

  ■ the employee does not have current valid leave to be in the UK; or

  ■ the employee's leave is subject to a condition which stops him from taking up that employment. (NB: The reference to 'that employment' is important since an employee who has a work permit, for example, will be entitled to work in the employment to which the permit relates, but not in any other job.)

b) In certain cases, even where the employee, *prima facie*, is not entitled to be in, or to work in, the UK, an employer may nonetheless employ him. The three situations in which this is permissible were introduced by the Immigration (Restrictions on Employment) Order 1996 (SI 1996 No. 3225)

  (i) where an employee, having made a claim for asylum which is still under consideration, has been given written permission to work by the Home Office

  (ii) where the employee has an appeal pending under Part II of the Immigration Act 1971 – provided that before the appeal was made the employee was entitled to work in the UK

  (iii) if the employee is entitled to work under the Immigration Rules.

6.2 The defence

An employer will have a defence to a potential prosecution for employing someone who is not entitled to be or to work in the UK if before that person's employment began:

a) the employer was shown a document that appeared to relate to the employee in question (ie it appeared to be both a genuine document and to relate to the employee)

b) the document was of a description specified by the Secretary of State as being appropriate for these purposes (**see 6.3 below**)

c) the employer either kept the document itself or a copy of it (a copy can be either a paper copy or a copy kept on a 'Write Once Read Many' times [WORM] CD: these CDs can only be written on once, so a true, unalterable copy is kept); and

d) the employer did not know that employing the employee would be unlawful under these provisions.

6.3 Acceptable documents

The Home Office has issued a guide to employers dealing with the requirements under these provisions. A full list of the types of document that are acceptable for purposes of the defence in 6.2 above is contained in the guide which has been sent to all employers. The main documents are:

a) a 'documented National Insurance number' (an official document on which the person's National Insurance number is stated), as usually provided by a new employee for employers. This could be:

- a document issued by a previous employer, such as a P45, a pay slip or a P60

- a document issued by the Inland Revenue, the Benefits Agency, the Contributions Agency or the Employment Service (or their Northern Ireland equivalents) such as a NINO card (the newer plastic cards or the older-style cards) or a letter issued by one of the government bodies mentioned above.

It should be noted that a document showing a National Insurance number with a 'TN' prefix is a temporary National Insurance number and is not acceptable.

b) a passport which shows that the person is a British or EU citizen or which has a stamp on it showing that the person has a right to be or to remain in the UK

c) naturalisation papers

d) a work permit or a letter from the immigration authorities saying that the person has a right to work in the UK.

6.4 Race discrimination

It is obviously important that all job applicants are treated the same so that there are no accusations or feelings that people are being discriminated against on grounds of their race. One way of dealing with this is to ask for the same documents from all those who are going to be offered a job. Employers may have their own list of documents which employees are required to produce. These might include, for example, a P45, P60, other documented NI number, passport, etc. 'The Code of Practice for employers on the avoidance of race discrimination in recruitment practice while seeking to prevent illegal working' now makes it clear that all applicants, regardless of race, should be told that the successful applicant will be required to provide one of the relevant forms of proof. Although a breach of this Code does not give an applicant a right to claim race discrimination, a failure to follow its provisions may be taken into account by an employment tribunal in deciding whether or not a prospective employer has discriminated against an applicant.

6.5 Further information

There is a telephone helpline available to anyone with a query on these requirements: 020-8649 7878. The Employer's Guide is also available on the Internet at http://www.open.gov.uk/home_off/ind.htm

7 Attachment of Earnings Act 1971

Empowers a court to order that a judgment debt be paid directly by the employer, from the employee's earnings, to the court.

8 Banking and Financial Dealings Act 1971

Amended by Employment Act 1989.

   Repeals previous legislation relating to bank holidays and substitutes a schedule of bank holidays.

9 Children (Protection at Work) Regulations 1998 (SI 1998 No 276)

Amend the Children and Young Persons Act 1933 and 1963. These Regulations were brought in to give effect to the 1994 EC Directive on the Protection of Young People at Work (94/33/EC).

- The lowest age at which a child can be employed is raised from 13 to 14.

- The prohibition against employing children on work that might harm them is replaced with a prohibition against their undertaking anything other than 'light work'. Light work is work that does not jeopardise a child's safety, health, development, attendance at school or participation in work experience.

- Hours of work and required rest breaks for children at work are also brought into line with those required by the Directive, and a requirement is introduced that a child must have at least one two-week period in his school holidays when he does no work.

- The requirement to obtain a local authority licence before children can take part in public performances for profit or go abroad to perform for profit is extended to children taking part in sports or modelling for money whether in this country or abroad.

9a Children (Protection at Work) Regulations 2000 (SI 2000 No 1333)

Amend the Children and Young Persons Act 1933 and give further effect to the 1994 EC Directive on the Protection of Young People at Work (94/33/EC).

These Regulations provide that a Local Authority cannot authorise a child under 13 to be engaged in light agricultural work or horticulture. They also provide that a Local Authority can make Regulations restricting the days, hours and places at which any person under school leaving age can be engaged in street trading.

9b Children (Protection at Work) (No 2) Regulations 2000 (SI 2000 No 2548)

Amend the Children and Young Persons Act 1933 and give further effect to the 1994 EC Directive on the Protection of Young People at Work (94/33/EC).

These Regulations provide that a child cannot be employed for more than 12 hours during any school week.

10 Collective Redundancies and Transfer of Undertakings (Protection of Employment) (Amendment) Regulations (SI 1995 No 2587)

Amend the EPCA (now consolidated into ERA), TULRA and TUPE.

These regulations provide for representation by employee representatives as an alternative to trade union representation in relation to:

- consultation about proposed redundancies (**see also 153.10**); and

- consultation about transfers of undertakings (**see also 156.1**).

10a Collective Redundancies and Transfer of Undertakings (Protection of Employment) (Amendment Regulations) 1999 (SI 1999 No 1925) and Transfer of Undertakings (Protection of Employment) (Amendment) Regulations 1999 (SI 1999 No 2402)

The Collective Redundancies and Transfer of Undertakings (Protection of Employment) (Amendment Regulations) 1999 amend TUPE and Trade Union, Labour Relations (Consolidation) Act 1992 and ERA. The Regulations came into effect on 28 July 1999. They were almost immediately amended by the Transfer of Undertakings (Protection of Employment) (Amendment) Regulations 1999 (SI 1999 No 2402) to correct a minor drafting fault in the first Regulations.

10a.1 Collective redundancies

a) An extension of consultation requirements to those who are not going to be dismissed

Where an employer is proposing to dismiss 20 or more employees at the same establishment within a period of 90 days, the requirement for consultation is extended so that the employer must now consult with the appropriate representatives not merely of those whom it is proposed to dismiss, as was previously the case, but also with representatives of all those who may be affected

- by the proposed dismissals; or

- by measures taken in connection with those dismissals.

b) A requirement to consult with recognised trade unions if there are any

The ability of the employer to choose whether to consult with a recognised trade union or employee representatives is removed. The employee must consult with any trade union that is recognised. If there is no recognised trade union, the employer must consult with employee representatives.

c) Employee representatives

Employee representatives for these purposes may be:

- representatives who were appointed or elected by the affected employees for a reason other than redundancy consultation. This can happen only if, having regard to the purposes for which they were elected and to the way in which they were elected or appointed, they can be considered to have the authority of the employees in question to receive information and to be consulted about the redundancy on their behalf

- representatives appointed or elected by the affected employees specifically for the redundancy consultation. Any such election must satisfy the following specific requirements:

  - *the employer must ensure that the election is fair;

  - the employer must decide on the number of representatives to be elected so that there are enough representatives to represent the interests of all the affected employees. In deciding on the number of representatives the employer must take into account

    - the number; and

    - types of employees affected;

  - the employer must decide whether the employee representatives should represent just one class of employees or all the employees;

  - before the election the employer must decide for how long the representatives are to hold office (it must be long enough for them to be given the information required by statute and to complete the statutory consultation);

  - *the candidates for election must themselves be affected by the redundancy at the date of election;

  - *no affected employee may be unreasonably excluded from standing for election;

  - all employees who are affected at the date of election must be entitled to vote;

  - all affected employees must be allowed to vote for as many candidates as represent them or the particular class of employee that they fall into;

  - *the election must be by secret ballot;

  - *the votes must be counted accurately.

- If an employee representative, elected under the above criteria, ceases to act as such then there must be an election to replace him which meets the requirements that are asterisked in the above list

d) If the employees fail to elect representatives

If the affected employees fail to elect representatives within a reasonable time, the information required to be given to representatives to start consultation under s 188(4) TULR(C)A is to be given individually to each of the affected employees.

e) Those who can claim a protective award (ie an award to compensate each employee for a number of days to reflect the lack of consultation) are amended in line with the additional duties that have been imposed on the employer under these Regulations. Who can bring a complaint still depends on the nature of the employer's particular failure in relation to the appointment of employee representatives or consultation requirements.

- In the case of any failure relating to election of an employee representative, any of the employees who are affected by the redundancy or dismissed as redundant can present a complaint.

- In the case of any other failure relating to employee representatives, the employee representative to whom the failure relates can present a complaint.

- In the case of any failure to fulfil any requirement relating to a trade union representative, the trade union is the appropriate complainant.

- In any other case an affected employee or one who has been or may be dismissed as redundant can complain.

f) The Regulations change the burden of proof in relation to two situations. In both the burden is put on to the employer:

- In relation to the question of whether or not the employee representative was 'appropriate' the employer must prove that the employee representative had authority to represent the affected employees; and

- It is for the employer to prove that the requirements concerning the election of employee representatives have been complied with.

g) The lower maximum level of protective award is revoked.

If the tribunal finds a complaint well founded, it can make a protective award. This is payable to each of the employees in respect of whom there has been a failure in relation to employee representatives or consultation. The protected period still continues for such time as the tribunal considers just and equitable having regard to the seriousness of the employer's default, subject to a maximum of 90 days regardless of the number of employees made redundant. The erstwhile lower limit of 30 days for cases where between 30 and 100 employees were made redundant has been removed by the Regulations.

10a.2 Transfers of undertakings

a) The requirements concerning:

- the need to consult a recognised trade union, rather than employee representatives;

- employee representatives and their elections;

- the need to consult employees directly in the absence of any employee representatives;

- who may present a claim in respect of any failure by the employer; and

- the reversal of the burden of proof;

are all the same as in relation to Collective redundancies (**see 10a.1 above**).

b) The maximum award that a tribunal can make if the employer has failed to meet any of the election or consultation requirements in relation to the transfer of an undertaking is increased from four weeks' to 13 weeks' pay.

11 Companies Acts 1985

The Companies Act 1985 is a consolidation of the previous Companies Acts. The Companies Act 1985 is of great importance to the employment, duties and liabilities of company directors.

Matters of particular concern in the personnel field:

a) The Act obliges companies to keep a copy or memorandum of their directors' contracts of employment for inspection by members of the company (ie shareholders).

b) A contract of employment with a director that is to be for more than five years and which includes any restriction on the company's ability to terminate the contract by notice, may be made only if approved by a general meeting of the company following due notification of the terms of the agreement.

c) The Act puts directors under a duty to perform their functions so as to promote the interests of the company's employees as well as its shareholders. It also includes within the powers of a company, where this is not specified, a power for the company to make adequate provision for its employees (or those of a subsidiary company) where the company is winding up or being transferred.

d) The Act requires certain matters to be disclosed in directors' reports where the average number of employees in a company in each week of the relevant financial year is more than 250. These are:

(i) the policy that has been applied in relation to disabled employees during that year:

- for giving full and fair consideration to applications for employment from disabled people

- for continuing the employment of and retraining of those who become disabled while in the company's employment

- for the training, career development and promotion of disabled employees generally within the company.

(ii) the action taken during that year to introduce, maintain or develop arrangements aimed at:

- systematically providing employees with information on matters of concern to them as employees

- consulting employees/their representatives on a regular basis so that employees' views can be taken into account in making decisions that are likely to affect employees' interests

- encouraging employee involvement in the company's performance through employee share schemes or by other means

- achieving a common awareness on the part of all employees of the financial and economic factors affecting the performance of the company.

12 Companies Act 1989

Amends the Companies Act 1985 to require that all elements of remuneration paid to directors and any payments for loss of office be disclosed. This applies whether the payments are made by the company itself or by a holding or subsidiary company.

13 Company Securities (Insider Dealing) Act 1985

Repealed and replaced by Part V of the Criminal Justice Act 1993 (**see 22 below**).

14 Computer Misuse Act 1990

Makes it a criminal offence for a person knowingly to try to gain unauthorised access to a computer program or to any data held on a computer. The Act also makes it an offence to try to modify any of the contents of a computer without authority.

15 Conduct of Employment Agencies and Employment Businesses Regulations 2003 (SI 2003 No 3319)

Amends the Employment Agencies Act 1973 (**see 41 below**).

16 Contracts (Applicable Law) Act 1990

The Act provides that:

- Where an employee habitually carries out his or her work in a particular country, the contract of employment is governed by the laws of that country – even when the employee is not working in that country.

- If the employee works in different countries, it is the law of the place through which the employee is engaged which determines the law that governs the contract of employment.

Both of these provisions can, however, be overridden if the circumstances show that the contract is more closely connected with a different country.

- In this last case the contract will be interpreted by applying the law of that, different, country.

It should be noted, however, that this Act applies only to the contractual aspects of employment, and other statutory rights – eg discrimination and unfair dismissal rights – are independent of an employee's contractual base.

17 Contracts (Rights of Third Parties) Act 1999

The Act allows for third parties who are identified by a contract to enforce the terms of a contract that has been entered into on their behalf – even though they have not themselves provided consideration for the contract. In the employment field this can be relevant to compromise and confidentiality agreements entered into with employees and to post-termination restrictions imposed on employees.

18 Control of Asbestos at Work Regulations 2002 (SI 2002 No 2675)

Impose requirements to protect employees who might be exposed to asbestos at work and to protect other persons who might be affected by such work. Employees are also put under a duty to protect themselves from exposure to asbestos at work.

19 Control of Lead at Work Regulations 2002 (SI 2002 No 2676)

The Regulations impose requirements to protect employees who might be exposed to lead at work and to protect other persons who might be affected by such work. Employees are also put under a duty to protect themselves from exposure to lead at work.

20 Control of Substances Hazardous to Health Regulations 2002 (S1 2002 No 2675)

These Regulations revoke and re-enact, with modifications, the Control of Substances Hazardous to Health Regulations 1999 (S1 1999 No 437). The Regulations amend the Health and Safety at Work etc Act 1974.

20.1 Protection against substances hazardous to health

- Duties are imposed on employers to protect employees and others who may be exposed to substances hazardous to health.

- Personal protective equipment must be provided by an employer to comply with the Personal Protective Equipment (EC Directive) Regulations.

- A duty is placed on employees to use any protective equipment provided and any controls put in place by the employer to protect them from such exposure.

- Maximum exposure levels to substances may be set as approved by the Health and Safety Commission.

20.2 Import of substances hazardous to health

The Regulations prohibit the import into the United Kingdom of certain substances and articles from outside the European Economic Area.

21 Copyright, Designs and Patents Act 1988

The Act repeals the Copyright Act 1956 and consolidates the law of copyright. Amended by Patents Act 2004.

a) The Act determines the ownership of the copyright of literary, dramatic or other artistic works and provides that the copyright in such a work created by an employee in the course of his employment belongs to the employer, subject to any agreement to the contrary.

b) The copyright in anything done outside the course of the employee's duties belongs to the employee.

c) The ownership of a copyright may be determined by contract.

d) Computer software is subject to copyright.

e) The provisions concerning compensation of employees for inventions which are patented is dealt with under the Patents Act 2004 (**see 103 below**).

22 Criminal Justice Act 1993

Part V repeals and replaces the Company Securities (Insider Dealing) Act 1985.

a) The Act prohibits any individual from knowingly dealing in securities of any company when he has information 'as an insider'. It also prohibits him from encouraging anyone else to deal in such securities or disclosing the information which he has 'as an insider' to anyone else, other than in the proper performance of his employment or profession.

b) 'Inside information' is information which:

- relates to particular securities
- is specific
- is unpublished
- would be likely, if published, to have a significant effect on the price of any securities.

c) A person has information 'as an insider', *inter alia*, if

- it is inside information; and
- he has obtained it through his employment; or
- he has obtained it from someone who obtained it through his (the other person's) employment.

23 Data Protection Act 1998

Repealed the Data Protection Act 1984, Access to Personal Files Act 1987. Amends Access to Medical Reports Act 1988 and Access to Health Records Act 1990.

The Act came into force on 1 March 2000. It provides for the compulsory registration of users of personal data, for the protection of personal data and for individual access to an individual's personal data. The Act also provides for compensation for misuse of personal data and for compensation to data subjects for inaccuracies. The main framework of the Act is:

23.1 Definitions

a) 'Data' is information that is:

- recorded in a form in which it is or is intended to be processed automatically;

- held in a filing system which is structured in a way that information concerning individuals is readily accessible (this will encompass paper personnel systems); or

- part of an 'accessible record', most important of which are health records. A health record is one that has been made by a health professional in connection with the care of an individual and which concerns that individual's physical or mental state. Although 'health professional' is defined by the Act, 'care' is not. This may lead to some difficulties since 'care' has been given a specific meaning in the Access to Medical Reports Act 1988 (**see 2.1 above**).

b) 'Processing' is more widely defined under these provisions than it was under the 1984 Act. Processing now means obtaining, recording or holding information or carrying out any operations on the information or data, including by organising, adapting, or altering the data; retrieving or consulting it or disclosing or making it available.

c) 'Personal data' is data that relates to a living individual who is identifiable either from the data alone or with the aid of any other information in the data user's possession. Personal data includes any expression of opinion about the individual, but not any expression of intention the data user may have in respect of him.

d) A 'data subject' is an individual who is the subject of personal data. The Act introduces a new concept of 'sensitive personnel data'. This is data concerning:

- racial or ethnic origins of the data subject

- his political opinions

- religious beliefs or beliefs of a similar nature

- whether he is a member of a trade union

- his physical or mental health or condition

- his sexual life

- the commission or alleged commission by him of any offence

- any proceedings for any offence committed or alleged to have been committed by him, the disposal of such proceedings or the sentence of the court in any such proceedings.

23.2 Data protection principles

The Act lays down eight data protection principles. These are not all the same as the eight data protection principles in the 1984 Act, although there are similarities. The Act provides interpretation for the application of those principles. The principles are these:

a) The information contained in personal data must be obtained, and the personal data processed, fairly and lawfully.

   (i)   This principle also stipulates that personal data shall not be processed unless at least one of the following conditions has been met:

   ■ the data subject has consented to it; or

   ■ the processing is necessary for one of the following reasons:

      ■ the performance of a contract to which the data subject is a party

      ■ to take steps at the request of the data subject with a view to entering into a contract

      ■ for the data controller to comply with a legal obligation – other than a contractual obligation – on him

      ■ to protect the vital interests of the data subject

      ■ to comply with various public duties

      ■ for the legitimate interests of the data controller or a third party to whom they are disclosed, except where processing is not warranted in the particular case because of the prejudice to the rights and legitimate freedoms or interests of the data subject (the Secretary of State can specify circumstances in which this condition is, or is not, to be taken to be satisfied).

   (ii) Where the data in question is 'sensitive personnel data' (**see 23.1d above**), one of the following conditions must also be met:

   ■ the data subject has given explicit consent to the processing of the data

   ■ the processing is necessary for exercising any right conferred or performing any obligation imposed by law on the data controller in connection with employment

   ■ the processing is necessary to protect the vital interests of the data subject or another in a case where

      ■ the data controller cannot, or cannot reasonably, be expected to obtain the data subject's consent; or

      ■ the data subject has unreasonably withheld his consent

   ■ the data concerns members of a non-profit-making body or trade union and is processed for internal use in a way which protects the data subject's rights and freedoms

   ■ the information has been made public as a result of steps deliberately taken by the data subject

   ■ the processing is necessary

      ■ for the purposes of or in connection with any legal proceedings or prospective legal proceedings

      ■ for obtaining legal advice

- for the purpose otherwise of establishing, exercising or defending legal rights
- where the processing is necessary to fulfil one of a number of public functions
- where the processing is necessary for medical purposes and is carried out by someone owing a duty of confidentiality equivalent to that of a health professional
- where the processing is of information regarding racial or ethnic origins which is carried out with appropriate safeguards for data subjects, where the purpose is to monitor equal opportunities between those of different racial or ethnic origins with a view to promoting equality.

In terms of interpreting the first data protection principle, the Act says that in deciding whether data was obtained fairly and lawfully, the purpose for which it was obtained and used, and questions as to whether any person who provided the information was deceived or misled as to that purpose, must be taken into account.

b) Personal data is to be held for only one or more specified and lawful purposes and is not to be used or disclosed in a manner incompatible with the specified purpose/s.

c) Personal data must be adequate, relevant and not excessive in relation to the purposes for which it is held.

d) Personal data must be accurate and updated if necessary.

e) Personal data must not be kept for longer than is necessary to fulfil the purpose for which it is held. (This principle is subject to an exception where data is used for historical, statistical or research purposes. In such cases, provided the data subject is not likely to suffer any damage or distress thereby, the data may be kept indefinitely.)

f) Personal data is to be processed in accordance with the rights of data subjects under the Act.

g) Appropriate technical and organisational measures must be taken against unauthorised or unlawful processing of personal data and against accidental loss or destruction of or damage to personal data. (In considering whether this principle has been complied with, the state of technological development, the cost of any security measures and the damage that might result from any failure to take those measures have to be balanced against harm that might result from a breach. The organisational measures include assessment of the reliability of staff having access to the personal data.)

h) Personal data must not be transferred outside the European Economic Area (EEA) unless the place to which it is transferred ensures adequate protection for the rights and freedoms of data sheets in relation to the processing of personal data. (There are certain exemptions from this provision – most important, for these purposes, is where the data subject consents to the transfer of information.)

23.3 The registration of data controllers

The Act provides for the establishment of a Data Protection Commissioner who replaces the erstwhile position of Data Protection Registrar. All data controllers (with few exceptions) must register with the Commissioner, and must furnish him with:

- their name and address or the name of their nominated representative

- a description of the data being processed or to be processed and the categories of subject to which it relates

- a description of any recipients to whom the data controller intends or may wish to disclose the data

- the name and description of any countries or territories outside the EEA to which he intends or may wish directly or indirectly to transfer the data (ie to help enforce the data protection legislation which restricts personal data from being sent to countries outside the EEA where there is no similar protection)

- a statement where the personal data is of a type which is exempt from the notification requirements and where the notification does not extend to such data. (Personal data is exempt from the registration requirements where it consists only of paper files or health records. In such cases, under transitional arrangements, there is no need to register such data until 24 October 2001 or until the end of any current registration period, if earlier. Where paper records have not been processed since before 28 October 1998, registration is not required for those records until 24 October 2007. Some parts of the Act do, however, apply to such records.)

For those who are already registered under the 1984 Act, their registration continues for the time being.

23.4 Supervision

The Commissioner has some powers to refuse applications for registration, and orders may be made preventing data from being taken out of the UK. Enforcement notices may also be issued where any person appears to be in breach of the data protection principles.

A Data Protection Tribunal is established to hear appeals from any refusal by the Commissioner of an application for registration or alteration of registered particulars and from any order made by the Commissioner.

23.5 Individual rights

a) If the data subject makes a request in writing (including a request in electronic form) he is entitled:

   (i)   to be told by the data controller whether he or someone on his behalf is processing that individual's personal data

   (ii) where the data controller acknowledges that he does hold personal data, to be given

- a description of the personal data

- the purposes for which it is being processed

- a description of those to whom it is or may be disclosed

- a copy in permanent form except where:

    - the supply of a copy is not possible;

    - to supply a copy would cause disproportionate effort;

- the data subject agrees otherwise; or

- the disclosure of the data would disclose information relating to another individual unless

    - the other individual has consented to the disclosure of that information; or

    - it would be reasonable in all the circumstances to disclose that information without the consent of that other individual – whether or not this is the case will depend on

        - any duty of confidentiality owed to the other individual

        - any steps taken by the data controller to seek the consent of the other individual

        - whether or not the other individual is capable of giving consent; and

        - any express refusal of his consent by the other individual.

- any necessary explanation to make intelligible information given to the data subject that is unintelligible without explanation

- an explanation of the logic involved in the decision-taking process in relation to data that is or is likely to be the sole basis on which a decision has to be taken that significantly affects the data subject, unless that logic is itself a trade secret

- any information as to the source of that data.

Where the data comes from another identifiable individual, however, the source can be identified only if the other individual has consented or if it would be reasonable in all the circumstances to disclose that information without the consent of the other individual (see above).

b) An individual is entitled to serve a data controller with a written 'data subject notice' requiring the data controller to cease or not to begin processing (or processing for a specified purpose or in a specified manner) personal data regarding that individual. This can be done only where the processing is causing or is likely to cause unwarranted and substantial distress to the data subject or another. This right is unavailable if the individual has, *inter alia*, given his consent to the processing. It will therefore be important, having regard to the wide way in which 'processing' is defined under the Act, for employers to obtain the consent of their employees that they may process any personal information in such ways as may be deemed necessary.

c) An individual is entitled to serve a notice on the data controller requiring that no decision which significantly affects him be taken based solely on a system which automatically processes his personal data. Examples given by the Act include the data subject's performance at work. Presumably this would also include computerised attendance records and other more esoteric software that may be used for career and manpower planning purposes.

   The data controller must reply to the data subject within 21 days telling him what steps he intends to take to comply with the data subject notice.

d) A person who suffers damages or distress as a result of any breach of the Act can be awarded compensation against the data controller unless the data controller can prove that he took such care as was reasonable in the circumstances to comply with the requirement.

e) A data subject can also apply to the court for an order requiring a data controller to rectify, block, erase or destroy inaccurate information and any expression of opinion based on inaccurate information.

23.6 Exemptions

The following data are totally exempt from the provisions of the Act:

a) data held for purposes of safeguarding national security

b) certain data concerned with crime and taxation

c) since the facility for data subjects to have access to data now encompasses medical reports, there are provisions under which the Secretary of State can introduce exemptions from the subject access provisions of the Act in respect of matters concerning, *inter alia*, the mental and physical health or condition of the data subject. No such provisions have yet been brought into force; however, it seems likely that such provisions will be made at least to reflect the erstwhile restrictions on subject access that were contained in the Access to Health Records Act 1990. These allowed disclosure to be refused where it might cause serious harm to any individual

d) data held by unincorporated clubs regarding their members

e) data that is required by law to be publicly available

f) data held by an individual for domestic or recreational purposes.

24 Deregulation and Contracting Out Act 1994

Amends the Employment Agencies Act 1973, Betting Gaming and Lotteries Act 1963 and Shops Act 1950.

The Act is in part repealed by and consolidated into the ERA (**see 53 below**).

24.1 Employment agencies

a) The Act removes the requirement for employment agencies and employment businesses to be licensed.

b) Prohibition Orders

   (i)   The Act introduces a system through which an employment tribunal can, on the application of the Secretary of State, make an order either:

   ■ prohibiting an individual from being involved in an employment agency or business; or

   ■ imposing conditions on their involvement.

   (ii) Before making any such order the tribunal must be satisfied that the individual was responsible, or partly responsible, for the improper conduct of the business. Where there is more than one person who manages the business, all are equally responsible for any misconduct of the business unless they can show that it happened without their connivance or consent and without negligence on their part.

(iii)   A prohibition or condition imposed by an employment tribunal can last for a period of up to 10 years.

(iv)   A person on whom an order is made can apply to have the order varied or can appeal to the EAT against the tribunal's decision (on a point of law only).

(v)   Failure to comply with a Prohibition Order is dealt with by criminal law sanctions.

24.2 Sunday working

Betting shop workers were given similar rights to those given to other shop workers under the Sunday Trading Act 1994 (the provisions for both betting shop and other shop workers are now consolidated into the ERA – **see 53.5 below**).

Ss 17 and 22 of the Shops Act 1950 are both repealed. These sections

- gave shop workers time off in lieu for Sunday working; and

- restricted shop workers from having to work more than three Sundays in any month.

25 Deregulation (Deduction from Pay of Union Subscriptions) Order 1998 (SI 1998 No 1529)

Amends TULRA.

The Order removes the rather cumbersome machinery instituted by TURERA in relation to the check-off system. The amendments have been inserted into the relevant section of the TULRA (**see 153.9 below**).

26 Disability Discrimination Acts 1995 and 2005

The Act repeals much of the Disabled Persons (Employment) Act 1944 and amends Disabled Persons (Employment) Act 1958, Chronically Sick and Disabled Persons Act 1970, EPCA, Local Government and Housing Act 1989, Education Act 1993. Amended by Disability Rights Commission Act 1999 and Disability Discrimination (Exemption for Small Employers) Order 1998, Disability Discrimination Act 1995, Employment Rights (Disputes Resolutions) Act 1998, Equal Opportunities (Employment Legislation)(Territorial Limits) Regulations 1999 (SI 1999 No 3163), Disability Discrimination (Blind and Partially Sighted Persons) Regulations 2003 (SI 2003 No 712), Disability Discrimination Act (Amendment) Regulations 2003 (SI 2003 No 1673) and Disability Discrimination Act 1995 (Pensions) Regulations 2003 (SI 2003 No 2770).

26.1 Disability

A person who has a physical or mental impairment which has a long-term and substantial adverse effect on his ability to carry out normal day-to-day activities has a disability for purposes of the Act. It should be remembered that the rights under the Act affect people with disabilities individually so that if a person with one leg is discriminated against by being refused a job because of his disability, it is no defence for an employer to have hired a person with one arm to do that job. The 2003 Regulations amended the definition of disability to include not only direct discrimination but also indirect discrimination. Harassment on grounds of disability was also introduced as a cause of action by the Regulations. The protection of the Regulations extends to contract workers and office holders as well as to employees.

'Impairment'

a) There is no general definition of what an impairment is. (Although under the 2005 Act those with HIV, cancer and multiple sclerosis are deemed to be disabled.)

b) The requirement that a mental impairment only amounted to a disability if it resulted from an illness which is clinically well recognised was removed by the 2005 Act.

c) Specific conditions may be declared by regulations to be or not to be impairments for the purposes of the Act. The Disability Discrimination (Meaning of Disability) Regulations 1996 (SI 1996 No 1455) specify certain matters as not being impairments:

   - addictions – unless they originally arose from medically prescribed drugs

   - tendencies to setting fires, stealing, physical or sexual abuse, exhibitionism or voyeurism

   - hay fever – although this can be taken into account where its effects aggravate another impairment

   - tattoos and body piercing that have been done for non-medical purposes.

'Substantial adverse effect'

d) There is no definition of what amounts to a 'substantial adverse effect'.

e) Regulations can prescribe that a particular kind of effect on the ability of a person to perform normal day-to-day activities shall or shall not be considered to be 'substantial'.

f) Severe disfigurement

   (i) An impairment which consists of severe disfigurement is to be treated as having a long-term substantial adverse effect on a person's ability to carry out normal day-to-day activities.

   (ii) Cases where severe disfigurement is not to be treated as having that effect may be prescribed by Regulations. Tattoos and voluntary body piercing have already been proscribed for these purposes (see Disability Discrimination (Meaning of Disability) Regulations 1996 (SI 1996 No 1455)).

g) The impact of medical treatment

   Where an impairment would be likely to have a substantial adverse effect on a person but for the fact that measures are being taken to correct or to treat it, the impairment is nonetheless treated as having a substantial adverse effect.

   (i) 'Measures' include medical treatment and the use of prostheses or other aids.

   (ii) This does not apply to people whose eyesight is correctable by glasses or contact lenses.

   (iii) Regulations can be made to exclude other cases where a person receiving treatment or subject to other measures is not to be considered substantially adversely affected by the impairment in question.

Long-term effect

h) An impairment is considered to have a long-term effect if:

- it has lasted 12 months or more

- it is likely to last for at least 12 months; or

- it is likely to last for the rest of that person's life.

i) Guidance may be issued by the Secretary of State (which must be taken into account by any court or tribunal, where it is relevant) as to whether any impairment may or may not be considered as having a long-term effect.

j) Recurrence

(i) If the condition ceases to have a substantial adverse effect on the person's ability to carry out normal day-to-day activities but the effect is expected to recur, it is to be treated as continuing to have that effect.

(ii) Regulations can prescribe

- when the threat of recurrence is to be ignored for these purposes; and

- circumstances where an effect that would not otherwise be considered long-term is to be considered to be long-term and vice versa.

Normal day-to-day activities

k) The impairment must affect one or more of the following if it is to affect 'normal day-to-day activities':

- mobility

- manual dexterity

- physical co-ordination

- continence

- ability to lift, carry or otherwise move day-to-day objects

- speech, hearing or eyesight

- memory or ability to concentrate, learn or understand; or

- perception of the risk of physical danger.

l) Regulations may prescribe where an impairment does or does not have any of the above effects or where it is to be taken as not affecting the person's ability to carry out normal day-to-day activities.

Deemed disability

m) Registered disabled: A person who was registered as disabled on 12 January 1995 is to be taken to be disabled for three years from that date and is thereafter treated as having been disabled during that period. Under the new provisions disabled people are no longer registered as such.

n) Progressive conditions: A person who is suffering from a progressive condition which is likely to result in his having a substantial impairment is to be treated as having a substantial impairment (examples of such conditions include cancer, MS, muscular dystrophy, and HIV infection).

o) Past disabilities: The Act applies to those with past disabilities as it, with some modifications, applies to those who are currently disabled.

p) Under the Disability Discrimination (Blind and Partially Sighted Persons) Regulations 2003 (SI 2003 No 712), those who are registered as blind or partially sighted are deemed to be disabled.

26.2 Small employers

Employers with fewer than 20 employees were originally exempt from the Act. This number was reduced and the exemption finally removed completely by the 2003 Regulations.

26.3 Discrimination by employers

It is unlawful for an employer to discriminate against a disabled person:

a) at the pre-employment stage:

    (i) in the arrangements he makes for determining who should be offered that employment

    (ii) in the terms on which he offers that employment

    (iii) by refusing to offer, or deliberately not offering, that employment; or

b) who is an employee of his:

    (i) in the terms of employment that he offers

    (ii) in the opportunities that he affords him for

- promotion
- transfer
- training; or
- receiving any other benefit.
  - 'Benefits' include facilities or services.
  - This does not apply where the employer is concerned with the provision of benefits of that description for the public (whether or not for payment) or for a section of the public which includes the employee unless:
    - what is provided for the public is materially different from what is provided for his employees; or
    - the provision of the benefit in question is regulated by the employee's contract of employment; or
    - the benefits relate to training (s 4(3)).

    (iii) by refusing/failing to afford him any of the above opportunities

c) by dismissing the employee or subjecting him to any other detriment.

'Employment'

As with the sex and race discrimination legislation, 'employment' is widely defined. It means employment under a contract of apprenticeship or employment or under a contract personally to do any work. As such, it includes those who are self-employed and who are working through employment agencies provided they are hired to do the work personally. Contract workers and office holders are specifically protected under the Regulations.

'Discrimination'

An amended definition of discrimination, for the purposes of the Act, was provided by the Disability Discrimination Act (Amendment) Regulations 2003 (SI 2003 No 1673).

d) An employer discriminates against a disabled person if for a reason related to that person's disability he treats the disabled person less favourably than he treats a person not having that particular disability whose relevant circumstances, including his abilities, are not materially different from those of the disabled person.

e) An employer discriminates against a disabled person if for a reason related to that disability (NB this is concerned with the individual's particular disability, not with the fact that the person is disabled in general terms):

- he treats him less favourably than he treats or would treat others to whom that reason does not or would not apply; and

- he cannot show that the treatment in question is justified.

(i) *'Justification'*

Treatment is 'justified' only if the reason for it:

- is material to the circumstances of the particular case; and

- is substantial.

Regulations can be made to provide when any treatment is and is not to be taken to be justified. Such regulations may make provision

- by reference to the cost of providing any benefit; and

- in relation to benefits under an occupational pension scheme with a view to enabling uniform rates of contributions to be maintained (see Disability Discrimination (Employment) Regulations 1996 (SI 1996 No 1456)).

Where an employer has failed to comply with the duty to make reasonable adjustments to accommodate a disabled person (**see 26.4 below**), any question of whether or not the employer was justified in any discrimination against that person has to be approached as if the employer had made all reasonable adjustments that were necessary. Or, put another way, the employer cannot rely on his failure to make reasonable adjustments as justification for discriminating on grounds of disability.

(ii)   Apart from the requirement to make reasonable adjustments (**see 26.4 below**), the Act does not require an employer to give a disabled person better treatment than he would give to any other person.

(f)   An employer also discriminates against a disabled person if:

(i)   he fails to comply with any duty to make reasonable adjustments (**see 26.4**); and

(ii)   he cannot show that his failure to comply with the duty in question is justified (for 'justification', **see 26.3e(i) above**).

26.4 The employer's duty to make adjustments

The duty to make adjustments is enshrined in s 4A of the Act as amended, to the effect that where:

- a provision, criterion or practice applied by or on behalf of an employer; or
- any physical feature of premises occupied by the employer

places the disabled person concerned at a substantial disadvantage by comparison with people who are not disabled, the employer is under a duty to take such steps as it is reasonable for him to take in all the circumstances of the case, to prevent the arrangements or feature from having that effect.

An employer has no duty to take steps if he did not know and could not reasonably be expected to know that a person who is or may be an applicant for employment is in fact a disabled applicant or potential applicant for employment. Or, in the case of an employee, if the employer could not reasonably be expected to know that the person has a disability and is likely to be put at a substantial disadvantage by any of the above.

'The disabled person concerned' for the purposes of s 4A is:

a)   in the case of discriminatory arrangements for determining to whom employment should be offered, any disabled person:

(i)   who is a job applicant; or

(ii)   who has notified the employer that he might be an applicant for the job; or

b)   in any other case a person who is:

(i)   an applicant for the job; or

(ii)   an employee, contract worker or office holder.

Reasonable steps

c)   The type of steps that it may be reasonable for an employer to take to obviate the adverse impact of any discriminatory effect are exemplified by the Act itself. These include:

- making adjustments to premises
- allocating some of the disabled person's duties to another person
- transferring the disabled person to fill an existing vacancy
- altering his hours of work

- assigning him to a different place of work

- allowing him to be absent during working hours for rehabilitation, assessment or treatment

- giving him or arranging for him to be given training

- acquiring or modifying equipment for his use

- modifying instructions or reference manuals

- modifying procedures for the testing or assessment of the disabled person

- providing a reader or interpreter

- providing supervision or other support.

However, these are only examples and the steps which it may be reasonable for an employer to take will depend on the circumstances. For example, in the case of a job applicant it would normally be reasonable to hold the interviews in a place that is accessible to the candidate and at a time that does not prevent him, because of his disability, from attending the interview.

d) In determining whether it is reasonable for an employer to have to take a particular step in order to prevent a disabled person being put at a substantial disadvantage as compared with a person who is not disabled, the following must be considered:

- the extent to which the step would prevent the effect in question

- the extent to which it is practicable for the employer to take the step

- the financial and other costs that would be incurred by the employer in taking the step and the extent to which taking it would disrupt his activities

- the extent of the employer's financial and other resources

- the availability to the employer of financial or other assistance with respect to taking the step

- the nature of his activities and the size of his undertaking

- where steps would be taken in relation to a private household, the extent to which making the adjustment would disrupt the household or disturb any person residing there.

26.5 Victimisation

a) A person victimises another if he treats that other less favourably because he has:

- brought proceedings against any person under the DDA

- given evidence or information in connection with any such proceedings

- otherwise done anything under the DDA in relation to any person

- alleged that anyone has contravened the DDA.

b) A person victimises another if he treats that other less favourably because he believes or suspects that the other has done or intends to do any of the things set out in the bullet list in 26.5a above.

c) A person cannot claim victimisation if he has made a false allegation.

26.6 Disability discrimination and pensions

Under the Act as originally drafted one of the specific exclusions from the requirement to make adjustments was in relation to occupational pension schemes. The Disability Discrimination Act 1995 (Pensions) Regulations 2003 (SI 2003 No 2770) replace this erstwhile exclusion with positive duties placed on pension scheme managers and trustees not to discriminate on grounds of disability. This is achieved by putting new sections 4G–4K into the DDA. These rules apply equally to pension scheme trustees and managers.

Non-discrimination rule

a) Every occupational pension scheme is deemed to contain 'the non-discrimination rule'. This is a requirement that the trustees must not discriminate against or harass disabled members or potential members of a pension scheme in carrying out their functions. It is also made unlawful for the trustees of the scheme to discriminate against or to harass any members or potential members of the scheme.

b) The other rules of the pension scheme are to have effect subject to this non-discrimination rule and the new provisions include a mechanism whereby the scheme rules can be changed by resolution to accommodate these requirements if the rules would otherwise be impossible, difficult or cumbersome for the trustees to change.

Duty to make adjustments

c) Where any provision, criterion or practice (including a scheme rules) applies or any physical feature of the premises occupied by the trustees puts a disabled member or prospective member at a substantial disadvantage compared with those who are not disabled, the trustees must take such steps as are reasonable in all the circumstances of the case to prevent the provision, criterion, practice or feature from having that effect.

d) One of the adjustments the new provisions might require the trustees to make are alterations to the pension scheme rules. The duty to adjust pensions is the same as the duty on employers to make adjustments to their premises.

e) The requirement to make adjustments does not apply if the trustees do not know and could not reasonably be expected to know that the disabled person is a member/prospective member of the scheme and that he or she is likely to be adversely affected by the provision, criterion, practice or feature in question.

26.7 Enforcement

Enforcement in the employment field is through the tribunal system. A case must be brought within three months of the discrimination complained of. As with sex and race discrimination claims, the tribunal can extend time for presenting a complaint if it considers that it is just and equitable to do so in the circumstances of the case. In the case of complaints brought against the managers or trustees of a pension scheme, the employer is to be treated as a party to the proceedings and is entitled to be heard.

Where a tribunal finds that a complaint is well founded, it can:

a) make a declaration as to the claimant's and the employer's rights in relation to the matters complained of (in relation to a claim under the pension scheme this may include a declaration that the employee be admitted to the scheme)

b) order the employer to pay compensation (the compensation in these cases, as with sex and race discrimination, is without limit and can include damages for injury to feelings caused by the discrimination)

c) recommend that the employer takes such action as the tribunal considers reasonable to obviate or reduce the adverse effect on the claimant of the matter complained of. The tribunal can also specify the time within which such action must be taken. If the employer fails to take the recommended action, the tribunal can award additional compensation.

Disability Rights Commission Code of Practice 2004
The Disability Rights Commission's Code of Practice replaces the 1996 DfEE Code of Practice for the elimination of discrimination in the field of employment against disabled persons or persons who have had a disability. The Code is not legally binding in its own right, but its provisions are admissible in evidence before a tribunal or a court. The Code, as well as going through the law on disabilities and employment and giving helpful examples of the provisions of the DDA, makes a few fundamental suggestions which employers should take into account:

1 Understand the social dimension of disability. Disabled peoples' impairments would often not restrict them if it were not for environmental factors.

2 Recognise the diverse nature of disability. To avoid discrimination it is important to understand the range of disabilities there are. It is also important for employers to understand the effects of their own actions.

3 Do not make assumptions. Find out about disabled peoples' needs – talk to the individual disabled person to see what the effects of his disability might be. In most cases he will have a better idea than you as to what his limitations are and how any limitations can be got round.

4 Seek expert advice. Although there is no obligation to obtain expert advice, it may be helpful to do so, especially where the person is newly disabled and therefore less likely to know what his limitations (if any) now are.

5 Plan ahead. Where changes are being made in buildings, etc, consider the possible effect on potential disabled job applicants.

6 Have equal opportunities policies and procedures. Employers who have equal opportunities policies are more likely to comply with their duties under the Act, and therefore are less likely to have cases brought against them.

7 Audit policies and monitor employees. Again, although there is no statutory requirement to do so, it is important to review the policies and to monitor employees to make sure that the policies are effective.

Employers who need specialist help regarding the employment of people with disabilities should contact their local Placing, Assessment and Counselling Team (PACT). PACTs are part of the Employment Service.

27 Disability Discrimination Act 1995 (Amendment) Regulations 2003 (SI 2003 No 1673)

Amends the Disability Discrimination Act 1995 – **see 26 above**.

28 Disability Discrimination Act 1995 (Pensions) Regulations 2003 (SI 2003 No 2770)

Amends the Disability Discrimination Act 1995 – **see 26 above**.

29 Disability Discrimination (Blind and Partially Sighted Persons) Regulations 2003 (SI 2003 No 712)

A person who is registered as blind or partially sighted is deemed to be disabled.

30 Disability Rights Commission Act 1999

Amends the Disability Discrimination Act 1995.

The Act sets up the Disability Rights Commission (DRC). The DRC's main duties will be similar to those of the EOC and the CRE in relation to sex and race discrimination respectively, ie:

- to work towards the elimination of discrimination against disabled people;

- to provide assistance for disabled people;

- to promote equal opportunities for the disabled;

- to provide a central source of information and advice to key sets of people including disabled people and employers;

- to encourage good practice in the treatment of the disabled;

- to advise the government on the operation of the Disability Discrimination Act 1995;

- to prepare and review statutory codes of practice; and

- to undertake formal investigations.

31 Dock Work Act 1989

Abolished the Dock Workers Employment Scheme and the National Dock Labour Board.

The Act provides for redundancy payments for dock workers who are made redundant and provides that those registered as dock workers at the date that the Act was passed are to have their previous service while registered count towards their period of continuous employment.

32 Education Act 1996

Consolidates and repeals much of the earlier Education legislation. Repeals Education Acts 1944, 1946, 1959, 1964, 1968, 1975, 1976, 1979 1981, 1993, Education (Work Experience) Act 1973 and the

Education (School-leaving Dates) Act 1976. Amends Children and Young Persons Act 1963, Education Act 1962, 1967, 1973, 1980 and 1994, Employment Act 1990, Disability Discrimination Act 1995, ERA, SDA and SDA.

Amended by Education Act 1997.

32.1 Compulsory school age

The Act sets down when a person is of compulsory school age. A person ceases to be of compulsory school age if he attains the age of 16:

- on the school-leaving date for that year; or

- after the school-leaving date for that year, but before the beginning of the following school year.

Otherwise, the end of compulsory school age is the school-leaving date that immediately follows his 16th birthday.

32.2 The employment of children

a) Any individual who is not over compulsory school age is a 'child' for the purposes of statute.

b) The Act gives the local education authority certain powers to oversee the employment of children in local authority education:

(i) The authority can require a parent or employer to provide it with information so that the authority can determine whether the child is being employed in a manner which renders him unfit to obtain the full benefit of his education.

(ii) If it appears to the authority that the child is being employed in such a manner, it can serve a notice on the employer:

- prohibiting him from employing the child; or

- imposing any restrictions on the child's employment that the authority considers expedient.

(iii) An employer who fails to comply with any prohibition or restrictions imposed by a local education authority is liable to prosecution.

(iv) The local education authority is given powers of entry to enforce any restrictions or prohibitions it may have imposed on an employer.

32.3 Work experience in last year of compulsory schooling

During the last year of compulsory schooling the local education authority or the governing body of a grant-maintained school can make arrangements to provide children with work experience as part of their education.

33 Education Act 1997

Amends the Education Act 1996. Alters the definition of compulsory school age, but only in respect of when it begins.

34 Education (Restriction of Employment) Regulations 2000 (SI 2000 No 2419)

The Regulations provide for individuals to be prohibited or restricted from employment as a teacher or in employment which brings them into contact with children or young persons on any of four grounds:

- medical condition;

- misconduct;

- they are not fit and proper persons to be employed as teachers or in work that brings them into contact with children or young persons; or

- because they have been placed on the list of people considered unsuitable to work with children. (This list is 'the Department of Health List' which is kept by the Secretary of State for Health under section 1 of the Protection of Children Act 1999.)

a) Under the Regulations:

- the Secretary of State may direct an employer to terminate an employee's employment or make his continued employment subject to certain conditions where either of the first two grounds above applies.

- the Secretary of State must direct an employer to terminate a relevant person's employment if he is found not to be a fit and proper person to work with children or young persons or where he is on the Department of Health List.

b) If a person is dismissed (or resigns in circumstances in which he would have been dismissed) from relevant employment on grounds of misconduct, his employer must report the facts of the case and information regarding the circumstances of the dismissal or resignation to the Secretary of State.

35 Education (Restriction of Employment) (Wales) Regulations 2000 (SI 2000 No 2906)

The Regulations place a ban on engaging on a self-employed basis those whose employment with children and young persons is restricted or banned. This ban operates where their work would bring them into regular contact with children or young persons.

36 Employers' Liability (Compulsory Insurance) Act 1969

Amended by Police Act 1997, Employers' Liability (Compulsory Insurance) Regulations 1998 (SI 1998 No 2573) and Employers' Liability (Compulsory Insurance) Regulations 2004 (SI 2004 No 2882).

The Act prescribes that all employers must insure against liability for personal injury and disease sustained by their employees and arising out of, or in the course of, their employment in Great Britain.

37 Employers' Liability (Defective Equipment) Act 1969

Amended by Police Act 1997.

The Act makes an employer liable, without proof of fault on his part, in all cases where an employee sustains personal injury in the course of his employment 'in consequence of a defect in equipment provided by his employer for the purposes of the employer's business'.

38 Employment Act 1989

Amended by Employment Act 1990, Further and Higher Education Act 1992 and Education Act 1993.

Amends Employment of Women, Young Persons and Children Act 1920, Shops Act 1950, Factories Act 1961, Children and Young Persons Act 1963, Employment and Training Act 1973, Health and Safety at Work etc Act 1974, Employment Protection Act 1975, Social Security Act 1975, Sex Discrimination Acts 1975 and 1986, SDA, EPCA, Employment and Training Act 1981, Agricultural Training Board Act 1982, Industrial Training Act 1982, Employment Act 1988. Repeals Young Persons (Employment) Acts 1938 and 1964.

38.1 Sex discrimination law amendments

Unusually for an 'Employment Act', the 1989 Act is primarily concerned with updating the SDA to bring it into line with the European Directive on sex discrimination.

a) Removing the effects of discriminatory legislation passed before the SDA

Where any provision of an Act passed before the SDA imposes a requirement to do anything which would be discriminatory under the SDA 1975, that provision is 'of no effect'. This provision extends to cover post-1975 re-enactments of pre-1975 Acts and also includes any statutory instrument made under any such Act – whether the statutory instrument was made before or after the 1975 Act was passed.

The Secretary of State for Employment is also given power to amend, revoke or repeal any such provision of any such Act or of any statutory instrument made under any such Act.

b) Circumstances in which discrimination is permissible

The Act provides that discrimination against women is not unlawful insofar as it is necessary:

(i) to comply with any existing (ie pre-SDA 1975) statutory provision (or any statutory instrument passed under any such statute) concerning the protection of women in relation to pregnancy, maternity, or risks specifically affecting women; or

(ii) to comply with the requirement to take care of the health and safety of women in relation to pregnancy, maternity, or risks specifically affecting women.

c) Exemptions from the provisions of the SDA 1975

(i) employment as a head teacher or principal of an educational establishment where any instrument relating to the establishment requires that its head be of a particular religious order

(ii) employment as the head, a fellow or any other member of the academic staff of any college or similar institution where any instrument relating to the establishment requires that the position in question be filled by a woman.

d) Discrimination as regards training

(i)   Section 14 of the SDA, which was concerned with the provision of training by vocational training bodies, is re-enacted with amendments (the equivalent provision of the SDA is similarly amended).

(ii)   The Secretary of State is empowered to allow for discrimination in favour of single parents in relation to certain types of training.

38.2 Working conditions for women and young persons

The Act removes restrictions on hours of work, etc, in respect of women and young persons.

Most of the restrictions on the hours of employment for women and young persons are lifted. This legislation does not, however, affect the restrictions on the employment of 'children' (ie those under minimum school-leaving age).

38.3 Race discrimination

a) Discrimination as regards training

Section 13 of the RRA, which was concerned with the provision of training by vocational training bodies, is re-enacted with amendments (the equivalent provision of the SDA is similarly amended).

b) Safety helmets

A Sikh who is wearing a turban is exempted from any legal requirement to wear a safety helmet on a construction site. If he is injured, however, any liability on the person causing the injury is limited to the damage that would have been done if the employee had been wearing a safety helmet.

39 Employment Act 2002

Amends TULRA, Employment Tribunals Act 1996, ERA, Employment Relations Act 1999, Social Security Contribution Benefits Act 1992, Equal Pay Act 1970, Social Security Administration Act 1992, SDA, Disability Discrimination Act 1995.

39.1 Paternity and adoption leave

The Act provides a skeleton set of rights in relation to certain matters to be filled in by Regulations for paid paternity and adoption leave – see Paternity and Adoption Leave Regulations 2002 (**104 below**).

39.2 Maternity and Maternity Pay

The Act makes certain amendments to the maternity and maternity pay provisions in the ERA.

■ The Ordinary maternity leave period and the period for which basic statutory maternity pay (SMP) is paid are extended from 18 to 26 weeks.

■ The way in which SMP is calculated is changed slightly so that the higher-rate SMP, which is paid for the first six weeks of maternity leave, is based on 90 per cent of a woman's earnings in the last eight weeks prior to the 14th week before the expected week of confinement. This is called the 'earnings-related rate'. The remainder of SMP is paid at whichever is the lower of the earnings-related rate or the weekly lower statutory maternity pay rate.

- The job to which a woman is entitled to return is of a job of a 'prescribed kind'. What a job of a 'prescribed kind' amounts to is left to be filled in by Regulations.

39.3 Tribunal reform

See mainly under Employment Tribunals (Constitution and Rules of Procedure) Regulations 2004 (**57 below**).

- The Act allows for Regulations to be made to allow employment tribunals and the EAT to award costs against parties' representatives by reason of the representative's conduct of the proceedings.

- Where a tribunal awards costs in favour of a party, it can reduce those costs or award costs against that party's representative in respect of his or her conduct of the proceedings.

- Regulations can also be made to allow an award to be made by an employment tribunal in respect of the time taken by a party to prepare its case.

- Cases may also be postponed by a tribunal to give parties an opportunity to try to settle proceedings. Where it exercises this power the tribunal may also warn the parties that if they do not settle during this period, the services of a conciliation officer may no longer be available to them.

- The Act allows for matters to be determined without hearing in circumstances which Regulations may provide for. This gives tribunals the power to weed out hopeless cases.

- The Presidents of employment tribunals in England and Wales and in Scotland are given power to make practice directions to regulate their procedure. This is a power similar to that already enjoyed by many courts including the EAT.

39.4 Statutory disputes resolution

The provisions of the Act are supplemented by the Employment Act 2002 (Disputes Resolution) Regulations 2004 (SI 2004 No 752) which took effect from 1 October 2004. The following analysis includes the effect of those Regulations.

The Act sets out a statutory disputes resolution procedure which must be followed in all cases of discipline and dismissal and in relation to grievances.

These procedures are minimum requirements which employers and employees must follow where they are relevant.

a) Dismissal and disciplinary procedure

The statutory dismissal and disciplinary procedure applies to all dismissals other than constructive dismissal.

It also applies to any action short of dismissal that is being taken because of an employee's conduct or capability, other than giving oral or written warnings or suspending the employee on full pay.

(i) *The standard dismissal and disciplinary procedure*

Step 1: The statement:

- The employer must send the employee a written statement which sets out the conduct or other matters which have led to him to contemplate dismissing or disciplining the employee.

- The statement must say why the employer is contemplating dismissing or disciplining the employee on those grounds.

- The employee must be invited to a meeting to discuss the matters at issue.

- Before this meeting the employee must be given a given a reasonable opportunity to consider his response to the employer's statement.

Step 2: The meeting:

- Except where the disciplinary action consists of suspension no action may be taken until after there has been a meeting.

- The employee is under a duty take all reasonable steps to attend the meeting.

- After the meeting has been held the employer must inform the employee of his decision, and if the decision is to dismiss or to take disciplinary action he must also inform the employee of the employee's right to appeal against the disciplinary action if he is not satisfied with it.

Step 3: Appeal:

- If the employee wishes to appeal, he must inform the employer.

- Another meeting must be set up (which need not be prior to the employee's dismissal taking effect).

- The appeal should normally be heard by a more senior manager than the one who was present at the original disciplinary hearing.

- Again the employee is under a duty to make all reasonable efforts to attend the appeal hearing and the employer must give the employee his final decision following that hearing.

(ii) *The modified procedure*

The modified procedure applies where:

- the employer dismissed the employee without notice because of his conduct;

- the dismissal occurred as soon as the employer became aware of the employee's misconduct or immediately afterwards;

- the employer was entitled to treat the employee's conduct as gross misconduct; and

- it was reasonable, in the circumstances, for the employer to dismiss the employee before enquiring into the circumstances in which the conduct took place;

but this procedure does not apply where the employee has lodged an unfair dismissal claim before the employer has sent the employee the statement required in Step 1 below.

Step 1: The statement:

The employer must send the employee a written statement which sets out:

- the conduct that has led to the employee's dismissal;

- the employer's basis for believing at the time of the employee's dismissal that he was guilty of that misconduct; and

- the employee's right of appeal against the dismissal decision.

Step 2: Appeal:

- If the employee wishes to appeal he must inform the employer and the employer must set up an appeal hearing.

- The employee is under a duty to make all reasonable efforts to attend the appeal.

- After the appeal the employer must give his final decision.

(iii) General

- The meetings must be held at times and places which are reasonable and must be conducted in such a way as to enable both parties to explain their cases.

- All these meetings are 'disciplinary hearings' for the purposes of the statutory right to be accompanied under s 10 Employment Relations Act 1999.

- There is a requirement that all steps must be taken without unreasonable delay.

- Wherever possible, the modified procedure should be avoided.

- Neither procedure applies to cases where:

  - all employees of a particular category are dismissed on the basis of an offer of re-engagement either during or at the end of their employment

  - the dismissal is one of a number of redundancy dismissals in respect of which there is a requirement to consult with the employees' representatives under s 188 TULRA

  - the employee is taking part in unofficial strike or other industrial action such that an employment tribunal is not entitled to determine the fairness of his dismissal

  - the employee is dismissed for taking part in protected industrial action

  - the employer's business suddenly ceases to function because of an unforeseeable event that makes it impractical for him to employ any employees

  - the employee's continued employment would be in breach of a statutory restriction

  - the employee is subject to a separate dismissal procedures agreement made between trade union/s and employers or employers' association/s.

b) Grievance procedures

The statutory disputes resolution procedures require the employee to follow the statutory grievance procedure.

- A 'grievance' is a complaint by the employee bringing a grievance about any action his employer has taken or is contemplating taking in relation to him.

- If the procedure has not been followed, the employee cannot make a complaint to an employment tribunal about that action or proposed action under a number of jurisdictions including: discrimination under all the relevant statutes, detriments in employment, complaints about deductions from pay, complaints about breach of contract which is amenable to tribunal jurisdiction and unfair dismissal. (This will only apply where the employee's complaint is of constructive dismissal – where the employee complains of a normal dismissal, any 'grievance' regarding this need not be taken through the statutory disputes resolution grievance procedure.)

- The rationale behind this provision is to make sure that an employer knows that an employee has a complaint and has an opportunity to deal with it before it gets to the employment tribunal.

(i)   *The standard procedure*

Step 1: The statement:

The employee must set out his grievance in writing and send it to the employer.

Step 2: The meeting:

The employer must invite the employee to attend a meeting to discuss the grievance.

- The employer must have a reasonable opportunity to consider his response to the information contained in the grievance, but should otherwise set up the grievance meeting as quickly as possible.

- The employee must take all reasonable steps to attend the meeting and is entitled to be accompanied – as per s 10 Employment Relations Act 1999.

- The meeting must be conducted in such a way as to enable both parties to explain their positions as far as possible.

- After hearing the grievance the employer must inform the employee of his decision and must inform the employee of the employee's right to appeal against that decision if he is not satisfied with it.

Step 3: Appeal:

If the employee wishes to appeal he should inform the employer of this.

- The employer must then set up an appeal meeting, if possible with a more senior manager than heard the original grievance.

  - The hearing must be set up as soon as possible.

  - The employee is entitled to be accompanied at the hearing.

  - The employee is under a duty to take all reasonable steps to attend the hearing.

- After the appeal the employer must inform the employee of his decision.

(ii)   *The modified procedure*

There is again a modified two-step procedure which is available to an employee to deal with grievances.

The modified procedure applies where:

- the employee is no longer employed by the employer in question;

- the employer was either not aware of the employee's grievance, or was aware of it but the standard grievance procedure had not been completed before the employee's employment ended (this includes cases where the standard grievance procedure has not been started prior to the employee's employment ending); and

- the employer and the employee have agreed that the modified procedure should apply. (This agreement may be reached after the employee's employment has terminated.)

Step 1: Written statement:

The employee must set out his grievance and the reasons for it in writing and send them to his employer.

Step 2: Response:

The employer must set out his response in writing and send it to the employee.

(iii) General

- The meetings, which form part of the grievance procedure,

    - must be held at times and places which are reasonable; and

    - must be conducted in such a way as to enable both parties to explain their cases.

- All the meetings are 'grievance hearings' for the purposes of the statutory right to be accompanied under s 10 Employment Relations Act 1999.

- All steps must be taken without unreasonable delay.

- Using the statutory discrimination questionnaire procedures does not constitute a statement by the employee of his grievance for the purposes of the statutory grievance procedures.

- Neither grievance procedure applies where the employee's employment terminated before either procedure was started and since his employment terminated it has ceased to be reasonably practicable to put in a grievance under either the standard or the modified procedure.

- Where the grievance is that the employer is contemplating taking or has taken disciplinary action against the employee, then prima facie neither procedure applies ('disciplinary action' for these purposes is action short of dismissal, other than paid suspension or warning which is taken because of the employee's conduct or capability).

    - The grievance procedures do apply in such cases, however, if the basis of the employee's grievance is that the disciplinary action would amount to unlawful discrimination or that the disciplinary action is being taken for reasons other than the reasons which the employer has given for taking that action.

    - Where the employee's grievance is of unlawful discrimination or that the employer's reasons for taking action are bogus, he is treated as having complied with the procedure:

- if he sets out his grievance and sends it to the employer before any appeal meeting is held under the statutory dismissal and disciplinary procedure; or

- if neither of the statutory dismissal and disciplinary procedures are being followed, he is taken to have complied with the grievance procedure requirements if he sets out his grievance and sends it to the employer before presenting any complaint arising out of the grievance to an employment tribunal.

- Where the employee's employment has terminated in a case where the standard grievance procedure applies and the employee has put his grievance in writing and sent it to the employer, then:

  - if it ceases to be reasonably practicable for the employer or the employee to comply with the remainder of the requirements of the grievance procedure, they are taken to have complied with it.

  - The only exception is where there has been an initial meeting and it is only the employer's decision that is awaited. In such cases there is no 'deemed compliance' until the employer gives his decision to the employee in writing.

- If a grievance is brought by an independent trade union official or an elected employee representative on behalf of the employee and at least one other employee, the grievance procedure is deemed to have been complied with if the representative writes to the employer setting out the grievance and the names of the employees on whose behalf it is brought.

c) Circumstances where statutory procedures are deemed not to apply or are treated as having been complied with

These exceptions apply equally to both the dismissal and disciplinary and to the grievance procedures where relevant.

(i) Threat or harassment

If the relevant procedure is not started for either of the following reasons, that procedure is treated as not applying to the 'innocent' party, but as applying and therefore as having been breached by the 'guilty' party. The reasons are:

- The party reasonably believes that starting the procedure would result in a significant threat to himself or another or to his property or that of another;

- The party has been subjected to harassment and reasonably believes that starting the procedure would result in further harassment. ('Harassment' is conduct which has the purpose, or can reasonably be taken to have the effect, of violating the person's dignity or creating an intimidating, hostile, degrading, humiliating or offensive environment for that person.)

If the relevant procedure has been started, but for either of the the reasons set out above a party has not complied with any of the subsequent requirements, that procedure is treated as having been complied with by the 'innocent' party, but as not having been complied with by the 'guilty' party.

(ii)   Starting the complete procedure is impracticable

- If the relevant procedure is not started because it is not practicable for the party to commence the procedure within a reasonable time, that procedure is treated as not applying.

- If the relevant procedure has been started, but it is not practicable for the party to complete the procedure within a reasonable time, that procedure is treated as having been complied with.

(iii)   Failure to attend a meeting

- If the employee, his companion (if he is exercising his right to be accompanied), or the employer are unable to attend a meeting for a reason which was not foreseeable at the time when the meeting was arranged, the side which failed to attend is not to be treated as being in breach of the relevant procedure. In such cases the employer must invite the employee (and his companion if applicable) to a second meeting.

- If because of unforeseen circumstances any of the invited attendees are not able to attend the second meeting, the parties are to be treated as having complied with the applicable statutory procedure.

d)   The effect of a failure to comply with statutory dispute resolution procedures

(i)   If an employer fails to complete the statutory dismissal and disciplinary procedure, the dismissal is treated as being automatically procedurally unfair.

- Unless the tribunal considers that it would result in an injustice to the employer it must make a basic award of no less than four weeks' pay (this is subject to reduction on the basis of an employee's contributory conduct).

- Unless there are exceptional circumstances the tribunal must increase the employee's award by 10 per cent and may increase it by up to 50 per cent. If there are exceptional circumstances the tribunal may increase the award by such lesser amount as it considers just and equitable or it can decide not to increase the amount at all.

(ii)   The employee fails to comply with the statutory disputes grievance procedure

- If the employee fails to take a grievance where the statutory disputes grievance procedure applies, he will not be allowed to bring a tribunal claim about any matter which should have been made the subject of a grievance.

- The employee is also required to allow 28 days to elapse between putting in a grievance under the statutory disputes procedure and bringing a complaint based on any matter which is the subject of the grievance.

- The tribunal's jurisdiction under these provisions is only affected if:

  - the failure is apparent to the tribunal from the information provided by the employee in bringing proceedings; or

- the employer specifically raises the issue of jurisdiction – although it is not clear whether this must be raised by the employer in his response to the claim or if it may be raised at the hearing itself.

- If the case does go ahead where the employee is in breach of the statutory disputes procedures, unless there are exceptional circumstances the tribunal must reduce the employee's award by 10 per cent and may reduce it by up to 50 per cent. If there are exceptional circumstances the tribunal may reduce the award by such lesser amount as it considers just and equitable or it can decide not to reduce the amount at all.

e) Extension of time limits where statutory procedures apply

- When a complaint is presented to a employment tribunal to which one of the statutory procedures applies, in certain circumstances the time limit for presenting the complaint is extended by a further three months starting with the day after the expiry of the original time limit.

- Where it is the statutory dismissal and disciplinary procedure that is the relevant procedure, time is extended if, when the original time limit expired, the employee had reasonable grounds for believing that a dismissal and disciplinary procedure – whether the statutory one or not – was being followed in respect of any matter included in the employee's complaint.

- Where it is the statutory grievance procedure which is the relevant procedure, time can be extended for a further three months starting with the day after the expiry of the normal time limit in a number of situations:

(i) *Employee not allowed to present his claim*

- The employee is not allowed to present his claim because it is one to which the statutory grievance procedure applies and he has not begun that procedure; or

- The employee is not allowed to present his claim because it is one to which the statutory grievance procedure applies, he has begun the procedure, but less than 28 days have passed since he put in his statement of grievance.

(ii) *Employee has started the grievance procedure*

- The claim is presented after the expiry of the normal time limit but the employee sent a statement of his grievance to his employer within the normal time limit.

- For these purposes the 'normal time limit' is taken as the time limit laid down by statute which is applicable to a claim without any extension of time needing to be granted.

f) The requirement to notify employees of procedures related to grievance dismissal and discipline and grievance

- Section 3 of the ERA is amended so that employers are required to notify employees not only of disciplinary and grievance procedures but also of dismissal procedures.

- The exemption from the requirement to notify of disciplinary procedures for employers who employ fewer than 20 employees is removed.

g) Procedurally unfair dismissal

- Where the statutory dismissal and disciplinary procedures apply and there has been a failure to go through them which is attributable to the employer, the employee's dismissal is considered as being procedurally unfair.

- Apart from any failure to follow the statutory disputes procedure, which gives rise to an automatic procedurally unfair dismissal, any other procedural unfairness can be overcome if the employer is able to show that had he gone through the procedure correctly he would still have decided to dismiss the employee.

39.5 New award for failure to provide a statutory statement of terms and conditions or of changes

- If an employer fails to provide a statutory statement of terms and conditions prior to certain types of case being brought against him by an employee, the tribunal must make an award of two weeks' pay. It can increase the award to up to four weeks' pay where it considers it just and equitable to do so.

- The types of case to which this power applies include unfair dismissal, discrimination, breach of contract and detrimental treatment cases, but strangely do not include cases where the employee is bringing a claim against a defaulting employer to obtain a declaration as to what terms and conditions should be contained in his statement of terms and conditions of employment under s 1 ERA.

39.6 Equal pay questionnaires

The Act allows for Regulations to be made to introduce a questionnaire procedure for equal pay claimants. These have been introduced by the Equal Pay (Questions and Replies) Order 2003 (SI 2003 No 722) and are similar to the other discrimination questionnaires.

39.7 Fixed-term work

The Act provides for Regulations to be made to ensure that those on fixed-term contracts are treated no less favourably than those in permanent employment 'for such purposes and to such an extent as the regulations may provide'. (See the Fixed-term Employees (Prevention of Less Favourable Treatment) Regulations 2002 (SI 2002 No 2034) – **72 below**.)

39.8 Flexible working

The Act amends the ERA. These provisions are fleshed out by the Flexible Working (Eligibility, Complaints and Remedies) Regulations 2002 (SI 2002 No 3236) and the Flexible Working (Procedural Requirements) Regulations 2002 (SI 2002 No 3207). The effects of these Regulations are included below.

a) General

The Act provides for flexible working where the employee wants to change:

- his hours of work;

- his times of work; or

- his place of work (as between home and the employer's place of business); or

- such other terms and conditions as may be specified by regulations;

or where the purpose of a request for flexible working is for the employee to look after a child.

b) Entitlement to apply for flexible working

The employee:

- must have been continuously employed for not less than 26 weeks;

- must be:

  - the mother, father, adopter, guardian of foster parent of the child; or

  - married to, or the partner of, the mother, father, adopter, guardian or foster parent of the child (for the purposes of this provision partners can be same-sex partners, but not close relatives – ie: parent, grandparent, brother, sister, aunt or uncle of the child's parents)

- must have responsibility for the upbringing of the child

- The child must be:

  - under the age of six; or

  - if disabled, under the age of 18.

c) Application for flexible working

An application for flexible working must be in writing, be dated, and must state:

- that it is an application for flexible working;

- the change/s of terms sought;

- the date when those changes are to take effect;

- the impact that the proposed changes will have on the employer and the employee's view of how any such impact can be dealt with;

- details of the relevant relationship with the child in question;

- the date when any previous application was made to the employer for flexible working;

- the date of the application.

The application must be made at least two weeks before the child reaches the relevant birthday.

An employee who has made an application for flexible working may not make a further application to the same employer within 12 months of the first application. (For the purposes of this provision an application is made when it is received by the employer.)

d) Employer's action on receiving an application for flexible working

Within 28 days of receiving the employee's application the employer must arrange a meeting with the employee to discuss his application unless he agrees to the employee's application prior to the expiry of the 28-day period.

The employee is entitled to be accompanied at the meeting by a fellow worker who is:

- chosen by the employee;

- permitted to address the meeting, but not to answer questions on behalf of the employee; and

- permitted to confer with the employee during the meeting.

If the employee's companion is not available on the day set for the hearing, the employer must postpone the meeting provided the employee is able to propose an alternative time that is:

- convenient for the employer, employee and companion; and

- within seven days of the date of the original meeting.

e) Refusing the employee's application and employer's decision

An employer may only refuse an application made by an employee if he considers that one of the following grounds applies:

- it will involve additional cost;

- it will have a detrimental effect on:

    - his ability to meet customer demands;

    - quality; or

    - performance;

- he is unable to reorganise the work amongst other staff;

- he is unable to recruit additional staff; or

- there is an insufficiency of work during the period during which the employee proposes to work.

The employer's decision regarding the employee's application must be given within 14 days after the meeting. The decision must be:

- in writing; and

- dated.

If the employer agrees to the contract change, the decision must also:

- specify the contract change agreed; and

- state the date from which the variation is to take effect.

If the employer's decision is not to allow the contract change, the decision must:

- state which of the above grounds apply to the refusal;

- contain a sufficient explanation of why the employer considers those grounds apply; and

- set out the appeal procedure.

f) Appeal against refusal of flexible working application

The employee is entitled to appeal against the employer's decision to refuse his application for a change in contract terms within 14 days after the date of the employer's decision.

The employee's appeal:

- must be in writing;

- must state the grounds of appeal; and

- must be dated.

Unless the employer decides to uphold the employee's appeal beforehand, there must be an appeal meeting within 14 days after the employee's notice of appeal.

The employer must notify the employee of his decision on the appeal within 14 days of the hearing.

The decision must be:

- in writing and dated.

If the employer upholds the appeal, the decision must also:

- specify the contract change agreed; and

- state the date from which the variation is to take effect.

If the employer dismisses the appeal, the decision must:

- state the grounds for that decision; and

- contain a sufficient explanation of why the employer considers that those grounds apply.

g) Withdrawal of flexible working application

An employer must treat an employee's application as withdrawn if the employee has:

- notified him orally or in writing that he is withdrawing his application;

- failed to attend either the initial meeting or the appeal meeting on more than one occasion without reasonable cause; or

- without reasonable cause refused to provide the employer with information the employer requires to assess whether the contract variation should be agreed to.

If the employee has withdrawn his application orally, the employer must confirm that withdrawal to the employee in writing.

h) Application to an employment tribunal

- An employee can bring a complaint to an employment tribunal within three months of the employer's refusal to grant his request for flexible working. In such cases the tribunal may order the employer to reconsider a flexible working application and may make an award up to a maximum of eight weeks' pay.

- An employee can also complain if the employer fails to allow him to be accompanied at any of the meetings or refuses to fix an alternative meeting date. The tribunal can award up to two weeks' pay in respect of any such refusal.

- As with most other provisions an employee may also present a claim to an employment tribunal if he suffers a detriment because of a flexible working application. Dismissal because of such an application is also made automatically unfair.

- Note that an alternative form of dispute resolution is provided by the ACAS (Flexible Working) Arbitration Scheme (Great Britain) Order 2004 (SI 2004 No 2333).

39.9 Paid time off for learning representatives

These have been put into the text under TULRA – **see 153.9g below**.

40 Employment Act (Disputes Resolution) Regulations 2004 (SI 2004 No 752)

The effect of these Regulations is dealt with in the text under the Employment Act 2002 on statutory disputes resolution procedures (**see 39.4 above**).

41 Employment Agencies Act 1973

Amended by Employment Protection Act 1975, Deregulation and Contracting Out Act 1994, Police Act 1997 and the Conduct of Employment Agencies and Employment Businesses Regulations 2003.

The Act lays down rules for running employment agencies and employment businesses. The former requirement for employment agencies to be licensed was removed by the Deregulation and Contracting Out Act 1994. The Conduct of Employment Agencies and Employment Businesses Regulations 2003 provide a number of protective measures for the benefit of those who use employment agencies, whether to find them work or to find them workers.

42 Employment Appeal Tribunal Rules 1993 (SI 1993 No 2854)

Amended by Employment Appeal Tribunal (Amendment) Rules 2001 (SI 2001 No 1128), Employment Appeal Tribunal (Amendment) Rules 2004 (SI 2004 No 2526) and by the Employment Appeal Tribunal Practice Direction (Employment Appeal Tribunal Procedure) 2004.

The Rules lay down the basic procedure for appeals, primarily from employment tribunals. The Employment Appeal Tribunal (Amendment) Rules 2001 provide for appeals from the CAC and deal with appeals affecting national security. The procedure under the rules is set out in the EAT Practice Direction.

43 Employment Appeal Tribunal (Amendment) Rules 2004 (SI 2004 No 2526)

Amend Employment Appeal Tribunal Rules 1993 (SI 1993 No 2854).

Took effect from 1 October 2004, the same date as the new Employment Tribunal Rules. The main changes to the rules are:

- drafting changes to reflect the changes in the terminology used for the parties to employment tribunal proceedings from 'applicant' and 'respondent' to 'claimant' and 'respondent';

- the introduction of the overriding objective into the rules;

- amendments to the rules regarding costs and expenses.

A new EAT Practice Direction was also issued in December 2004 which took immediate effect and which deals with the EAT procedure in more detail.

44 Employment (Continental Shelf) Act 1978

Amended by TULRA.

The Oil and Gas (Enterprise) Act 1982 contains provisions repealing the following extensions of the sex and race discrimination legislation. An Order will have to be made under the 1982 Act to give effect to these repeals.

The Act extends the rights under the SDA and RRA to those working on 'cross-boundary' oil fields in the North Sea. A 'cross-boundary' oil field is one that is partly inside and partly outside United Kingdom territorial waters.

45 Employment Equality (Religion or Belief) Regulations 2003 (SI 2003 No 1660)

The Regulations provide that it is unlawful to discriminate directly or indirectly or to harass an employee on grounds of his religion or belief. The Regulations also provide that it is unlawful to victimise anyone for having done anything under or in relation to the Regulations.

- 'Religion or belief' is defined by the Regulations as including 'any religion, religious belief, or similar philosophical belief'.

- As with the sex and race discrimination legislation 'employment' includes those working under contracts of employment, apprenticeship or contracts for personal work. The protection of the Regulations is also extended to contract workers and office holders.

- The 'occasions of discrimination' are the same as in relation to sex and race discrimination and include prohibitions against: pre-employment discrimination, offering less favourable terms, not offering training, promotion or other benefits, dismissing the individual or subjecting him to some other detriment.

45.1 Genuine occupational qualification (GOQ)

Where the nature and the context in which the employment is carried requires that the employee to be of a particular religion, provided it is proportionate to apply this requirement in the particular case, the employer may refuse to take on someone who is not of the relevant religion.

■ Being of a particular religion or belief can also be a genuine occupational qualification where the employer has an ethos based on religion or belief. In such cases regard must be had not only to that ethos but also to the nature of the job and context in which it is carried out, as well as to the requirement of proportionality to determine whether being of a particular religion or belief is a GOQ in any particular case.

46 Employment Equality (Sexual Orientation) Regulations 2003 (SI 2003 No 1661)

The Regulations provide that it is unlawful to discriminate directly or indirectly or to harass an employee on grounds of a person's sexual orientation. The Regulations also provide that it is unlawful to victimise anyone for having done anything under or in relation to the Regulations.

■ As with the sex and race discrimination legislation 'employee' is defined to include those in employment or on an apprenticeship and those under a contract for personal work. The protection of the Regulations is also extended to contract workers and office holders.

■ The 'occasions of discrimination' are the same as in relation to the sex and race discrimination provisions and include prohibitions against: pre-employment discrimination, offering less favourable terms, not offering training, promotion or other benefits, dismissing the individual or subjecting him to some other detriment.

46.1 Genuine occupational qualification (GOQ)

The only genuine occupational qualification that is relevant in this case is where the nature and the context in which the employment is carried out requires the employee to be of a particular sexual orientation and the requirement is proportionate.

47 Employment Medical Advisory Services Act 1972

Amends Factories Act 1961.

The Act sets up the Employment Medical Advisory Service (EMAS). Allows an EMAS medical adviser to serve notice on a factory occupier requiring the occupier to allow for medical examination of employees in factories where the medical adviser is of the opinion that an employee's health has been, is being or may be, injured by reason of the work he is being, or may be, called upon to do. Provides for EMAS medical advisers to take over medical examinations required by the Factories Act 1961. Payment for these services is made to the Secretary of State.

48 Employment of Women, Young Persons and Children Act 1920

Amended by Employment of Women, Young Persons and Children Act 1936 and Employment Act 1989.
The Act restricts the employment of children in industrial undertakings.

49 Employment Protection (Continuity of Employment) Regulations 1996 (SI 1996 No 3147)

Amended by Employment Protection (Continuity of Employment) (Amendment) Regulations 2001 (SI 2001 No 1188).

The Regulations provide for an employee to be treated as having continuous service where he is re-engaged after having made an unfair dismissal claim under ERA, SDA, RRA or DDA, or where the re-engagement follows action having been taken by an ACAS conciliation officer or a compromise agreement having been reached. The Regulations also apply where the employee has made a claim under a designated disputes procedure under the ERA. The Employment Protection (Continuity of Employment) (Amendment) Regulations 2001 (SI 2001 No 1188) extend the circumstances in which an employee's employment is to be counted as being continuous to include re-engagement following an ACAS arbitration. (For ACAS arbitration see ACAS Arbitration Scheme (Great Britain) Order (SI 2004 No 753) – **1 above**.) If an employee is reinstated, there is no need for any statutory protection for his or her continuity of employment: the effect of reinstatement is to treat employment as if it had never been terminated.

50 Employment Protection (Continuity of Employment) (Amendment) Regulations 2001 (SI 2001 No 1188)

Amend Employment Protection (Continuity of Employment) Regulations 1996 (SI 1996 No 3147) – **see 49 above**.

51 Employment Relations Act 1999

Amends Employment Agencies Act 1973, SDA, SDA, TULRA, TURERA, Disability Discrimination Act 1995, ERA, Employment Tribunals Act 1996, Employment Rights (Dispute Resolution) Act 1998, National Minimum Wage Act 1998, Public Interest Disclosure Act 1998.

Much of this Act consists of 'enabling legislation' which simply allows for the Secretary of State to make Regulations to make law in a particular areas; this, for example, is the case with family and domestic leave. Even where the Regulations are not to create the law, they are still required to give effect to the provisions of the Act.

51.1 Trade union matters

The right not to be subjected to a detriment on grounds of trade union activities or membership is redefined – **see 153.9c**.

51.2 Certification Officer

The duties of the Certification Officer are considerably extended by the Act.

- The posts of Commissioner for the Rights of Trade Union Members and Commissioner for Protection Against Unlawful Industrial Action are abolished.

- The duties of the Certification Officer are widened to encompass some of the functions of the Commissioner for the Rights of Trade Union Members.

51.3 Changes in unfair dismissal awards

- The maximum compensatory award for unfair dismissal is raised to £50,000 and annual increases are index-linked.

- The upper limit for unfair dismissal compensation does not apply where the dismissal is for a health and safety reason or because of a protected disclosure.

- The maximum amount of a 'week's pay' for calculation of an employee's basic award for unfair dismissal and redundancy payment entitlement, the maximum daily amount of a guarantee payment and the new upper limit for the unfair dismissal compensatory award are all index-linked from December 1999.

51.4 National Minimum Wage for those in religious communities

From 25 October 1999 those who are members of residential religious communities are excluded from the right to receive the National Minimum Wage.

51.5 Time off to care for dependants

A new provision is introduced as s 57A ERA, with effect from 15 December 1999, which allows employees reasonable time off during working hours to take care of, or to arrange for care to be taken for dependants of theirs.

Time off may be taken to effect any action necessary:

- to provide assistance when a dependant falls ill, gives birth, is injured or assaulted;

- to make arrangements for care to be provided for a dependant who is ill or injured;

- as a consequence of the death of a dependant; or

- to deal with an incident involving a child of the employee during the school term.

To be entitled to take time off under this provision, the employee must tell his employer:

- the reason for any absence as soon as is reasonably practicable; and

- how long the absence is expected to last (this does not apply where the employee is unable to tell his employer the reason for his absence prior to returning to work).

A 'dependant' for these purposes is:

- a spouse;

- a child;

- a parent;

- a person who lives in the same household as the employee – other than as the employee's employee, tenant, lodger or boarder – unless that person reasonably relies on the employee to make arrangements for the provision of care for them.

A 'spouse or child' includes any person who reasonably relies on the employee:

- for assistance if that person is ill, injured or assaulted; or

- to make arrangements for the provision of care if they are ill or injured.

If the employer fails to allow reasonable time off, the employee can complain to an employment tribunal within three months of the employer's refusal and the employment tribunal may award the employee such compensation as it considers just and equitable in the circumstances having regard to the employer's default and to the losses sustained by the employee by reason of the employer's refusal to allow time off.

51.6 Part-time working

The Act provides for Regulations to be made to prevent employees being discriminated against on grounds of part-time working.

- The Part-Time Workers (Prevention of Less Favourable Treatment) Regulations 2000 (SI 2000 No 1551) give effect to these provisions (**see 102 below**).

- Section 20 ERelA 1999 allows for the Secretary of State to issue Codes of Practice.

- Such Codes of practice may be issued for the purposes of:

    - eliminating discrimination against part-time workers in employment;

    - facilitating opportunities for part-time work;

    - facilitating the development of opportunities for part-time work;

    - facilitating the flexible organisation of working time taking into account the needs of workers and employees; and

    - any matter dealt with in the framework agreement on part-time work annexed to Council Directive 97/81/EC.

- Failure to comply with any such Codes of practice will not make a person liable to any proceedings but, as other Codes of practice, any such failure may be taken into account as evidence by an employment tribunal.

- No Codes have been issued to date.

51.7 Maternity and Parental Leave

These provisions were largely left by the Act to be fleshed out by Regulations (see Maternity and Parental Leave etc Regulations 1999 – **95 below**).

51.8 Dismissal or redundancy for taking part in protected industrial action

These amendments have been put into the relevant part of the ERA and TULRA – **see 53 and 153 below**.

51.9 Collective bargaining recognition

These amendments have been put into the relevant part of the TULRA – **see 153 below**.

51.10 The right to be accompanied at disciplinary and grievance hearings

a) Definitions

These provisions were amended by the Employment Relations Act 2004. The amendments are included below.

A 'disciplinary hearing' is defined as a hearing which could result in:

- the administration of a formal warning to a worker;
- the employer's taking some other action in respect of the worker; or
- confirming either of the above.

A 'grievance hearing' is one which concerns the performance of a duty by an employer in relation to a worker.

b) The right

The right to be accompanied arises where a worker is invited to attend a disciplinary or grievance hearing and reasonably requests to be accompanied at the hearing.

Where this right applies the employee is entitled to choose one of the following as his companion:

- an employed official of a trade union;
- an official of a trade union whom the union has reasonably certified in writing as having experience of, or as having had training in, acting as a worker's companion at disciplinary or grievance hearings; or
- another of the employer's workers.

c) The role of the companion

The employer must permit the worker's companion to address the hearing for the following purposes:

- to put the worker's case;
- to sum up the worker's case;
- to respond on the worker's behalf to any view expressed at the hearing.

The companion must also be allowed to confer with the worker during the hearing.

But the employer is not required to permit the companion to:

- answer questions on behalf of the worker;
- address the hearing if the worker does not wish it; or
- use any of the above powers at the hearing in such a way as to prevent the employer from putting his case or preventing anyone else from contributing to the hearing.

d) Arrangements to attend the hearing

- Where the worker's companion is not available at the time set by the employer for the hearing, the hearing must be postponed to a later time provided:

- the time is reasonable; and

- the proposed date is within five working days (ie Monday to Friday – other than bank holidays).

- A worker who attends as another worker's companion is entitled to time off.

- If the companion is a trade union representative, this constitutes a trade union duty and he will be entitled to paid time off to accompany the worker.

e) Complaint to an employment tribunal

- A complaint may be brought to an employment tribunal within three months or, if that is not reasonably practicable, such longer period as the tribunal considers reasonable.

- The tribunal may award up to two weeks' pay for an employer's failure to allow the worker to be accompanied under these provisions. But if the tribunal makes a supplementary award under the statutory disputes resolution procedures in an unfair dismissal case, the tribunal cannot also make a separate award under this provision.

f) Protection from detriment or dismissal

A worker is entitled not to suffer any detriment or to be dismissed because he has sought to exercise his rights under these provisions or because he has accompanied or sought to accompany another worker at a hearing.

- Where a worker is dismissed for enforcing his rights of accompanying a fellow worker, the qualifying period for claiming dismissal and the upper age limit do not apply and the dismissal is to be regarded as automatically unfair.

52 Employment Relations Act 2004

Amends TULRA, Employment Relations Act 1999. The amendments have been inserted in the relevant Acts.

52.1 Information and consultation

The Act provides for information and consultation Regulations to be made by the Secretary of State for the purpose of providing rights for employees to be informed and consulted about prescribed matters. These are the Information and Consultation of Employees Regulations 2004 (SI 2004 No 3426) which took effect from 6 April 2005 – **see 86 below**.

52.2 Protection of employees in respect of jury service

a) Subjection to a detriment

An employee is entitled not to be subjected to a detriment on the grounds that:

- he has been summoned to act as a juror; or

- has been absent from work because he has acted as a juror.

An employee is not to be regarded as having suffered a detriment where he is not paid for any period of absence while away on jury duty unless he is contractually entitled to be paid for any such period.

b) Dismissal or redundancy by reason of jury service

An employee is to be treated as having been unfairly dismissed if the reason or principal reason for dismissal or selection for redundancy is that:

- he has been summoned to act as a juror; or

- has been absent from work because he has acted as a juror.

This protection does not apply, however, where

- the employee's absence for jury duty was likely to cause substantial injury to the employer's undertaking;

- the employer brought this to the employee's attention; and

- the employee unreasonably refused or failed to apply to an appropriate officer of the court to be excused from jury duty or for jury duty to be deferred.

53 Employment Rights Act 1996 (ERA)

Repeals and consolidates in part or in whole *inter alia*: Betting, Gaming and Lotteries Act 1963, SDA, EPCA, Education Act 1980, Employment Act 1980, Magistrates' Courts Act 1980, Finance Act 1980, New Towns Act 1981, Civil Aviation Act 1982, Oil and Gas Enterprise Act 1982, Social Security and Housing Benefits Act 1982, Employment Act 1982, Water Act 1983, Reserve Forces (Safeguard of Employment) Act 1985, Local Government Act 1985, Insolvency Act 1985, Housing (Consequential Provisions) Act 1986, Insolvency Act 1986, Wages Act 1986, Social Security Act 1986, Sex Discrimination Act 1986, Income and Corporation Taxes Act 1988, Norfolk and Suffolk Broads Act 1988, Legal Aid Act 1988, Education Reform Act 1988, Housing Act 1988, Dock Work Act 1989, Water Act 1989, Electricity Act 1989, Employment Act 1989, National Health Service and Community Care Act 1990, Employment Act 1990, Environmental Protection Act 1990, Social Security (Consequential Provisions) Act 1992, Further and Higher Education Act 1992, TULRA, TURERA, Pension Schemes Act 1993, Race Relations (Remedies) Act 1994, Social Security (Incapacity for Work) Act 1994, Sunday Trading Act 1994, Deregulation and Contracting Out Act 1994, Health Authorities Act 1995, Environment Act 1995, Pensions Act 1995, Disability Discrimination Act 1995, Reserve Forces Act 1996, Time Off for Public Duties Order 1990 (SI 1990 No 1870), Sex Discrimination and Equal Pay (Remedies) Regulations 1993 (SI 1993 No 2798), Employment Protection (Part-time Employees) Regulations 1995 (SI 1995 No 31), Time Off for Public Duties Order 1995 (SI 1995 No 694), Collective Redundancies and Transfer of Undertakings (Protection of Employment) (Amendment) Regulations 1995 (SI 1995 No 2587), Environment Act 1995 (Consequential Amendments) Regulations 1996 (SI 1996 No 593), Environment Act 1995 (Consequential and Transitional Provisions) (Scotland) Regulations 1996 (SI 1996 No 973).

Amended by Police Act 1997, Police (Health and Safety) Act 1997, Employment Rights (Disputes Resolutions) Act 1998, National Minimum Wage Act 1998, Public Interest Disclosure Act 1998, Teaching and Higher Education Act 1998, Working Time Regulations 1998, Collective Redundancies and Transfer of Undertakings (Protection of Employment)(Amendment) Regulations 1999, Unfair Dismissal and Statement of Reasons for Dismissal (Variation of Qualifying Period) Order 1999, Maternity and Parental

Leave Regulations 1999 (SI 1999 No 3312), Employment Act 2000, Employment Act 2002 and Sunday Working (Scotland) Act 2003.

53.1 Statement of terms and conditions of employment

Originally ss 1 to 7 EPCA (and s 11 re enforcement) as amended by TURERA. Now ss 1–6 ERA (and ss 11 and 12 re enforcement).

a) The right

   (i) An employee is entitled to be given a written statement of the main terms and conditions of employment within two months of beginning employment (the reduction from three months within which to give the statement to two months was brought about by TURERA). If the employee is going to be sent abroad for a period of more than a month within this initial two-month period, the statement must be given before he leaves. The employee is entitled to a statement of terms and conditions if his employment is terminated after he has been employed for more than one but less than two months.

   (ii) Certain of the terms must be included in a single document (these are asterisked in the list in b) below). The facility, allowed by the EPCA, to refer to other documents for these terms was severely curtailed by TURERA.

   (iii) If there are no particulars to be entered under any particular head in the particulars set out in b) below, this fact must be specified.

   (iv) The Employment Act 2002 provides that a contract given to the employee which contains the information required to be given under this provision and/or under the requirement to give details of the employer's rules, disciplinary, dismissal, grievance procedures and a note regarding pensions is to be taken as fulfilling this requirement.

b) Particulars to be specified

   (i) the names of the employer and employee*

   (ii) the date when the employment began*

   (iii) the date on which the employee's period of continuous employment began (taking into account any employment with a previous employer which counts towards that period)*

   (iv) the scale or rate of remuneration or the method of calculating remuneration*

   (v) intervals at which remuneration is paid (ie weekly, monthly or other specified intervals)*

   (vi) any terms and conditions relating to hours of work (including any terms and conditions relating to normal working hours)*

   (vii) any terms and conditions relating to

- entitlement to holidays, public holidays and holiday pay (the particulars must be sufficient to enable the employee's entitlement, including entitlement to accrued holiday pay on termination of employment, to be calculated)*

- incapacity for work due to sickness or injury, including any sick pay; and

- pensions and pension schemes (the requirement to notify this item is excluded in relation to certain pension schemes set up by statute).

(viii) the length of notice required from each party to terminate the employee's employment

(ix) job title or a brief description of the employee's work* (amended by TURERA – previously only job title was allowed)

(x) where the employment is not intended to be permanent, the period for which it is expected to continue or, if it is for a fixed term, the date when it is to end (amended by TURERA – previously there was no reference to the period for which a temporary job was expected to last). It should be noted that where the employment is for less than one month there is no entitlement to a s 1 statement (this was reduced from three months by TURERA)

(xi) the place of work or, if the employee is required or permitted to work at various places, an indication of that fact and of the employer's address* (introduced by TURERA)

(xii) any collective agreements which directly affect the terms and conditions of the employment including, where the employer was not a party, the persons by whom they were made (introduced by TURERA)

(xiii) where the employee is required to work outside the UK for more than one month

- the period for which he is to work outside the United Kingdom
- the currency in which his remuneration will be paid while working outside the UK
- any additional remuneration payable/benefits to be provided to or in respect of him, by reason of his being required to work outside the UK; and
- any terms and conditions relating to his return to the United Kingdom (introduced by TURERA).

c) Reference to other documents

(i) The section 1 statement may refer the employee for particulars to do with incapacity for work due to sickness or injury, including sick pay provisions, and for details of pensions and pension schemes to another document that is reasonably accessible to the employee.

(ii) The section 1 statement may refer to the law or to the provisions of any collective agreement directly affecting the employee's terms and conditions which is reasonably accessible to the employee, for the length of notice to be given by either party to terminate his employment.

This very limited facility to refer the employee to other documentation, brought in by TURERA, can be contrasted to the original provisions of the EPCA which allowed the employer to refer the employee to other documents for all the items which had to be notified to him under s 1.

d) Disciplinary, dismissal and grievance procedures and pensions

A section 1 statement must also include:

(i) in relation to discipline and grievance

- details of the disciplinary rules applicable to the employee (the employee can be referred to another document for this)

- the disciplinary, dismissal and grievance statutory disputes procedures are now the basic minimum procedural requirements in employment, and the Employment Act 2002 makes these a contractual minimum

- a note of any further steps available in the grievance or disciplinary procedures

- the erstwhile exclusion of the requirement for an employer who employs fewer than 20 employees to provide details of the disciplinary and grievance procedure was removed by Employment Act 2002

(ii) a note saying whether there is a contracting-out certificate (under the Pension Schemes Act 1993) in force.

e) Statement of changes

If there are changes in any items of which particulars are required to be given, the employer must give the employee a written statement containing particulars of the change at the earliest opportunity, and in any event not later than one month after the change in question (or before the employee goes abroad if he is leaving to work outside the UK for more than a month before the statement of changes would otherwise be due).

Where the employer changes its name or there is a change of employer which does not affect the employee's continuity of employment, that change can be noted in a statement of change rather than supplying a new statement. If a statement of change is given where there is a change of employer, that statement must also give the employee's original continuity date.

f) Enforcement

(i) If the employer does not give an employee a section 1 statement or a statement of changes of particulars of employment, or gives an incomplete statement, the employee can ask a tribunal to determine what particulars ought to have been included in the statement.

(ii) If there is a question regarding the accuracy of the terms in a section 1 statement or in a statement of changes of particulars of employment, either the employer or the employee can refer the matter to a tribunal. The tribunal can confirm or amend the particulars that have been given or substitute other particulars.

(iii) A claim can be brought at any time up to three months after the employment to which the question relates has finished or, if that is not reasonably practicable, within such further period as is reasonably practicable. (The 'not reasonably practicable' escape clause was inserted by TURERA.)

(iv) Where, at the time a claim is brought against an employer other than for failure to provide a section 1 statement, the employer is in breach of any of the notification requirements, a new remedy is provided for by the Employment Act 2002. Under this provision if the tribunal makes no award against the employer in relation to the specific case brought, it must make an award of two weeks' pay to the employee and may make an award of up to a total of four weeks' pay.

53.2 Itemised pay statement

Originally ss 8 to 10 EPCA (and s 11 re enforcement) as amended by TURERA. Now ss 8 to 10 ERA (and ss 11 and 12 re enforcement).

a) The right

An employee is entitled to be given a written itemised pay statement. This must be given either before or at the time he is to be paid and must contain the following information:

(i)   gross pay;

(ii)   the amounts of any deductions and the reasons why they have been made (where there are fixed deductions which are made from the employee's pay, a separate statement of these can be given to the employee in advance and the global amount of the fixed deductions is then noted on individual pay statements);

(iii) net pay; and

(iv)   if different parts of the net amount are paid in different ways, the amount and method of payment of each bit.

b) Enforcement

(i)   If the employee is not given an itemised pay statement or if the statement is incomplete, the employee can refer the matter to a tribunal and the tribunal can decide what particulars ought to have been included in the statement.

(ii)   Where a question arises as to the accuracy of an itemised pay statement or a statement of fixed deductions, either the employer or the employee can refer the matter to a tribunal. A tribunal cannot solely question the accuracy of an amount stated in the statement. In other words, the tribunal can look at the reasons for mistakes but not at the accuracy of the mathematics (although it can consider this under the Protection of wages provisions – **see 53.3 below**).

(iii) A claim can be brought at any time up to three months after the employee's employment finishes or, if that is not reasonably practicable, within such further period as is practical. (The 'not reasonably practicable' escape clause was inserted by TURERA.)

(iv)   If the employee was not given a pay statement or if a pay statement or statement of fixed deductions did not contain the particulars required, the tribunal can make a declaration to that effect and can require the employer to pay the employee a sum not exceeding the amount of all the unnotified deductions that the employer made from the employee's pay during the 13 weeks immediately preceding the date when the application to the tribunal was made.

53.3 Protection of wages – unlawful deductions/payments to employers

Originally contained in the Wages Act 1986. Now ss 13 to 27 ERA. These provisions apply to payments employees make to employers as well as to deductions *per se*.

a) The meaning of 'wages'

Wages are broadly any monetary sums paid by an employer payable by reference to the employee's employment other than items such as repayment of expenses. Both SSP and SMP are deemed to be 'wages' for these purposes.

b) The meaning of 'deduction'

(i) Definition: a 'deduction' is, broadly, any shortfall between the amount that an employee is entitled to receive, after any lawful deductions have been made, and the amount he actually receives.

(ii) Exclusions from the definition of 'deduction'

- errors of computation

- deductions in respect of overpayment of wages or expenses

- deductions made following any statutory disciplinary procedure

- any requirement on the employer to deduct monies that have been determined to be due to a public authority

- agreed deductions from an employee's wages for the benefit of a third party

- deductions made by the employer in respect of strike or other industrial action taken by an employee

- any amount that the employee has agreed to repay to the employer by deduction from his wages pursuant to a court or tribunal order.

It should be noted that the above items are not necessarily lawful deductions – they are simply excluded from consideration under these particular statutory provisions.

c) When deductions are allowable

For a deduction, which is caught by the Act, to be allowable it must satisfy one of the following criteria. It must either:

(i) be required or authorised by statute; or

(ii) be required or authorised by a provision of the worker's contract – which must have existed at the date when the matter giving rise to the deduction occurred; or

(iii) be a deduction to which the worker has previously signified his written agreement or consent. (Previous consent, in this context, means that consent must be given before the event which gives rise to the deduction being made rather than just pre-dating the deduction itself.)

d) Retail employment

Where an employee is in 'retail employment', no more than 10 per cent of his gross pay can be deducted from his wages on any pay day, in respect of cash shortages or stock losses. This limit is lifted in respect of wages paid for the employee's final period of employment – where there is no limit on the amount of any such deductions.

e) Bringing a claim

A claim for wrongful deduction may be brought to an employment tribunal within three months of the deduction complained of.

53.4 Guarantee payments

Originally ss 12–18 EPCA, now ss 28–35 ERA.

a) The right

(i) Where an employer is unable to provide an employee with work throughout the whole of a day when the employee would normally be working because of either:

■ a lack of work of the type which the employee is employed to do, or

■ any other occurrence affecting the work that the employee is employed to do,

the employee is entitled to a guarantee payment in respect of that day.

(NB Where the employee's work spans midnight, the day on which the employee must be 'workless' is the day in which the greater number of hours are normally worked. If the employee is employed for the same number of hours on both days, it is the second day that must be workless.)

(ii) The amount of a guarantee payment is the employee's daily rate of pay subject to a statutory maximum, which is updated from time to time and is currently £18.40 per day. Any contractual pay which the employee is entitled to receive in respect of the same day goes towards discharging the employer's liability to pay a guarantee payment for that day and vice versa.

(iii) The maximum number of days for which guarantee payments can be made in any three-month period is the same as the number of days per week (not exceeding five) which the employee normally works.

b) Exclusions from the right to guarantee payments

(i) employees who have not had at least one month's continuous service

(ii) employees employed:

■ under fixed-term contracts for less than three months; or

■ to do a specific task that is not expected to take more than three months unless they have been employed for three months

(iii) if the failure to provide work is because of a strike or lock-out

(iv) if the employee unreasonably refuses suitable alternative employment on the day in question; or if he fails to comply with his employer's reasonable requirements to ensure that his services are available on the day in question

(v) where there is an exemption order, approved by the Secretary of State, in force in respect of the employee.

c) Enforcement

A complaint regarding an employer's failure to pay all or part of an employee's guarantee payment entitlement can be presented to a tribunal within three months of the employer's failure or, where that is not reasonably practicable, within such further time as is reasonably practicable.

53.5 Sunday working

When Sunday betting was legalised by the Deregulation and Contracting Out Act 1994, statutory protection similar to that in Schedule 4 of the Sunday Trading Act 1994, which covered shop workers, was enacted for betting workers by the Deregulation and Contracting Out Act 1994. This Act inserted a new Sch 5A into the Betting, Gaming and Lotteries Act 1963. The Sunday working provisions are now contained in ss 36 to 43, 45, 101, 104, 105(a), 108 and 197(2) ERA.

a) Who is covered?

  (i) These provisions originally applied only to those who work in England and Wales. They were extended to include those working in Scotland by the Sunday Working (Scotland) Act 2003.

  (ii) A 'betting worker' is a worker in England or Wales who can be required to do work either:

- for a bookmaker at a track which includes dealing with betting transactions; or

- in a licensed betting office on a day on which the office is open for betting transactions.

  (iii) A 'shop worker' is one who can be required to work in or about a shop on a day when the shop is open for serving customers.

b) 'Protected shop/betting worker'

  (i) A 'protected shop/betting worker' is either:

- one who was employed as a shop worker on 26 August 1994 or as a betting worker on 5 January 1995 (the commencement dates of the relevant provisions of the Sunday Trading Act 1994 and the Deregulation and Contracting Out Act 1994), but not to work only on Sundays, and has throughout his service from that date, until the date at which any particular right falls to be determined, continued to be a shop/betting worker; or

- one who cannot be required under his contract of employment to work on Sundays (independently of any right to refuse to work on Sundays he may have under the Act).

  (ii) While the employee remains a protected shop worker, however, the employer is entitled not to pay the employee for Sunday work. If there is no specific amount which is referable to the employee's Sunday work, the employer is entitled to reduce the employee's remuneration by the proportion of the week that the employee loses by no longer working on Sundays. If the work is made up during the remainder of the week, there will be no loss to the employee in such cases, but employers are entitled to reduce the protected employee's weekly hours by the number of hours that he normally worked on a Sunday.

  (iii) A protected employee can be required to work on Sundays only if he has opted in to working on Sundays.

c) Opting in

(i)   A shop/betting worker is not a protected worker if

- he has given his employer an opting-in notice on or after the commencement date of the relevant statute; and

- after giving the notice, he has expressly agreed with his employer to do shop work, or betting work, on Sunday or on a particular Sunday.

(ii) An 'opting-in notice' is a written notice, signed and dated by the shop/betting worker, in which the worker expressly states that he wishes to work on Sunday or that he does not object to Sunday working.

d)   Opting out

(i)   Any shop/betting worker who is not employed purely to work on Sundays, but who, under his contract, may be required to work on Sundays, is entitled to give his employer an opting-out notice. This is so even if the employee opted in to Sunday work.

(ii) An opting-out notice is a written notice, signed and dated by the employee, saying that the employee objects to Sunday working.

(iii) A shop/betting worker who is entitled to opt out of Sunday working must be given a notice in the following statutory form by his employer:

STATUTORY RIGHTS IN RELATION TO
SUNDAY [*SHOP/BETTING*] WORK

[*You have become employed as a shop worker and are or can be required under your contract of employment to do the Sunday work your contract provides for.*]

[*You have become employed under a contract of employment under which you are or can be required to do Sunday betting work, that is to say, work*

at a track on a Sunday on which your employer is taking bets at the track, or

in a licensed betting office on a Sunday on which it is open for business.]

However, if you wish, you can give notice, as described in the next paragraph, to your employer and you will then have the right not to [*work in or about a shop on any Sunday on which the shop is open*] [*do Sunday betting work on any Sunday*] once three months have passed from the date on which you gave notice.

Your notice must

be in writing;

be signed and dated by you;

say that you object to [*Sunday working*]

[*doing Sunday betting work*].

For three months after you give the notice, your employer can still require you to do all the Sunday work your contract provides for. After the three-month period has ended, you have the right to complain to an employment tribunal if, because of your refusal to [*work on Sundays on which the shop is open*] [*do Sunday betting work*], your employer

dismisses you, or

does something else detrimental to you, for example, failing to promote you.

Once you have the rights described, you can surrender them only by giving your employer a further notice, signed and dated by you, saying that you wish to [*work on Sunday*] [*do Sunday betting work*] or that you do not object to [*Sunday working*] [*doing Sunday betting work*] and then agreeing with your employer to [*work on Sundays*] [*do such work on Sundays*] or on a particular Sunday.

(iv) The above statement must be given to the employee within two months of the employee's becoming an eligible shop/betting worker. If the employer fails to provide the statutory statement within two months, the three months' notice period during which the employee can normally be required to continue to work on Sundays is reduced to one month. This does not apply if the employee gives an opting-out notice before the two-month period for giving the statement expires.

(v) An employee who opts out of Sunday working can still be required to work on Sundays during the three months' (or one month's – **see iv above**) statutory notice period before his opt-out takes effect.

(vi) Where an employee has opted out of Sunday work, he can still opt back in again, but unless he does, any contractual requirement for Sunday work becomes unenforceable after the end of the notice period.

e) The rights

(i) Dismissal for refusal to work on Sunday

A protected or opted-out shop/betting worker is to be regarded as having been unfairly dismissed if the principal reason for dismissal is that he:

- refused, or proposed to refuse, to work on Sundays or a particular Sunday (provided that the Sunday in question is not during the notice period after the opting-out certificate has been given, but before it takes effect); or

- gave, or proposed to give, an opting-out notice to the employer.

There is no minimum qualifying period of employment before the employee is entitled to bring such cases.

(ii) Selection for redundancy for refusal to work on Sunday

A protected or opted-out shop/betting worker is to be regarded as having been unfairly dismissed if:

- the principal reason for dismissal is redundancy

- there are others holding similar positions who have not been dismissed; and

- the principal reason for his selection for dismissal was that he

  - refused, or proposed to refuse, to work on Sundays or a particular Sunday (provided that the Sunday in question is not during the notice period after the opting-out certificate has been given, but before it takes effect); or

- gave, or proposed to give, an opting-out notice to the employer.

There is no minimum qualifying period of employment before the employee is entitled to bring such cases.

(iii) The right not to be subjected to a detriment for refusal to work on Sunday

A protected or opted-out shop/betting worker has the right not to be subjected to any detriment by his employer because the employee:

- refused, or proposed to refuse, to work on Sundays or on a particular Sunday (other than a Sunday during the notice period after an opting-out certificate has been given to an employer, but before it takes effect); or

- gave, or proposed to give, an opting-out notice to the employer.

These provisions do not apply where the detriment in question is the employee's dismissal, where the employee will have to claim unfair dismissal rather than a detriment. A detriment for these purposes includes any act, or deliberate failure to act, by the employer.

None of the following can amount to a detriment for these purposes:

- failure to pay the employee or to provide benefits in respect of Sunday work he has not done

- failure to provide the employee with work where the employer is statutorily allowed not to provide work (where a protected worker was obliged to work on Sunday but now does not, the employer is not obliged to provide alternative work or remuneration in lieu)

- the employer can offer to pay other protected or opted-out employees a premium for working on Sunday without either the failure to pay or the failure to offer the work being a detriment to anyone who is not made this offer

- the employer can offer to pay a protected or opted-out employee a premium for working on Sunday without either the failure to pay or the failure to offer being a detriment to anyone who refuses the offer.

Where an action continues over a period, it is the beginning of that period which is relevant for deciding when that action occurred.

A deliberate failure to act is treated as having been done when it was either decided on or when the employer does an act inconsistent with the act he has failed to do.

(iv) Dismissal for asserting a statutory right

If an employee is dismissed for having brought a claim against the employer under these provisions, then, provided:

- that the claim was brought in good faith, regardless of the merits of the claim, and

- that the employee made it clear in general terms what he was claiming,

the dismissal will be considered to be unfair.

53.6 Protection for health and safety representatives, trustees of pension schemes and employee representatives

a) Health and safety representatives

Protection for health and safety representatives was originally introduced by Sch 5 of TURERA to comply with the employment protection aspects of the Health and Safety European 'Framework Directive' (Directive 89/391/EEC). These rights were introduced by way of amendments to the EPCA mainly in ss 22A to C, 57A and 59 – now ss 44, 48, 49, 100, 105, 108, 109 ERA and 117, 120, 125, 128, 130 and 132 ERA re remedies. These provisions were amended by the Health and Safety (Consultation with Employees) Regulations 1996 (SI 1996 No 1513).

(i)   To whom and in what circumstances is protection afforded?

- Anyone designated by the employer to do anything connected with reducing or preventing health and safety risks, where the action taken by the employer is because they did anything to reduce or prevent a risk, or proposed to.

- Health and safety representatives and members of Safety Committees, who are either designated as such or who are acknowledged as such by the employer (under the Safety Representatives and Safety Committees Regulations 1977 [SRSCR] (SI 1977 No 500)) and representatives of employee safety appointed under the Health and Safety (Consultation with Employees) Regulations (HSCER) 1996 (SI 1996 No 1513). Health and safety representatives and members of safety committees can be appointed, under SRSCR, where trade unions are recognised by the employer. Representatives of employee safety can be appointed under HSCER where no union is recognised.

- An employee who has action taken against him because he has brought something which he reasonably believes to be harmful or potentially harmful to health and safety to his employer's attention.

  An action in this type of case is available only where there are either no health and safety representatives or safety committees, or where it is not reasonably practicable for the employee to raise the matter through a safety representative or committee.

- An employee who has action taken against him because he left or proposed to leave, or refused to return to his place of work, or a dangerous part of it, because he reasonably believed there to be a serious and imminent danger which he could not have been expected to avert.

- An employee who has action taken against him because he took, or proposed to take, appropriate steps to protect himself or others in circumstances of danger which he reasonably believed to be serious and imminent.

  In judging whether the steps the employee took were appropriate all the circumstances of the case must be looked at, including the employee's knowledge and the facilities and advice available to the employee. The employee loses his protection under this provision if the employer is able to show that the steps that the employee took were so negligent that the employer's treatment of him was reasonable in the circumstances.

(ii)   Rights

■ Not to suffer a detriment by any deliberate act or inaction on the part of the employer.

Dismissal for any of the above reasons is automatically unfair, as is selection for redundancy for those reasons where there are others holding similar positions who have not been dismissed. There is no qualifying period for entitlement to claim unfair dismissal, nor is there an upper age cut-off for entitlement to claim.

(iii) Remedies

A complaint must be brought within three months of the action complained of.

Detriment

■ It is for the employer to show the reason for any action or failure to act.

■ If the tribunal is satisfied that the employee has been treated detrimentally, the tribunal will make a declaration to that effect and award such compensation as is just and equitable.

Dismissal

Where the employee has been designated by the employer to look after health and safety matters, is a health and safety representative or is a member of a safety committee, then:

■ as in the case of whistleblowers, there is no upper limit to the compensation that can be awarded in health and safety cases

b) Trustees of occupational pension schemes

The rights and protection for trustees of occupational pension schemes were originally introduced by ss 42 to 46 of the Pensions Act 1995. These rights were introduced by way of amendments to the EPCA mainly in ss 22A to C, 31A, 57, 57A, 59, 64, 71(2A and B), 72, 73, 75A and 77 to 79. These provisions are now ss 44, 48, 49, 58 to 60, 98(6), 100, 105, 108, 109, 117 to 122, 125, 128, 130 and 132 ERA.

(i)   The right not to suffer a detriment or to be dismissed

Employee trustees of occupational pension schemes related to their employment are entitled not to have any detrimental action taken against them by their employer (including any deliberate inaction), because they performed or proposed to perform any duties as trustees.

The dismissal of employee trustees of occupational pension schemes or their selection for redundancy on those grounds (where there are others holding similar positions who have not been dismissed) will be automatically unfair and will attract special basic and compensatory awards (see under Health and safety representatives **53.6a above**). There is no qualifying period for entitlement to claim unfair dismissal on these grounds.

The general pattern of this protection is similar to the protection afforded in the case of health and safety representatives (**see 53.6a above**)

(ii)   The right to time off for occupational pension scheme trustees

Employee occupational pension scheme trustees are entitled to be permitted reasonable paid time off:

- to carry out their duties as trustees; or

- for training relevant to their duties as trustees.

The employee is entitled to be paid for time off under this provision as if he had been at work normally.

The employee can complain to an employment tribunal if he is either refused time off or is not paid, or paid fully, for it.

c) Employee representatives

The Collective Redundancies and Transfers of Undertaking (Protection of Employment) Regulations 1995 (SI 1995 No 2587) introduced a new concept of elected 'employee representatives' whom the employer must consult on collective redundancies (see TULRA) and proposed transfers of undertakings (see TUPE) where no trade union is recognised. The regulations originally added protection for employee representatives into the EPCA by adding ss 22AA, 31AA and 57AA and making various amendments to other parts of the EPCA. These changes have now become ss 47, 61 to 63, 103, 105(6) ERA.

(i) The right not to suffer a detriment or to be dismissed

An employee representative, or someone who is a candidate to become an employee representative, is entitled not to suffer a detriment because of anything that is done by him in carrying out his duties in respect of consultation with the employer either under TULRA or TUPE or as a candidate for election as an employee representative.

The dismissal of employee representatives or their selection for redundancy on those grounds (where there are others holding similar positions who have not been dismissed) will be automatically unfair and will attract special basic and compensatory awards. There is no qualifying period for entitlement to claim unfair dismissal on these grounds.

The general pattern of this protection is similar to the protection afforded in the case of health and safety representatives (**see 53.6a above**).

(ii) The right to time off

Employee representatives and candidates for election as employee representatives are entitled to be permitted reasonable paid time off:

- to carry out their duties as employee representatives; or

- in connection with their candidacy.

The employee can complain to an employment tribunal if he is either refused time off or is not paid, or paid fully, for it.

53.7 Time off for public duties

Originally s 29 EPCA (and s 30 re enforcement). Now ss 50 ERA (and s 51 re enforcement).

a) JPs are entitled to time off to perform any of the duties of their office.

b) Members of

- local authorities

- statutory tribunals

- police authorities including the Service Authority for National Criminal Intelligence Service and the Service Authority for the Crime Squad (this extended meaning of 'police authority' was brought in by the Police Act 1997)

- boards of prison visitors or prison visiting committees

- certain health bodies

- certain education bodies

- the Environment Agency or the Scottish Environment Protection Agency

are allowed to have time off to attend meetings of the body (including committees and sub-committees) and to do anything else for the purpose of discharging the functions of the body in question or its committees.

c) The amount of time that an employee is allowed is what is reasonable, and depends *inter alia* on:

- the amount of time off that an employee has for trade union activities and duties;

- the amount of time off required for the public duties in question; and

- the needs of the employer's business.

d) Time off under this provision is unpaid.

53.8 Suspension on medical grounds

Originally ss 19 to 22 EPCA. Now ss 64, 65 and 69 ERA (and s 70 re enforcement).

a) Who is entitled

An employee who is suspended because of a requirement imposed by

(i) Control of Lead at Work Regulations 2002;

(ii) Ionising Radiation Regulations 1999; or

(iii) Control of Substances Hazardous to Health Regulations 2002.

b) The rights

(i) The employee is entitled to be paid his normal remuneration for up to 26 weeks.

(ii) An employee who is dismissed because of a requirement to suspend him on medical grounds can claim unfair dismissal if he had one month's continuous service before the date of dismissal.

(iii) Where an employer dismisses a replacement who has been hired to cover for such an employee, then provided

- that the employer informed the replacement in writing that he was being hired to cover for someone on medical suspension and would be dismissed when that person returned, and

- that the employer dismisses the replacement to take the suspended employee back,

the employer will be deemed to have a 'substantial' reason for dismissal. The employer will still have to satisfy the tribunal that he acted reasonably in dismissing the replacement in the circumstances.

c) Exclusions from the right to remuneration

The following are excluded from entitlement to remuneration while under medical suspension:

(i) those who have been continuously employed for less than one month before being suspended

(ii) those on a fixed-term contract of three months or less, provided they have not been employed for more than three months

(iii) those hired for a job that is expected to take three months or less, provided they have not been employed for more than three months

(iv) an employee who is sick

(v) an employee who unreasonably refuses to undertake suitable alternative employment

(vi) an employee who unreasonably refuses to comply with the employer's reasonable requirements for keeping his services available.

53.9 Rights connected with pregnancy and maternity

a) Time off for ante-natal care

Introduced by the Employment Act 1980, originally adding a new s 31A to the EPCA. These provisions are now contained in ss 55 to 57 ERA.

(i) An employee who is pregnant and who has made an appointment to attend for ante-natal care on the advice of a medical practitioner, midwife or health visitor, is entitled to take paid time off during working hours to keep the appointment.

(ii) Except for the first ante-natal appointment, the employee must show the employer, if he asks for it:

- a certificate from a medical practitioner, midwife or health visitor to say that she is pregnant; and

- an appointment card or document showing that an ante-natal appointment has been made.

(iii) An employee can complain to an employment tribunal

- that she has unreasonably been refused time off; or

- that her employer has refused to pay her fully or at all for the time she has taken off for ante-natal care.

(iv) If a tribunal finds that a woman has been unreasonably refused time off, then, as well as declaring that to be the case, it must also award the woman the remuneration that the employer would have paid her if she had not been refused the time off.

b) Suspension on maternity grounds

The right to payment on suspension on maternity grounds was added to the EPCA by TURERA as ss 45 to 47 EPCA The provisions are now contained in ss 66 to 70 ERA.

(i) An employee is suspended on maternity grounds if she is suspended pursuant to an Order specified under s 66(2) ERA on the ground that she is pregnant, has recently given birth or is breast-feeding a child. Currently there is one Order made under this provision – Suspension From Work (On Maternity Grounds) Order 1994 (SI 1994 No 2930) – which in turn refers to a list of reasons for suspension under this heading. The reasons for suspension are contained in Management of Health and Safety at Work Regulations 1999 and in Annexes 1 and 2 of EC Directive 92/85/EEC, the Pregnant Workers Directive.

(ii) As an alternative to suspension, the employee has a right to be offered any alternative employment that the employer has available. For alternative employment to be 'suitable' for these purposes it must be

- suitable in relation to the employee;

- appropriate for her to do in the circumstances; and

- on terms and conditions not substantially less favourable than her existing terms and conditions.

(iii) An employee is entitled to be paid while she is suspended on maternity grounds. Any contractual payment made by the employer goes towards discharging the employer's liability to pay the woman while on suspension so that if the employee does any work for the employer, the remuneration due to her on suspension will 'top up' her pay to the extent that it is less than her normal 'week's pay'.

(iv) It should be noted that if an employee is dismissed in circumstances where she ought to be suspended under these provisions, she will be able to claim that her dismissal is automatically unfair. It will also be automatically unfair to select a woman for redundancy because of her entitlement to be suspended because of pregnancy where there are others holding similar positions who have not been dismissed.

c) Maternity leave and Parental leave

The right to maternity leave was restated in amended form by the Maternity and Parental Leave Regulations 1999 (SI 1999 No 3312) amended by the Maternity and Parental Leave Regulations (Amendment) Regulations 2002 (SI 2002 No 2789). These Regulations also introduced the right to parental leave. Current maternity and parental leave rights are dealt with under the Maternity and Parental Leave Regulations 1999 – **see 95 below**.

d) Dismissal of a temporary replacement

This right, as amended by TURERA and the Employment Act 2002, is now contained in s 106 ERA. Where a temporary replacement is engaged to do the work of an employee who is:

- suspended on maternity grounds; or

   ■ absent because of pregnancy or confinement or on adoption leave

then, provided:

   ■ that the replacement is informed of this fact when she or he takes the job on, and

   ■ that the replacement is dismissed to allow for the woman to return to work,

the employer will be seen to have a substantial reason for dismissing the employee in relation to unfair dismissal legislation. The employer will still have to show, of course, that he acted fairly in treating that reason as a sufficient reason for dismissal.

e) The right not to be dismissed for family leave

A limited right in the EPCA, making dismissal for pregnancy automatically unfair in certain circumstances, was amended by TURERA and later substituted by EReIA 1999 and again amended by Employment Act 2002 to create this general protection for employees who take family leave. This extended right is contained in s 99 ERA.

An employee is considered to be automatically unfairly dismissed if dismissed for any reason related to her pregnancy, maternity leave, parental leave, paternity leave or family leave.

f) The right to pay in lieu of notice while absent due to the pregnancy or maternity

Employees who are given notice when they are away from work due to pregnancy or confinement are entitled to be paid in lieu of notice provided that their notice entitlement is not over a week more than the statutory minimum notice entitlement.

Any sick pay, SSP, maternity pay, SMP or holiday pay goes towards discharging the employer's obligations as do state sickness benefits.

Where it was the employee who gave notice, the requirement for the employer to pay for the notice period in such cases only applies if the employee actually leaves the employer's employment.

g) The automatic right to written reasons for dismissal in pregnancy, maternity and adoption cases

This provision became s 53(2A) EPCA by an amendment made by TURERA and is now s 92(4) ERA.

An employee who is dismissed while pregnant or on adoption leave or in trying to exercise a right to return to work after such leave is entitled to be given written reasons for dismissal without asking for them.

53.10 Notice rights

Originally contained in ss 49 to 52 and Schedule 3 EPCA, Social Security and Housing Benefits Act 1982, Social Security (Incapacity for Work) Act 1994 and TURERA. These are now contained in ss 86 to 91 ERA.

a) General right

   (i) Employees who have been employed for more than four weeks and less than two years are entitled to a minimum of one week's notice to terminate their contracts of employment. After completing two years' continuous employment an employee is entitled to minimum of two weeks' notice with an extra week per completed year of service up to 12 weeks after 12 completed years of service.

(ii) Employees who have been employed for more than four weeks must give a minimum of one week's notice to terminate their contracts of employment.

b) The right to pay in lieu of notice

(i) An employee who gives or who is given notice and who

- is ready and willing to work, but is not given any work by his employer

- is incapable of work because of sickness or injury

- is absent from work wholly or partly because of pregnancy or childbirth, or

- is absent from work on holiday

is entitled to be paid in lieu of notice provided that his notice entitlement is not over a week more than the statutory minimum notice entitlement.

(ii) Any sick pay, SSP, maternity pay, SMP or holiday pay goes towards discharging the employer's obligations as do state sickness benefits. If the employee gives notice of termination of employment, the requirement for the employer to pay for the notice period in such cases applies only if the employee actually leaves the employer's employment.

(iii) The right to be paid in lieu of notice ceases if, and when, an employee is guilty of gross misconduct and could therefore be summarily dismissed, or if the employee takes part in a strike.

53.11 Written reasons for dismissal

Previously s 53 EPCA as extended by TURERA in respect of pregnant women and those dismissed on maternity leave – now s 92 ERA.

a) General right

(i) An employee who has been employed for not less than one year before being dismissed is entitled to request written reasons for dismissal. (The erstwhile requirement for two years' continuous employment was reduced to one year with effect from 1 June 1999 by Unfair Dismissal and Statement of Reasons for Dismissal (Variation of Qualifying Period) Order 1999 (SI 1999 No 1436).)

(ii) Where such a request is made, the employer must provide written reasons within 14 days of the request.

b) Pregnancy, childbirth and adoption

An employee who is pregnant when dismissed or whose maternity or adoption leave period ends by reason of dismissal is entitled to be provided with written reasons for dismissal automatically.

53.12 Unfair dismissal

Provisions concerning unfair dismissal are derived from: Betting Gaming and Lotteries Act 1963, EPCA, Employment Acts 1980, 1982 and 1989, Sex Discrimination Act 1986, TURERA, Sunday Trading Act 1994, Deregulation and Contracting Out Act 1994, TULRA, Collective Redundancies, Transfer of Undertakings

(Protection of Employment) (Amendment) Regulations 1995 (SI 1995 No 2587), Pensions Act 1995 and Employment Relations Act 1999 and Employment Act 2002. These rights are now contained in:

- ss 94 to 110 dealing with qualification to claim and the circumstances in which an unfair dismissal claim can be brought

- ss 111 to 134 dealing with bringing an unfair dismissal claim and remedies for unfair dismissal.

a) General right

(i)   Entitlement to claim

There is a general right for employees not to be unfairly dismissed. To be entitled to claim unfair dismissal the employee:

- must have more than one year's continuous service (the erstwhile requirement for two years' continuous employment was reduced to one year with effect from 1 June 1999 by Unfair Dismissal and Statement of Reasons for Dismissal (Variation of Qualifying Period) Order 1999 (SI 1999 No 1436))

- must be under 'normal retirement age' for an employee in that organisation or, there is no normal retirement age, under 65

- The requirement that employees must normally be employed to work in Great Britain was removed by the Employment Relations Act 1999 with effect from October 1999. The effect of this change, for those employed overseas, is still being litigated.

- must not be dismissed while taking part in industrial action

- must be 'dismissed'. A dismissal occurs where:

  - an employee is dismissed with or without notice

  - a fixed-term contract expires without being renewed on the same terms

  - an employee is 'constructively dismissed' – ie he is entitled to leave because the employer fundamentally breaches his contract of employment

  - an employee who is under notice gives counter-notice to the employer which expires earlier than the employer's original notice.

(ii)   The elements of unfair dismissal

Where there is an unfair dismissal claim it is for the employer to show the tribunal:

- the principal reason for dismissing the employee;

- that the reason for dismissal was one of the following:

  - related to the employee's capability or qualifications to do the work for which he was employed

  - related to the employee's conduct

  - the employee was redundant, or

- there was a statutory bar on the employee's continuing to work in the position that he held or the reason was some other substantial reason that would justify the dismissal of an employee holding the position that that employee held.

It is then for the tribunal to decide (rather than the onus being on either party to satisfy it) that the employer acted fairly in dismissing the employee for that reason.

In determining

- what the principal reason for dismissal was,

- whether it was a sufficient reason to justify the dismissal of the employee, or

- whether the dismissal was fair or not,

no account is to be taken of any pressure exerted on the employer by way of industrial action or threatened industrial action.

b) Special cases

(i) Failure to allow a person to return after maternity or adoption leave

This is dealt with under maternity and adoption rights. In such cases the employee is treated as having been dismissed on the notified or due date of return.

Where the employee is dismissed in a redundancy situation without being offered alternative work which is available, that dismissal is automatically unfair.

In other cases the fairness of the dismissal must be judged by considering whether the employer would have been acting reasonably or unreasonably in treating [the reason for dismissal] as a sufficient reason for dismissing the employee if he had not been absent from work. It should be noted that the dismissal of a temporary replacement for a woman who has been on maternity leave or who is suspended on maternity grounds is deemed to be for a substantial reason provided:

- that the person was told in writing that she or he was going to be a temporary replacement; and

- that the person is dismissed so that the woman can resume work.

(The employer will still have to show that the dismissal of the temporary replacement was fair in all the circumstances of the case.)

(ii) Dismissal related to family reasons

An employee is considered to be automatically unfairly dismissed if dismissed for reasons related to pregnancy, childbirth or leave for family reasons.

(iii) Dismissal in health and safety cases

Employees who are dismissed because:

- they are health and safety representatives

- they are representatives of employee safety

- they are members of a health and safety committee

- they have brought a health and safety issue to the employer's notice

- they have taken steps to protect themselves or others, or

- they have left work where they perceive a serious danger to health and safety,

are treated as having been automatically unfairly dismissed. (See also the rights of Health and safety representatives, **53.6a above**.)

(iv) Shop workers/betting workers

Shop or betting workers who are dismissed for refusing to work on a Sunday or Sundays or for giving or proposing to give their employer an opting-out certificate are considered to be automatically unfairly dismissed (see mainly under Sunday working, **53.5 above**).

(v) Pension scheme trustees

Employees who are trustees of the occupational pension scheme who are dismissed for being trustees or for undertaking any of the duties as such are considered to be automatically unfairly dismissed (see mainly under Trustees of occupational pension schemes, **53.6b above**).

(vi) Employee representatives

Employees who are dismissed for being employee representatives (ie those elected for purposes of being consulted in relation to proposed redundancies or the transfer of an undertaking) or for standing for election as employee representatives are considered to be automatically unfairly dismissed (see mainly under Employee representatives, **53.6c above**).

(vii) The assertion of a statutory right

An employee who is dismissed because:

- he brought proceedings to enforce a relevant statutory right of his against the employer, or

- he alleged that the employer had infringed a relevant statutory right of his

is considered to be automatically unfairly dismissed. It does not matter for these purposes

- whether the employee actually has that statutory right or if it has been infringed provided that the claim is made in good faith

- if a specific claim is not made – provided it is reasonably clear to the employer what right it is being claimed was infringed.

The relevant statutory rights are:

- any right under the ERA for which the remedy is by way of complaint to an employment tribunal

- a claim for minimum notice

- the right not to have unauthorised deductions of TU subscriptions or contributions to the union's political fund made

- action short of dismissal for trade union membership

- time off for trade union duties or activities or payment for time off for trade union duties.

(viii) Selection for redundancy for certain reasons

The employee's dismissal is automatically unfair

- where an employee is selected for redundancy in circumstances where the redundancy applies to other employees who have not been dismissed, or

- where the reason for selection is one of a number of unacceptable reasons.

  The unacceptable reasons for these purposes are, broadly, those set out in paragraphs (i) to (vii) above:

- The employee was selected for redundancy because of a reason related to maternity or pregnancy.

- The employee was selected for redundancy for health and safety reasons.

- The employee was a shop or betting worker and was selected for redundancy for a reason related to not wishing to work on Sundays.

- The employee was a trustee of an occupational pension scheme and was selected for redundancy for a reason related to carrying out his duties in respect of the scheme.

- The employee was an employee representative or seeking election as such and was selected for redundancy for a reason related to carrying out his duties as an employee representative or in connection with seeking election.

- The employee was selected for redundancy because he had asserted a relevant statutory right against his employer.

- The employee was selected for redundancy because he had taken part in protected industrial action.

c) Complaint to a tribunal

An employee may present an unfair dismissal complaint to an employment tribunal within three months of the date of dismissal or, if that is not reasonably practicable, within such further time as the tribunal considers to be reasonably practicable.

d) Remedies

(i)   Reinstatement and re-engagement

If a tribunal finds that an unfair dismissal complaint is borne out, it must explain to the employee the orders that it can make for reinstatement and re-engagement and ask the employee if he wishes the tribunal to make such an order.

- reinstatement
  An order for reinstatement is that the employee be put back into the position in which he would have been if he had not been dismissed.

- re-engagement

  An order for re-engagement is that the employee be put into a different job from that from which he was dismissed. In the case of re-engagement the tribunal will set out the terms on which the employee is to be re-engaged.

If the employer unreasonably fails to comply with an order for reinstatement or re-engagement, the tribunal will award compensation. The amount that is awarded can be increased by an additional award, which will be:

- in a case where the dismissal amounted to unlawful sex or race discrimination, an extra 26 to 52 weeks' pay; and

- in any other case, an extra 13 to 26 weeks' pay.

An additional award cannot be made where the employee is entitled to a 'special' basic and compensatory award.

(ii) Compensation

Compensation is broadly of two types – the basic award, and the compensatory award. In some cases where the employer unreasonably fails to comply with a reinstatement or re-engagement order, the tribunal can award an additional award.

The basic award

The basic award is equivalent to a redundancy payment, ie:

- 1½ week's pay for each year of service over the age of 41

- 1 week's pay for each year of service over the age of 22

- ½ week's pay per year of service at any lower age.

The statutory limit for a week's pay applies.

Only the best 20 years of service can be counted under this provision.

From the age of 64 the complainant loses $^1/_{12}$ of this entitlement per month over 64 – this is to allow for the fact that at age 65 there would be no entitlement.

The compensatory award

The compensatory award is to compensate the complainant for the loss that he has suffered by being unfairly dismissed insofar as that loss is attributable to action taken by the employer.

The compensatory award is subject to an upper limit. The Employment Relations Act provided for the upper limit to be set at £50,000 and for it to be index-linked from 1999.

The losses that can be compensated include:

- any expenses incurred by the employee as a result of his dismissal; and

- the loss of any benefit that the employee might have expected to have had if it were not for the dismissal, including any redundancy payment in excess of the statutory amount that the employee might otherwise have expected to have.

Some factors may reduce the compensation that the employee is ultimately awarded:

- The complainant is under a duty to mitigate the losses arising from the dismissal.

- The tribunal can reduce the compensatory award, to such degree as it considers just and equitable, where the employee has in any way contributed to his own dismissal.

If the employer has given the employee any payment on the grounds that the dismissal was on account of redundancy, the amount by which that payment exceeds the basic award is to be taken to reduce the compensatory award.

53.13 Redundancy payments

Previously Part VI EPCA amended by Employment Acts 1982 and 1989 and TURERA. Now ss 136 to 181 ERA.

a) General right

(i) Dismissal for redundancy

An employee is dismissed for redundancy if he is dismissed wholly or mainly because:

- the employer stops running the business for which the employee was employed;

- the employer moves it to a different place; or

- the requirement for employees to carry out the type of work that the employee can be asked to do ceases or diminishes.

(ii) Lay-off and short-time working as redundancy

There are complex provisions under which an employee who has been laid off or kept on 'short time' (ie earning less than half his normal weekly wage because of lay-off) can give notice to his employer claiming a redundancy payment if that situation continues for four weeks or for six weeks in a 13-week period. The employer can give a counter-notice disputing liability to pay a redundancy payment. The most usual case in which this is relevant is where the employer informs the employee that there is a likelihood of not less than 13 weeks' full employment, that will begin within four weeks of the date of the employer's counter-notice. Where such full-time employment is available, the employee will not be entitled to a redundancy payment.

b) Qualifications for entitlement

- The employee must be continuously employed for two years.

- The employee must be either:

  - below normal retiring age for employees of that type in the business in question; or

  - below 65.

Where the employee is over 64 he loses $^{1}/_{12}$ of his redundancy payment for every month over 64.

c) Amount of redundancy payment

A redundancy payment is 1½ week's pay for each year of employment over the age of 41; 1 week's pay for every year over the age of 22; and ½ week's pay for any year below 22. The maximum number of years that can be taken into account in calculating a redundancy payment is 20, and the amount of 'a week's pay' is limited by statute.

d) Exclusions from entitlement

(i) Summary dismissal

An employee is not entitled to a redundancy payment if he is or could be summarily dismissed unless:

- the reason for dismissal is that he has taken part in a strike; or
- he is dismissed during the minimum notice which he is entitled to be given by the employer by statute, in which case it is for the tribunal to decide what redundancy payment, if any, the employee ought to get.

(ii) New employment and the trial period

If the employee accepts or unreasonably refuses suitable alternative employment then he is not entitled to a redundancy payment.

Where, before the employee's employment terminates, he is offered new employment to begin within four weeks of the end of his current employment, then

- if the terms and conditions of the new contract are different from the old contract the employee has a four-week statutory trial period in which to decide whether or not to continue in the job. If he does not, or if the employer dismisses him for a reason arising out of the new terms and conditions, he is considered to have been dismissed from the original redundancy date
- where the employee needs retraining, a longer trial period can be agreed in writing between the employer and the employee.

e) Claiming a redundancy payment

A claim for a redundancy payment must be made within six months of dismissal to a tribunal or to the employer. If a claim is made late, within a year of the dismissal, then the tribunal can award a redundancy payment if it appears to the tribunal to be just and equitable that the payment should be made. It should be noted that if the employer becomes insolvent or fails to pay the employee a redundancy payment to which he is entitled, a claim may be made directly to the Secretary of State for a redundancy payment to be paid.

53.14 Insolvency

Originally in EPCA as amended by Insolvency Act 1985 and 1986, Bankruptcy (Scotland) Act 1985, Employment Acts 1989 and 1990 and TURERA, now ss 182 to 190 ERA.

These provisions allow for certain debts owed to an employee by an employer who becomes insolvent to be paid by the Secretary of State.

53.15 Compromise agreements

Introduced by TURERA.

Generally, the rights under employment legislation, including those under the ERA, cannot be contracted out of. TURERA introduced a new system whereby a valid agreement can be reached to exclude an employee's rights to claim provided that a solicitor or barrister is involved and that certain specific statutory requirements are adhered to. The list of those who can advise on compromise agreements was extended by the Employment Rights (Dispute Resolution) Act 1998 to include trade union officials and those working in advice centres. (A settlement of a case can still be validly reached with the assistance of a Conciliation Officer.)

54 Employment Rights (Dispute Resolution) Act 1998

Amends Courts Act 1971, SDA, SDA, TULRA, Disability Discrimination Act 1995, Employment Tribunals Act 1996, ERA, TURER.

The Act changes the title 'industrial tribunals' to 'employment tribunals'.

The Act makes provisions allowing unfair dismissal cases to be dealt with by binding arbitration if both parties agree to this way of dealing with them.

The Act allows for trade union officials and those working in advice centres to advise on compromise agreements, as well as qualified lawyers, provided:

- that they are certified by the union or advice centre as competent to give advice and as competent to do so on behalf of the union or advice centre; and

- that the claim being compromised is not against the union or advice centre in question.

55 Employment Subsidies Act 1978

Repealed by Statute Law (Repeal) Act 2004.

56 Employment Tribunals Act 1996

Name changed by Employment Rights (Dispute Resolution) Act 1998 from Industrial Tribunals Act 1996. Repeals and consolidates various provisions from EPCA, TULRA and TURERA. Amended by the Employment Rights (Dispute Resolution) Act 1998, National Minimum Wage Act 1998.

Consolidates the legislation dealing with the powers and constitution of employment tribunals and the Employment Appeals Tribunal (EAT) and with conciliation and compromise agreements in tribunal cases.

57 Employment Tribunals (Constitution and Rules of Procedure) Regulations 2004 (SI 2004 No 1861)

The Regulations replace the Employment Tribunals (Constitution and Rules of Procedure) Regulations 2001 and the Employment Tribunals (Constitution and Rules of Procedure) (Scotland) Regulations 2001. Amended by the Employment Tribunals (Constitution and Rules of Procedure) Amendment Regulations 2005 (SI 2005 No 435).

The Regulations set down the procedure through which claims may be brought and defended at employment tribunals.

The main innovations in the new rules, which came into effect from 1 October 2004, are:

■ One set of rules covers the whole of Great Britain: previously, Scottish tribunals had a separate set of rules.

■ The President of Employment Tribunals is empowered to make practice directions. These may be different for different areas.

■ From 1 October 2005 both claims and responses must be made on the correct, prescribed, form, or they will not be accepted. (The original date for this requirement to take effect, 1 April 2005, was changed by Employment Tribunals (Constitution and Rules of Procedure) Amendment Regulations 2005 (SI 2005 No 435) because the forms had not been sufficiently developed in time.)

■ A claimant's claim may also be rejected if it is clear to the tribunal that it does not have power to deal with it or a part of it. Where the applicant's claim is about a grievance, the tribunal is not to consider that claim unless the applicant has invoked the statutory disputes grievance procedure. Where the tribunal does not accept a claim, it must give the claimant reasons for its refusal. Where the refusal to accept the claim arises from the applicant's failure to go through the statutory disputes procedure, the tribunal must inform the applicant of the time limit that applies to the claim and the effect of not going through the statutory disputes grievance procedure.

■ The respondent's response to a claim must be put in within 28 days of the date on which the claim has been sent to the respondent. If no response, or application for an extension of time in which to present a response, is put in within the 28-day period, the respondent may be barred from defending the claim.

■ The time during which an ACAS Conciliation Officer can act is limited, other than in discrimination cases. Once the time has elapsed no COT3 settlement will be possible.

■ Tribunals are required to consider the means of a party when considering whether or not to order costs against that party. The tribunal may also make a 'preparation time order' in favour of a party who has not been legally represented. A preparation time order can be made where the paying party has asked for an adjournment and the receiving party is thereby involved in further preparation time or where in bringing or conducting the proceedings the conduct of a party has been vexatious, abusive, disruptive or otherwise unreasonable or where the bringing or conducting of proceedings has been misconceived. (These are the same grounds on which an order for costs may be made in an employment tribunal.) The tribunal cannot award costs and make a preparation time order in favour of the same party at the same proceedings.

■ An employment tribunal may make a 'wasted costs order' directly against a party's representative:

   ■ where a party has incurred costs as a result of any improper, unreasonable or negligent act or omission by a party's representative; or

   ■ if, after the costs were incurred, a party's representative has acted or failed to act, in such a way that it would be unjust for the party to pay the costs.

Costs may only be awarded against a legal representative or someone who is 'acting in pursuit of profit' with regard to those proceedings.

■ The limit on fixed costs or preparation expenses that a tribunal can award remains at £10,000.

58 Employment Tribunals (Constitution and Rules of Procedure) (Amendment) Regulations 2004 (SI 2004 No 2351)

Amend Employment Tribunals (Constitution and Rules of Procedure) Regulations 2004 (SI 2004 No 1861) with effect from 1 October 2004.

Add a new Schedule 6 to the rules which gives the tribunal new case management powers in respect of equal value claims and simplifies the rules applicable to equal value claims.

59 Employment Tribunals (Constitution and Rules of Procedure) Amendment Regulations 2005 (SI 2005 No 435)

Amend Employment Tribunals (Constitution and Rules of Procedure) Amendment Regulations 2004 (SI 2004 No 1861) – **see 57 above**.

60 Employment Tribunals Extension of Jurisdiction (England and Wales) Order 1994 (SI 1994 No 1623)/(Scotland)(SI 1994 No 1624)

Name changed by Employment Rights (Dispute Resolution) Act 1998 from Industrial Tribunals Extension of Jurisdiction (England and Wales) Order 1994.

The Order extends the jurisdiction of employment tribunals to allow for breach of contract claims to be brought to an employment tribunal where the claim arises or is in issue on termination of employment.

The limit on such claims is £25,000. Certain types of claim, such as those involving personal injuries and restraint of trade, are excluded from the tribunal's jurisdiction.

A claim under these provisions must be brought within three months of the date of dismissal or within such further time as is reasonably practicable where it is not reasonably practicable to meet the three-month time limit. The respondent can also make a counter-claim against the claimant within six weeks of receiving the notice of the claimant's originating application.

61 Equal Opportunities (Employment Legislation) (Territorial Limits) Regulations 1999 (SI 1999 No 3163)

Amend the Equal Pay Act 1970, SDA, SDA and Disability Discrimination Act 1995.

With effect from 16 December 1999 these Regulations change the territorial limit of the above anti-discrimination statutes. As originally drafted, an employee was covered by the requirements of these statutes unless his work was done 'wholly or mainly outside Great Britain'. The Regulations remove the words 'or mainly' so that employees are now protected by the anti-discrimination legislation unless their work is done 'wholly outside Great Britain'.

62 Equal Pay Act 1970

Amended by Sex Discrimination Acts 1975 and 1986, Equal Pay (Amendment) Regulations 1983, Pensions Act 1995, Armed Forces Act 1996 and Equal Opportunities (Employment Legislation)(Territorial Limits) Regulations 1999 (SI 1999 No 3163). Further amended by Equal Pay Act 1970 (Amendment) Regulations 2003 (SI 2003 No 1656) and Equal Pay Act 1970 (Amendment) Regulations 2004 (SI 2004 No 2352).

62.1 The equality clause

The Act provides that a woman's contract is to have an equality clause implied into it if it does not specifically contain one. The effect of the equality clause is to modify the woman's contractual conditions so that they are no less favourable than those of a man who is engaged on like work, on work rated as equivalent (under a job evaluation scheme) or on work of equal value to that of the comparator.

A material difference/material factor defence allows the employer to justify a difference on non-sex-based grounds – such as personal differences or market forces.

The Act applies equally to men, who can, therefore, claim equality of terms with a woman on like work, on work rated as equivalent or on work of equal value.

62.2 Time for the claim

The Equal Pay Act 1970 (Amendment) Regulations 2003 (SI 2003 No 1656) extend the time in which a claim can be brought under the Act to six months from the date on which the claimant's employment terminated.

- If the claimant was aged either less than 18 in England and Wales, or less than 16 in Scotland, at any time during the six months following termination of employment, the time limit for claim is extended until no more than six months after the claimant reached the relevant age. (A similar extension applies where at any time during the time limit the claimant was mentally incapable.)

- If the employer conceals any material fact from the claimant, the time limit is extended until six months from the date of discovery of that material fact.

62.3 Level of compensation

Under the Act as originally drafted a claimant could only be compensated for up to two years' worth of underpayments. The 2003 Regulations extend this to a maximum of six years' from the date of claim (or date of discovery of the material fact or the date on which the claimant reached the relevant age or appropriate state of mind).

63 Equal Pay Act 1970 (Amendment) Regulations 2003 (SI 2003 No 1656)

Amend Equal Pay Act 1970 – **see 62 above**.

64 Equal Pay Act 1970 (Amendment) Regulations 2004 (SI 2004 No 2352)

Amend Equal Pay Act 1970, s 2A.

The Regulations change the procedure for equal value claims. Under the new Regulations the employment tribunal can choose to determine the question of equal value itself or it can appoint an independent expert to prepare a report. Where there has been a job evaluation study that has resulted in different values being attributed to the work of the claimant and her comparator, the tribunal must determine that the work is not of equal value. The only exceptions are where it reasonably suspects that the study was itself discriminatory on grounds of sex, or that for other reasons the study should not be relied upon.

64.1 The equal pay Code of Practice

The EOC Code is brought into force by the Code of Practice on Equal Pay Order 2003 (SI 2003 No 2865) with effect from 1 December 2003 when it replaced the earlier Code of Practice on Equal Pay.

a) The background

As the Code itself notes: despite the fact that the equal pay legislation has been in effect for more than 30 years, the average wage for a full-time female employee is still only 81 per cent of that of a full-time male employee.

b) The legal effect of the Code

Compliance by an employer with the provisions of the Code, although not a legal requirement, may be taken into account by an employment tribunal in any proceedings under the Equal Pay Act 1970.

c) The Code's main recommendations

The Code's three main recommendations are that employers should:

- have transparent and non-discriminatory pay schemes;
- carry out equal pay reviews; and
- have an equal pay policy.

d) Non-discriminatory pay schemes

The Code suggests that pay systems should be transparent and structured – such as a job evaluated system. Not only is such a system more likely to provide equal pay but also it is easier to check such a system than one which relies primarily on managerial discretion. A proper balance must, however, be reached between transparency and confidentiality both in setting up pay systems and in implementing equal pay reviews. Transparency in this context requires that an employee be able to see the basis of calculation on his own pay – not what others might be earning.

In order to check that a scheme is non-discriminatory, an employer must look at such matters as:

- whether pay statistics are broken down by gender
- whether the scheme is appropriate to the jobs it will cover

- if a proprietary scheme is used, whether the supplier has equal opportunities guidelines

- if any groups of workers are excluded from the scheme, whether there are clear and justifiable reasons for their exclusion

- whether the composition of the job evaluation panel/steering committee is representative of the jobs covered by the scheme, and whether its members are trained in job evaluation and avoiding sex bias

- whether the job descriptions are written to an agreed format and assessed to a common standard; whether trained job analysts have been used and whether the job-holders have been involved in writing their own job descriptions

- where the scheme uses generic/benchmark jobs, whether these are free from sex bias

- whether the factor definitions and levels are exact, and whether detailed descriptions are provided for each factor; if the factors cover all the important job demands.

If a job evaluation scheme is to remain free of sex bias it should be monitored.

e) Equal pay reviews

(i) The equal pay review process

The essential features of an equal pay review are:

- It should compare the pay of men and women on the basis of one or more of the criteria laid down by the Equal Pay Act 1970 (ie like work, work rated as equivalent and/or work of equal value).

- It should identify any gaps in equal pay.

- It should eliminate gaps for which there is no satisfactory explanation. In the absence of a satisfactory explanation the employer should conclude that the difference is on grounds of sex.

Because an equal pay review entails a commitment on the part of the employer to put right any sex-based pay inequalities, the review must have the commitment of managers who have the authority to make the necessary changes.

The validity of the review and success of subsequent action taken will be enhanced if the pay system is understood and accepted not only by the managers who operate the system but by the employees and their unions. Employers should therefore aim to secure the involvement of employees and trade union representatives when carrying out an equal pay review.

(ii) The equal pay review model

The Code also sets out a model for carrying out an equal pay review. This model is supported by the 'EOC Equal Pay Review Kit', which sets out the recommended model in more detail and provides supporting guidance notes.

The model equal pay review involves five steps:

STEP 1: Decide the scope of the review and identify the data required.

STEP 2: Determine where men and women are doing equal work.

STEP 3: Collect pay data to identify any gaps in equal pay.

STEP 4: Establish the causes of any significant pay gaps and consider the reasons for them.

STEP 5: Develop an equal pay action plan and/or reviewing and monitoring scheme.

Each of these steps is further analysed in the Code itself and in the 'EOC Equal Pay Review Kit'.

65 European Communities Act 1972 – the Treaty of Rome

The European Communities Act 1972 brought into effect the application of certain European regulations to UK law. Certain provisions of the Treaty of Rome are important in employment.

a) Provisions allowing for free movement of labour across EC borders.

b) Equal access for EC nationals to social security benefits.

c) Equal pay.

Article 119, which provides for 'equal pay for equal work', is wider than the Equal Pay Act 1970 and has direct effect in the UK.

66 Factories Act 1961

Amended by Sex Discrimination Act 1986 and Employment Act 1989, Manual Handling Operations Regulations 1992 (SI 1992 No 2793), Provision and Use of Work Equipment Regulations 1992 (SI 1992 No 2932), Workplace (Health, Safety and Welfare) Regulations 1992 (SI 1992 No 3004), Personal Protective Equipment at Work Regulations 1992 (SI 1992 No 2966), Education Act 1993, Lifting Operations and Lifting Equipment Regulations 1998.

Consolidates previous Factories Acts of 1937, 1948 and 1959: establishes standards of health, safety and welfare in factories. It is intended, eventually, to bring all the health and safety provisions under the ambit of codes and regulations made under the Health and Safety at Work etc Act 1974.

Previous restrictions on the hours of work of women and young persons contained in the Factories Act were lifted by the Employment Act 1989.

67 Family Law Reform Act 1969

Reduced the age of majority from 21 to 18.

68 Finance Acts

The provisions of the Finance Acts, so far as they affect taxation of employment under Schedule 'E', are largely consolidated in the Income Tax (Earnings and Pensions) Act 2003.

69 Fire Precautions Act 1971

Amended by the Health and Safety at Work etc Act 1974, Fire Safety and Safety of Places of Sport Act 1987 and by the Fire Precautions (Workplace) Regulations 1997.

The Act governs fire precautions in all places of work. The provisions governing fire precautions contained in the Factories Act 1961 and the Offices, Shops and Railway Premises Act 1963 are repealed.

70 Fire Precautions (Workplace) Regulations 1997

Amend the Fire Precautions Act 1971.

The onus for ensuring compliance with the Regulations in respect of the workplace is placed on employers.

a) Appropriate fire-fighting equipment

   (i)   The employer must ensure that the workplace is equipped with 'appropriate':

   ■ fire-fighting equipment

   ■ fire detectors, and

   ■ alarms.

   (ii) What equipment is 'appropriate' depends on:

   ■ the dimensions of the building in which the workplace is situated

   ■ the equipment it contains

   ■ the physical and chemical properties of the substances likely to be present, and

   ■ the maximum number of people that may be present at any one time.

   (iii) Any non-automatic fire-fighting equipment must be:

   ■ easily accessible

   ■ simple to use, and

   ■ indicated by signs.

b) Other measures

   The employer must comply with as many of the following as necessary to safeguard his employees in case of fire:

   (i)   taking measures for fire-fighting in the workplace adapted to:

   ■ the nature of the activities carried on there

   ■ the size of the undertaking

   ■ the size of the workplace, and

   ■ the number of people other than employees who may be present.

(ii) nominating sufficient employees to implement the measures taken and ensuring that the training and equipment with which they are provided is adequate having regard to the size of the workplace and the hazards involved

(iii) arranging any necessary contacts with external emergency services, particularly as regards rescue work and fire-fighting

(iv) providing emergency routes and exits:

- ensuring that they are kept clear

- ensuring that they lead as directly as possible to a safe place

- ensuring that emergency routes and exits are such that it is possible to evacuate the building quickly and safely, taking into account the number of people who may be present

- providing emergency doors which

  - open in the direction of escape

  - are not sliding or revolving doors

  - are not to be locked or fastened so they cannot be opened easily by anyone trying to escape

- ensuring that emergency routes and exits

  - are indicated by signs; and

  - have emergency illumination available if illumination is needed.

Failure to comply with these Regulations in such a way as to cause a serious risk (ie one where death or serious injury is likely to result) is a criminal offence. Fire authorities can also serve enforcement notices on employers who have failed to comply with their obligations under the Regulations.

71 Fire Safety and Safety of Places of Sport Act 1987

Amends Fire Precautions Act 1971 and Health and Safety at Work etc Act 1974.

The Act tightens up on matters such as means of escape from premises in cases of fire and allows for improvement notices and prohibition notices to be served where an occupier of premises has inadequate provision either for escape in cases of fire, or for fire-fighting.

72 Fixed-term Employees (Prevention of Less Favourable Treatment) Regulations 2002 (SI 2002 No 2034)

Amend the ERA.

a) Definition of 'fixed-term contract' and exclusions

A 'fixed-term contract' is one that expires:

- at the end of a period of time;

- on the completion of a task; or

- on the happening of an event – other than attaining normal retirement age.

Agency workers and those on a government training scheme are among those excluded from these provisions.

b) The comparison

A fixed-term employee is compared to a comparable permanent employee. Employees are comparable if they:

- are engaged by the same employer;

- are engaged on broadly similar work – having regard to the level of qualifications and skills; and

- work at the same establishment or, if there are no employees on similar work at the same establishment, work at different establishments.

No comparison, however, can be made with past employees.

c) The rights of a fixed-term employee

A fixed-term employee has the right:

- not to be treated less favourably than a comparative permanent employee;

- not to be subjected to any detriment by his employer in relation to

    - service-related conditions;

    - training opportunities;

    - the opportunity to secure a permanent position (To support this right, fixed-term employees are given the right to be informed by their employer of available vacancies during the day-to-day course of their employment.)

- to request and to receive from his employer a written statement as to the reasons for any particular treatment where he considers that he has been less favourably treated. The fixed-term employee is entitled to be given this statement within 21 days of his request

- not to be unfairly dismissed or subjected to a detriment because he has done anything under the Regulations. Where the principal reason for dismissal is that the employee is a fixed-term employee, the dismissal is treated as automatically unfair.

A fixed-term employee is only entitled not to be treated less favourably

- on grounds of being a fixed-term employee;

- where the treatment is not justified on objective grounds.

    In assessing 'objective justification' the tribunal must compare the overall benefits which each employee receives under his contract of employment.

In deciding whether a fixed-term employee is being treated less favourably, the pro rata principle is to be applied – unless that is inappropriate.

d) Application to an employment tribunal

An application can be made to an employment tribunal on grounds of less favourable treatment or detriment. Where the complaint is of a series of acts or omissions, the three-month time limit runs from the last of those acts or omissions. There is power to extend the time limit for complaint where it is just and equitable to do so.

e) Successive fixed-term contracts

This rule applies where a fixed-term employee has had a previous fixed-term contract with the same employer – whether that previous contract was immediately prior to the current fixed-term or earlier. In such cases, unless the continuation of the fixed-term can be justified on objective grounds, the employee will become a permanent employee from the later of:

- the date when his current fixed-term term was entered into, or

- the date on which he has completed four years' service.

An employee who believes that he has become a permanent employee under this provision is entitled to ask his employer for a statement confirming this. The employer must give the employee a statement within 21 days of his request which either:

- confirms that he is a permanent employee, or

- gives reasons why his contract remains fixed-term.

The rights under this provision can be modified by a workforce agreement.

- A workforce agreement is an agreement which:

    - is in writing;

    - lasts for up to five years;

    - applies to all members of the workforce or to a particular group within the workforce; and

    - is signed:

    - by representatives of the workforce or of the group in question, or

    - where the employer has fewer than 20 employees, either by the appropriate representatives or by the majority of the employees.

Before the workforce agreement is signed, the employer must have provided all employees affected by it with the text of it. The employer must also give those employees any explanation which might be required to ensure that they understand the text of the agreement.

73 Flexible Working (Eligibility, Complaints and Remedies) Regulations 2002 (SI 2002 No 3236)

The effect of these Regulations is integrated into the text on 'flexible working' – see the Employment Act 2002, **39 above**.

74 Flexible Working (Procedural Requirements) Regulations 2002 (SI 2002 No 3207)

The effect of these Regulations is integrated into the text on 'flexible working' – see the Employment Act 2002, **39 above**.

75 Food Safety Act 1990

The Act gives local authorities powers to oversee company canteens to ensure that food safety standards are met.

76 Further and Higher Education Act 1992

Amends Education Act 1944, Chronically Sick and Disabled Persons Act 1970, SDA, Employment Act 1989.

The Act makes any provision in a contract of employment in the further education sector void insofar as it provides either:

- that the employee shall not be dismissed by reason of redundancy; or

- that if the employee is dismissed by reason of redundancy he shall receive a larger redundancy payment than would be payable under the ERA.

77 Gender Recognition Act 2004

Amends SDA. The effects are noted in the commentary on the Sex Discrimination (Gender Reassignment) Regulations 1999 (**see 131 below**).

78 Health and Safety at Work etc Act 1974

Amended by Sex Discrimination Act 1986, Fire Safety and Safety of Places of Sport Act 1987, Employment Act 1989, Police (Health and Safety) Act 1997, and Control of Substances Hazardous to Health Regulations 1999 (S1 1999 No 437).

It is ultimately intended to replace all existing safety legislation with regulations and codes of practice under this Act. To facilitate this transfer of jurisdiction, the Act absorbs the inspectorates provided for by a multitude of statutes dealing with safety matters (eg Factories Act 1961, Explosives Act 1875, Mines and Quarries Act 1954) into a single Health and Safety Executive which now deals with all such matters.

Part I of the Act has four purposes:

- securing the health, safety and welfare of persons at work

- protecting other persons against risks to health and safety arising out of, or in connection with, the activities of persons at work

- preventing the unlawful acquisition and possession of explosives and other highly flammable and dangerous substances, and controlling their use and storage

- controlling the emission of noxious substances into the atmosphere.

These purposes are to be achieved to some extent by the Act itself which puts a general duty on employers, employees, the self-employed and other people who are concerned with the premises to have regard for the safety of others and themselves. Sections 15 and 16, respectively, provide for regulations to be made and for codes of practice. It should be noted that breaches of Part I of the Act give rise to criminal liability but not to civil liability, which is, therefore, largely the province of existing statutory and common law duties.

Part II of the Act amends and repeals in part the Employment Medical Advisory Services Act 1972.

Part III of the Act widens the scope of building regulations made under the Public Health Act 1936. (The Act amends and repeals parts of the Fire Precautions Act 1971, the Employment Medical Advisory Services Act 1972 and the Employment and Training Act 1973.)

79 Health and Safety (Consultation with Employees) Regulations 1996 (SI 1996 No 1513)

Amends ERA and Safety Representatives and Safety Committees Regulations 1977 (SI 1977 No 500).

In 1994 the EC Commission successfully brought a case against the UK complaining of the UK's failure to implement the requirement for consultation in relation to collective redundancies and transfers of undertakings in cases where trade unions were not recognised. The HSCE Regulations are a spin-off of this in that the Framework Directive (Directive 89/391/EEC), articles 10 and 11, requires that there be consultation with employees on matters affecting health and safety. Until these regulations were brought in, the requirement for employers to consult with employees was restricted to employments in which trades unions were recognised (see Safety Representatives and Safety Committees Regulations 1977 (SI 1977 No 500), **126 below**).

79.1 Exclusions

Employment in domestic households is excluded.

> Where employees are represented by safety representatives under the Safety Representatives and Safety Committees Regulations (SRSCR) 1977 (SI 1977 No 500), the employer must consult with those safety representatives. Where there are no safety representatives the employer is required to consult under these regulations (cf. the Collective Redundancies and Transfer of Undertakings (Protection of Employment) (Amendment) Regulations 1995 (SI 1995 No 2587), where the employer has a choice as to whether to consult with a recognised trade union or with employee representatives).

79.2 Representatives of employee safety

Representatives of employee safety are elected by employees specifically to represent them on health and safety matters. They are entitled to paid time off for training, to carry out their functions and to stand for election. They are specifically protected from dismissal and action short of dismissal related to their functions under the ERA (**see 53.6 above**).

An employee representative's duties are:

- to make representations to the employer on general matters of health and safety and on potential hazards and dangerous occurrences at the workplace which affect, or could affect, the group of employees he represents; and

- to represent the group of employees he represents in consultations at the workplace with health and safety inspectors.

79.3 Consultation

a) With whom

The employer must consult either employees who are affected or representatives of employee safety who have been elected by the group of employees in question to represent them.

b) About what

The employer must consult in good time on matters regarding employees' health and safety at work, in particular on

- the introduction of:

  - measures which may substantially affect employees' health and safety, and

  - new technology;

- arrangements for:

  - appointing people to be responsible for statutory health and safety duties,

  - nominating people to deal with serious and imminent dangers at work, and danger areas;

- health and safety information which he is required to provide by statute;

- the planning of health and safety training he is required to provide by statute.

c) Requirement to provide information

The employer must provide for the employees or their representatives to have all relevant information he has available that will allow them to participate fully and effectively in consultation. Certain types of confidential information are excluded from this requirement.

80 Health and Safety (Display Screen Equipment) Regulations 1992 (SI 1992 No 2792)

This is one of the 'six-pack' Regulations introduced in 1992 arising from European health and safety Directives.

a) Display screen users

The requirements of these Regulations are limited to 'display screen users' – ie those employees to whom all or most of the following criteria apply:

- the employee requires display screen equipment (DSE) to do the job – other means are not readily available

- the employee has no discretion as to whether or not to use DSE

- the employee requires training in the use of DSE to do the job

- the employee normally uses DSE for continuous periods of an hour or more

- the employee uses DSE in this way more or less daily

- fast transfer of information between the employee/user and the screen is an important requirement of the job

- performance requirements demand high levels of attention and concentration by the employee/user – eg where the consequences of error may be critical.

b) Work stations for DSE users

(i) Work stations used by DSE users must be assessed for risks and reassessed if there has been a significant change. The matters that must be looked at range from the equipment itself (including the software) and the desk and chair the emplyee/user uses, to the surroundings in which he uses it – including consideration of such matters as glare and reflection on the screen, ambient noise, heat from equipment, etc.

(ii) By December 1996 all work stations were required to meet a specification laid down in the schedule to the Display Screen Equipment Regulations.

c) Daily work routine of DSE users

(i) The job of DSE users should be so designed as to ensure that they have regular breaks or changes in activity to reduce their workload on the equipment.

(ii) This may be done by:

- job design – putting natural breaks into the work itself; or

- providing for specific breaks (such breaks should be taken away from the screen where possible).

d) Eye tests

(i) Regular professional eye tests must be provided by the employer for DSE users at the employer's expense.

(ii) If there is a specific visual difficulty which may reasonably be considered to be caused by work on DSE, the employer must provide a further eye test if the employee so wishes.

(iii) The employer must provide spectacles where they are needed specifically for DSE work (but not if the problem with using DSE would be overcome by using spectacles which the person requires for normal use).

e) Health and safety training

(i) The employer must ensure that DSE users are trained in health and safety aspects of DSE.

(ii) The employer must ensure that DSE users are retrained in health and safety if their work station is modified significantly.

f) Health and safety information

(i) Employers must provide DSE users with information on all aspects of health and safety re DSE work stations.

(ii) Employers must provide DSE users with information on measures taken by them to comply with:

- the requirement to give breaks to DSE users

- the requirement to give health and safety training to DSE users

- the availability of eye testing and specialised spectacles where these are required.

81 Human Rights Act 1998

The Act provides a fundamental set of human rights to give effect to the European Convention on Human Rights.

Most important of the rights provided for, in employment terms, is the freedom of assembly and association.

The right includes:

- the right of peaceful assembly;

- the freedom to associate with others, including the right to form and join trade unions.

- Restrictions can be placed on these rights by law only

  - in the interests of public security and safety;

  - for the prevention of crime;

  - for the protection of the rights and freedoms of others.

82 Immigration Act 1971

Amends and replaces previous immigration laws. Amended by the Asylum and Immigration Act 1996.

Generally, except for certain occupations such as dentistry and medicine, any non-patrials require work permits to work in the UK. The provisions of the Act have now been amended to allow EC nationals to take up employment in the UK freely.

83 Immigration and Asylum Act 1999

Amends Asylum and Immigration Act 1996 by requiring the Secretary of State to provide a 'Code of Practice for all employers on the avoidance of race discrimination in recruitment practice while seeking to prevent illegal working'. This Code was brought into effect from 19 March 2001 by the Immigration (Restrictions on Employment) (Code of Practice) Order 2001 (SI 2001 No 1436). For the amendments see Asylum and Immigration Act 1996, **6 above**.

84 Income Tax (Earnings and Pensions) Act 2003

Repeals and consolidates, with modifications, Income and Corporation Taxes Act 1988 and the Finance Acts insofar as they concern taxation of employment, and the whole of the Employee Share Schemes Act 2002.

Section 403 allows for tax-free termination payments of up to £30,000.

85 Industrial Training Act 1982

Amended by Employment Act 1989.

The Act consolidates the law relating to industrial training boards.

86 Information and Consultation of Employees Regulations 2004 (SI 2004 No 3426)

The Regulations, which implement the EC Directive on Informing and Consulting Employees (2002/14/EC), give employees, or their representatives, the right to be informed and consulted by their employer on matters set down by the Regulations.

From 6 April 2005 the regulations apply to undertakings of at least 150 employees.

From 6 April 2007 the regulations apply to undertakings of at least 100 employees.

And from 6 April 2008 the regulations apply to undertakings of at least 50 employees.

a) Request to negotiate an information and consultation agreement

Where the employer receives a written request or requests from at least 10 per cent of his employees within a period of six months, he is obliged to initiate negotiations unless either:

■ he holds a ballot (in a case where he is entitled to do this); or

■ there is a dispute regarding the question of whether or not there has been a valid employee request and the employer has referred that dispute to the CAC.

An employee request is not valid if made within three years of:

■ the date of a negotiated agreement;

■ the date on which standard information and consultation provisions started to apply;

■ the date of an employee request which led to a ballot;

or where a negotiated agreement is terminated within the first three years, prior to its set termination.

The limitation on an employee request being made within three years is excluded:

■ where, following an unsuccessful ballot, there ceases to be a pre-existing agreement; or

■ where the negotiated agreement ceases to cover all the employees in the undertaking.

b) Ballots

Either an employer or a group of employers may hold a ballot where:

- there is a pre-existing information and consultation agreement; and

- the employee request comes from fewer than 40 per cent of the workforce.

A pre-existing information and consultation agreement for these purposes is an agreement which:

- is in writing;

- covers all the employees of the undertaking;

- has been approved by employees; and

- sets out how the employer is to give information to the employees or their representatives and seek their views on that information.

Where a ballot is held,

- it must be a fair, secret ballot

- the ballot is to be taken to have endorsed the employee request if at least:

  - 40 per cent of the workforce voted; and

  - the majority of those voting voted in favour of endorsing the employee request.

If the ballot is in favour of endorsing the employee request,

- the employer must inform the employees of the result as soon as is reasonably practicable after the ballot; and

- must initiate negotiations.

c) Initiating negotiations

An employer may either be forced to initiate negotiations under the Regulations or may decide to initiate them himself.

Where the employer initiates them himself he must issue a written notification which:

- states that he intends to start the negotiation process and is giving notification under the Regulations;

- states the date on which it is issued; and

- is published so as to bring it to the attention of the all the employees in the undertaking.

Whether the employer initiates negotiations voluntarily or is required to under the Regulations, the same requirements apply concerning those negotiations.

d) Steps in initiating negotiations to reach an agreement

The first step is to elect or appoint negotiating representatives. The requirements for this are that

- following the elections/appointments, all employees are represented by one or more of the representatives; and

- all employees in the undertaking must be entitled to take part in the appointments or vote in the elections.

Once the negotiating representative are appointed, the employees must be informed in writing of their identity.

The third step is to invite negotiating representatives to enter into negotiations to reach a negotiated agreement.

- These negotiations start three months after a valid employee request or from when the employer voluntarily initiated negotiations. (Time spent on ballots and disputes as to the validity of the employee request is not counted in deciding when the three-month period started).

- The negotiations then continue for a period of up to six months from this date.

- The period of negotiation can be extended by agreement between the employer and the negotiating representatives.

e) Negotiated agreements

A negotiated agreement must cover all the employees in the undertaking, although, provided that each of the requirements below is met in relation to each group of employees, there can be different requirements agreed for different groups of employees. The requirements for a negotiated agreement are that it must:

- set out the circumstances in which the employer must inform and consult the employees to whom it relates. These requirements can be different for different groups of employees

- be in writing

- be dated

- be approved. To be approved it must be:

  - signed by a majority of the negotiating representatives, and

  - approved either in writing or in a ballot by at least 50 per cent of the employees who vote;

- be signed by or on behalf of the employer, and

- provide either:

  - for the appointment or election of information and consultation representatives for the employer to disseminate information and consult with; or

  - for the employer to disseminate information directly to and consult directly with the employees themselves.

  This requirement too can be different for different parts of the workforce.

f) The appointment of information and consultation representatives (IC representatives)

Where the standard provisions are to apply, the employer is obliged to arrange a ballot for employees to elect IC representatives.

The number of IC representatives to be elected is one per 50 employees or any fraction of 50 employees subject to a minimum of 2 and a maximum of 25 representatives.

g) Standard information and consultation provisions

Where these apply the employer must provide IC representatives with information on:

- recent and probable developments of the undertaking's activities and economic situation;

- the situation, structure and probable development of employment within the undertaking;

- any anticipatory measures envisaged regarding employment – especially where there is a threat to employment within the undertaking;

- decisions likely to lead to substantial changes in work organisation or in contractual relations including potential redundancies and transfers of undertakings. (In relation to redundancies and transfers of undertakings, however, the requirement to inform and consult ceases under these regulations when the existing statutory duties to inform and consult under TULRA and TUPE come into operation and the employer informs the IC representatives that he has given the information required under the relevant legislation.)

The information required to be given to IC representatives must be given to them

- at such time;

- in such fashion; and

- with such content

as to enable the IC representatives to have time to study the information and prepare for consultation on it.

The employer must then consult with the IC representatives on the information provided. The consultation must be conducted:

- in such a way as to ensure the timing, method and content are appropriate;

- on the basis of the information supplied by the employer and any opinion expressed by the IC representatives to their employer;

- in such a way that the IC representatives can meet the appropriate level of management – depending on the subject under discussion – and obtain a reasoned response to their opinions; and

- in relation to any redundancy or TUPE issues with a view to reaching agreement on decisions which are within the employer's power.

h) The application of standard information and consultation provisions

These apply where either:

- the employer is under a duty to initiate negotiations, but doesn't. In this case the standard provisions apply from the sooner of:

    - the date of the valid employee request; or

- the date when the information and consultation representatives are elected;

- or no agreement is successfully negotiated, in which case the standard provisions apply from the sooner of:

  - six months from the date on which negotiations began, or

  - the date when the information and consultation representatives are elected.

Where the standard provisions apply, the information and consultation representatives and the employer can enter into a negotiated agreement at any time which will supersede the standard provisions – provided, of course, that it meets all the requirements of a negotiated agreement.

i) Duty of co-operation

The Regulations impose a duty of co-operation on the parties having regard to the interests of the undertaking and employees when negotiating or implementing either a negotiated agreement or the standard information and consultation provisions.

j) Compliance and enforcement

Where an employer fails to comply with the terms of a negotiated agreement or with the terms of the standard information and consultation provisions, where those apply, an application can be made to the CAC.

- If the CAC finds the complaint well founded it shall make a declaration which tells the employer what steps he is required to take and within what time.

- Where the CAC makes a declaration under this provision an application for a penalty can be made to the EAT which can award a penalty of up to £75,000.

k) Confidential information

(i) General

Where the employer provides a person with information (or document) pursuant to his duties under these Regulations on the basis that the information be held in confidence, the person to whom it is discloses must not disclose it.

Disclosure is a breach of a statutory duty and is actionable as such by the employer except where:

- the recipient reasonably believes the disclosure to be a protected disclosure;

- the individual applies to the CAC:

  - if the CAC decides that disclosure of the information would not be likely to harm the legitimate interests of the undertaking, it must make a declaration that it was not reasonable for the employer to require the information to be held in confidence.

In such cases the information is thereafter to be treated as not having been given to the individual in confidence.

(ii) Non-disclosure of information by the employer

An employer is not required to disclose any information (or document) where the nature of the information is such that judged objectively disclosure of that information:

- would seriously harm the functioning of the undertaking; or

- would be prejudicial to the undertaking.

An application can be made to the CAC for a declaration as to whether or not the information is of such a nature as to be within this protection.

l)   Rights for IC representatives and negotiating representatives

Negotiating representatives and IC representatives are entitled to reasonable paid time off to perform their functions.

They are also protected from being subjected to a detriment, unfair dismissal or redundancy because they are such representatives or have done (or intend to do) anything in the course of their duties as such representatives.

- There is no qualification period before an employee can bring a complaint under these provisions; and

- The upper age limit for claiming unfair dismissal does not apply.

87 Insolvency Act 1985

Amended EPCA. This amendment is now consolidated into s 184(2) ERA.

The Act introduced a list of items which are to be treated as arrears of pay for purposes of obtaining payment directly from the Secretary of State in an insolvency situation (see also Insolvency Act 1986, **88 below**). These are:

- a guarantee payment

- remuneration from suspension on medical grounds

- payment in respect of statutory time off

- payment under a protective award.

88 Insolvency Act 1986

Amended EPCA.

Certain employee debts are given priority over other debts:

- remuneration for up to eight weeks preceding the date when the employer became insolvent up to a statutory maximum;

- where an employee's employment was terminated before the employer became insolvent, arrears of holiday pay of up to six weeks can be recouped.

89 Jobseekers Act 1995

Amends the Social Security Contributions and Benefits Act 1992, Social Security Administration Act 1992, Social Security (Incapacity for Work) Act 1994.

The Act introduced Jobseeker's Allowance to replace unemployment benefit.

89.1 Statutory exclusions from entitlement

a) Trade dispute

An employee who is unemployed either because he has a direct interest or is taking part in a trade dispute is disqualified from receiving Jobseeker's Allowance.

b) Misconduct and voluntary leaving

An employee can be disqualified from entitlement to Jobseeker's Allowance for up to 26 weeks if he:

- loses his employment through misconduct; or

- voluntarily leaves employment without just cause.

A volunteer for redundancy is treated as not having left voluntarily.

89.2 Reduction for pension

The Act provides for regulations to be made to reduce Jobseeker's Allowance where the individual is entitled to a personal or occupational pension.

90 Lifting Operations and Lifting Equipment Regulations 1998 (SI 1998 No 2307)

Amend the Factories Act 1961.

Give effect, as respects lifting equipment, to the Council Directive on Minimum Health and Safety Requirements for the Use of Work Equipment by Workers at Work (89/655/EEC as amended by 95/63/EC)

The Regulations make provisions concerning the strength, stability, safety, installation, marking, inspecting and use of lifting equipment at work.

91 Local Government Act 1988

The Act restricts Local Authorities from having regard to 'non-commercial' considerations when awarding public supply or works contracts. Such non-commercial considerations include:

a) the terms and conditions of employment afforded by contractors to their employees

b) the composition of the workforce, and arrangements for promotion, transfer or training of the workforce – ie discrimination consideration

(While considerations of discrimination by a contractor on grounds of race may be looked at as a relevant factor by an authority when considering whether or not to award a contract to a contractor, considerations of sex discrimination may not be taken into account.)

'Contract compliance' – ie forcing contractors to have non-discriminatory policies and terms and conditions of employment which are as good as the local levels – is, in a general sense, outlawed by this provision.

c)   whether the contractor's workers are employed or self-employed

d)   the conduct of contractors or workers in any industrial disputes

e)   any interests a contractor may have in any other country

f)   any political affiliation or activities of the contractor.

92   Management of Health and Safety at Work and Fire Precautions (Workplace) (Amendment) Regulations 2003 (SI 2003 No 2457)

Amend Management of Health and Safety at Work Regulations 1999 (SI 1999 No 3242) – **see 93 below**.

93   Management of Health and Safety at Work Regulations 1999 (SI 1999 No 3242)

Re-enact with amendments the Management of Health and Safety at Work Regulations 1992 (SI 1992 No 2051). Revoke the Health and Safety (Young Persons) Regulations 1997.

Amended by Management of Health and Safety at Work and Fire Precautions (Workplace) (Amendment) Regulations 2003 (SI 2003 No 2457).

93.1   Risk assessment

a)   The Regulations require an employer to make a suitable and sufficient assessment of

- risks to the health and safety of employees at work; and

- risks to the health and safety of others who are affected by the conduct of his undertaking

so that appropriate protective and preventative measures which must be taken to comply with any statutory provision can be identified. This includes measures which must be taken under Control of Substances Hazardous to Health Regulations 1999 as well as the more general health and safety requirements under HASWA and the other 'six-pack' directives, etc.

b)   The employer must also identify:

- significant findings from the assessment that is made; and

- any groups of employees assessed as being at special risk

and record these findings in writing.

c)   The risk assessment must be reviewed if:

- there is reason to suspect that it is no longer valid; or

- there has been a significant change in the matters to which it relates.

d) Where a number of employers share a workplace, they must co-operate in fulfilling their statutory health and safety duties. They should also take all reasonable steps to co-ordinate their health and safety efforts, and they must provide each other with information about the risks to the other employers' employees arising from their operations.

93.2 Health and safety arrangements

a) The Regulations require employers to make and put into effect appropriate arrangements, having regard to the nature of their activities and the size of the undertaking, for the effective planning, organisation, control, monitoring and review of the preventative and protective measures shown by the risk assessment to be necessary. This requirement is aimed at ensuring some sort of system for the ongoing monitoring and review of health and safety measures in the workplace. Under the amended Regulations, Schedule 1 sets out General Principles of Prevention which an employer must adopt to implement preventative and protective measures. These principles, which derive from Council Directive 89/391/EEC, are:

- avoiding risks;

- evaluating risks that cannot be avoided;

- combating risks at source;

- adapting the work to the individual – especially as regards: workplace design, work equipment, work and production method – with a particular view to alleviating monotonous work and work at a fixed rate, and reducing the effects of this on health;

- adapting to technical progress;

- replacing the dangerous with the non-dangerous or less dangerous;

- developing a coherent overall prevention policy which covers technology, organisation of work, working conditions, social relationships and the influence of factors relating to the working environment;

- giving collective protective measures priority over individual protective measures; and

- giving appropriate instructions to employees.

b) Where the employer employs more than five people, these arrangements must also be recorded in writing.

93.3 Health surveillance

Employers are required to ensure that employees are provided with such health surveillance as is appropriate having regard to the risks to their health and safety identified by the risk assessment. If a particular type of operation could potentially have an adverse effect on an employee's health, the employer must assess the employee's health on an ongoing basis.

The type of health surveillance that would apply in the majority of employments is exemplified by providing eyesight tests for those using display screen equipment (DSE/VDUs).

93.4 Health and safety assistance

a) Employers must appoint one or more competent persons to assist in undertaking the measures they have to take to comply with the various statutory health and safety provisions. Where more than one person is appointed the employer must ensure that they all co-operate with each other. The 1999 Regulations specify that where there is a 'competent person' in the employer's employment, that person should be appointed in preference to a person who is not employed by the employer. (A new reg 21 limits the employer's ability to rely on the fact of appointment of a competent person as a defence in a health and safety case.)

b) The employer is required to consult with the appropriate people or the appropriate body about the appointment of his assistant under this provision. The appropriate people or bodies are:

- where a trade union is recognised, safety representatives under Safety Representatives and Safety Committees Regulations 1977 (SI 1977 No 500)

- where no trade union is recognised, either the employees themselves or representatives of employee safety appointed under Health and Safety (Consultation with Employees) Regulations 1996 (SI 1996 No 1513).

93.5 Procedures for serious and imminent danger and for danger areas

a) Employers must establish and where necessary give effect to appropriate procedures to be followed in the event of serious and imminent danger to employees. This includes procedures for:

- making sure that those who are exposed to serious and imminent danger are informed:

    - of the nature of the hazard; and

    - of the steps taken or to be taken to protect them from it

- enabling people to stop work and go to a safe place in the event of serious, imminent and unavoidable danger

- preventing people from returning to work while a serious and imminent danger continues.

b) Employers must nominate sufficient competent people to implement any evacuation procedures. Safety representatives, employees or representatives of employee safety must be consulted about these nominations (as per **93.4b above**). The most obvious situation to which this applies is evacuation in the case of fire or bomb threat.

c) Employers must also ensure that no employee has access to an area to which access is restricted on health and safety grounds unless that employee has received adequate health and safety training.

d) Employers are required to arrange any necessary contacts with external services with regard to particularly to first-aid, emergency medical care and rescue work.

93.6 Information for employees

Employers must give employees comprehensible and relevant information on:

- risks to their health and safety identified by the risk assessment

- preventative and protective measures taken following the assessment

- the procedures to be followed by the employees in cases of serious and imminent danger – in most cases this will entail having at least a set fire evacuation procedure

- any risks to employees arising out of the operations of another employer who shares premises with the employer.

93.7 Employees' duties and training

a) Employers must take into account an employee's capabilities to do a task, in health and safety terms, before entrusting that task to that employee.

b) Employers must also ensure that employees are provided with adequate health and safety training during working hours:

  - when they are recruited

  - when they are exposed to new or increased risks because of:

    - a transfer or change of responsibility

    - the introduction of a new system of work, new machinery or new technology

    - a change in the system of work or in the way in which existing machinery is used.

c) Employees must use any health and safety equipment provided for them by their employer, including machinery, materials and safety equipment, in accordance with any training and instruction given by the employer.

d) Employees must inform their employer or a fellow employee with health and safety responsibility of any situation or matter that affects them or their work:

  - which they reasonably consider to be a serious and imminent danger to health and safety; or

  - which they reasonably consider to be a shortcoming in the employer's arrangements for health and safety protection.

  This duty on an employee is limited to what his training and experience would make him realise was a serious risk or a shortcoming in health and safety arrangements.

93.8 Liability to employees

Under the Regulations as originally drafted, neither employees nor others could bring a civil action for any breach of the Management of Health and Safety at Work Regulations 1999. An amendment brought about by the Management of Health and Safety at Work and Fire Precautions (Workplace) (Amendment) Regulations 2003 now allows employees to sue for breaches of the 1999 Regulations – although non-employees are still not able to sue for such breaches.

93.9 Children and young persons

a) The requirements concerning children and young persons, formerly contained in the Health and Safety (Young Persons) Regulations 1997 are included in the new 2003 Regulations.

'Young person' is defined as anyone who has not attained the age of 18.

b) The 2003 Regulations disapply the Management of Health and Safety at Work Regulations 1999 to certain categories:

(i) those employed on sea-going ships

(ii) those engaged on short-term or occasional work in:

- domestic service in a private household; or

- a family undertaking where the work is not harmful, damaging or dangerous to young people.

c) The 2003 Regulations require an assessment of risks to young persons

Other than in the cases where the Regulations are disapplied an employer must make a risk assessment in relation to the health and safety of any young person/s employed by him, having particular regard to:

(i) the inexperience, lack of awareness of risks and immaturity of young persons;

(ii) the fitting out and layout of the workplace and the work station;

(iii) the nature, degree and duration of the exposure to physical, biological and chemical agents;

(iv) the form, range and use of work equipment and the way in which it is handled;

(v) the organisation of processes and activities;

(vi) the extent of the health and safety training that is provided for young persons; and

(vii) risks from agents, processes and types of work listed in the Annex to Council Directive 94/33/EC.

d) The 2003 Regulations require employers to provide the parents of any child they employ with comprehensible and relevant information on:

(i) the risks to the child's health and safety identified by the assessment;

(ii) the preventative and protective measures taken; and

(iii) the risks arising from any other employer in a shared workplace.

e) The 2003 Regulations impose a series of duties on employers in terms of the protection of young persons

(i) Employers have a general duty to ensure that young persons are protected from risks to their health and safety that are a consequence of inexperience, lack of awareness of risks or immaturity.

(ii) An employer, having considered the risk assessment, may not employ a young person for work:

- beyond his physical or physiological capabilities;

- which may in any way chronically affect human health;

- involving harmful radiation;

- involving risk of accidents which it may reasonably be assumed cannot be recognised or avoided by young persons because of insufficient attention to safety, or lack of experience or training; or

- where there is a risk to health from:

  - extremes of temperature,

  - noise, or

  - vibration.

(iii) These restrictions do not apply where:

- the person employed is no longer a child (ie is above school-leaving age);

- the work is necessary for his training;

- he will be supervised by a competent person; and

- the risk has been reduced to the lowest level that is reasonably practicable.

94 Manual Handling Operations Regulations 1992 (SI 1992 No 2793)

This is one of the 'six-pack' of regulations introduced in 1992 arising from European health and safety Directives.

Amend the Offices, Shops and Railway Premises Act 1963 and the Factories Act 1961.

a) 'Manual handling' is concerned with moving objects around usually by lifting, but also by pushing or pulling.

b) Manual handling which shows in the general risk assessment as potentially involving risk of injury should be avoided wherever possible.

c) If manual handling cannot be avoided, it should be automated as far as is practicable.

d) Where it is not possible to avoid manual handling, an assessment must be made of all manual handling which is necessary and which involves a risk of injury. The assessment must be repeated if it gets out of date.

e) Steps must be taken to reduce the risk to employees to the lowest possible level, including:

- increasing automation

- reducing weights to be carried

- putting the weights into smaller packages

- making the packages more manageable

- redesigning the workplace or the job where the lifting is carried out to minimise risks.

f) Employers must also provide guidance on:

- lifting techniques

- the weight of each load, and

- where the centre of gravity of a load is not central, on which side the load is heavier.

95 Maternity and Parental Leave etc Regulations 1999 (SI 1999 No 3312)

The amendments inserted by the Maternity and Parental Leave (Amendment) Regulations 2002 (SI 2002 No 2789) are included below.

95.1 Maternity leave

a) Entitlement to Ordinary Maternity Leave (OML)

A woman is entitled to Ordinary maternity leave provided:

- she informs her employer, in writing if he so requires, before the end of the 15th week before the expected week of childbirth (EWC) of:

  - her pregnancy;

  - the EWC;

  - the date on which she intends her Ordinary maternity leave to begin.

The date on which her Ordinary maternity leave is to begin must not be before the beginning of the 11th week before the EWC.

- A woman can change the date on which she is to start her ordinary maternity leave provided she gives her employer at least four weeks' notice of the new date.

- If requested by her employer she must also produce a certificate from a doctor or midwife to show the EWC.

If a woman is absent wholly or partly due to pregnancy or confinement at any time after the start of the 4th week before the EWC, her maternity leave automatically starts when she is absent. In such cases the woman must as soon as is reasonably practicable notify her employer, in writing if he requires, that she is off on maternity leave.

If a woman gives birth, that too will automatically trigger the start of her maternity leave. Again the woman must as soon as is reasonably practicable inform her employer, in writing if he requires, that she has given birth.

- Once the employer is notified of the date the woman intends go on maternity leave, he must inform her of the date on which her maternity leave will end. If he fails to do this:

  - he cannot prevent her from returning early;

  - the woman is protected against being subjected to a detriment or dismissal if she fails to return on the due date; and

  - the employer cannot require her to tell him whether or not she intends to return at the end of her Additional maternity leave (see below).

b) Ordinary Maternity Leave (OML)

Ordinary maternity leave continues for 26 weeks.

During ordinary maternity leave a woman remains subject to her terms and conditions of employment other than those to do with remuneration (for these purposes 'remuneration' is defined as being restricted to those sums payable to the employee by way of wages or salary).

c) Return from Ordinary Maternity Leave

A woman is not allowed to return to work within four weeks of childbirth.

Subject to this, provided the woman gives her employer at least 21 days' notice, she can return to work. (If the employer has not notified her of her return date, she can return at any time without notice.)

A woman who returns from a single period of Ordinary maternity leave is entitled to return to her original job unless redundancy makes that not practicable – in which case she is entitled to be offered suitable and appropriate alternative employment.

d) Entitlement to Additional Maternity Leave (AML)

A woman who has had more than 26 weeks' service at the beginning of the 14th week before the EWC is entitled to take Additional maternity leave (AML).

AML is a period of 26 weeks beginning immediately after OML ends.

A woman who is entitled to AML may be requested by her employer to notify him in writing of:

- the date of childbirth; and

- whether or not she intends to return to work after her Additional maternity leave period.

The request from the employer for this information must inform the employee that if she fails to provide it she will lose her protection against dismissal and action short of dismissal for having taken AML. An employer who has failed to notify a woman of her due return date, when he was first informed of when she intended to start her ordinary maternity leave, is not entitled to make such a request or to be informed of whether or not the employee intends to return to work following her maternity leave.

e) Return from Additional Maternity Leave

A woman who returns from AML is entitled to return to her old job, or, if that is not reasonably practicable, to a job which is both suitable to her and appropriate for her to do in the circumstances.

- If it would have been practicable for the woman to return to her original job at the end of her AML, but following a period of parental leave of less than four weeks immediately following her AML it has become impracticable for the woman to return to her original job, then her entitlement to return remains an entitlement to return to her original job.

f) Protection from dismissal and detriment in relation to pregnancy and maternity leave

A woman is entitled not to be subjected to any detrimental act or failure to act or to be dismissed on a number of grounds concerned with pregnancy and maternity leave including: pregnancy;

having given birth; having been suspended on maternity grounds; or having taken maternity or parental leave or time off to care for dependants.

95.2 Parental leave

a) Entitlement to Parental leave

To be entitled to parental leave, the employee:

- must have been employed for a year; and

- must have, or expect to have, responsibility for a child.

The amount of parental leave which the employee can take is 13 weeks' leave in respect of any individual child. (Parents with children who are entitled to disability living allowance are entitled to 18 rather than 13 weeks' parental leave.)

Parental leave can only be taken up to the date of the child's fifth birthday, or, in the case of a child entitled to disability living allowance, up to the date of the child's 18th birthday. Where parental leave is taken by adoptive parents of a child, parental leave can be taken up to five years from the date of placement or until the child is 18 – whichever is the earlier.

Schedule 2 of the Regulations sets out default provisions which provide for:

- the notice to be given to the employer;

- the evidence to be presented to the employer;

- contingencies concerning postponement of parental leave; and

- the minimum and maximum periods of parental leave that may be taken.

These provisions apply in the absence of a workforce agreement concerning such matters.

b) On return from Parental leave

- If the period of leave was less than four weeks, the employee is entitled to return to his original job.

- If the period of parental leave exceeds four weeks and it is not reasonably practicable for the employee to return to his original job, the employee is entitled to return to a job which is both suitable and appropriate for employee to do in the circumstances and which is no less favourable in terms of the pay and other conditions.

Equivalent provisions apply to protect those who take parental leave from detrimental treatment and from dismissal as apply to protect women who take maternity leave.

96 Maternity and Parental Leave (Amendment) Regulations 2001 (SI 2001 No 4010)

Amend Maternity and Parental Leave etc Regulations 1999 (SI 1999 No 3312). The amendments are noted in those Regulations – **see 95 above**.

97 Maternity and Parental Leave (Amendment) Regulations 2002 (SI 2002 No 2789)

Amend Maternity and Parental Leave etc Regulations 1999 (SI 1999 No 3312) – **see 95 above**.

98 National Minimum Wage Act 1998 and National Minimum Wage Regulations 1999 (SI 1999 No 584)

Amend the Agricultural Wages Act 1948, Employment Tribunals Act 1996 and ERA.

Amended by the Employment Relations Act 1999 and National Minimum Wage Regulations 1999 (Amendment) Regulations 2004 (SI 2004 No 1161) and National Minimum Wage Regulations 1999 (Amendment) (No 2) Regulations 2004 (SI 2004 No 1930).

The Act establishes a framework for the national minimum wage, which took effect from April 1999. Much of the substance concerning those who are not entitled to receive the national minimum wage, the rate of the national minimum wage, the times of work in respect of which it is payable, the remuneration to be set off against it and record-keeping are dealt with by the National Minimum Wage Regulations 1999. In this commentary no distinction is made between provisions arising directly under the Act and those provided by the Regulations.

98.1 Who is entitled?

a) A person is entitled to the national minimum wage if he:

- is a worker,

- is working or ordinarily works in the UK under his contract, and

- is aged over 18.

b) A 'worker' means

- a person who has entered into or works under a contract of employment;

- a person who works under a contract of apprenticeship;

- someone who is under a contract to perform work personally for the employer where the employer is not a customer or client of that person's business.

c) A 'worker' also includes

- someone who works through an employment agency – even if there is no contract directly between the company and the worker (the person who is liable to pay the national minimum wage is whoever is liable to pay the worker's pay);

- homeworkers, even if they are not under a contract to perform the work personally;

- mariners, but not share fishermen, employed on UK-registered ships unless:

  - all their duties are performed outside the UK, and

  - they are not resident in the UK.

People in offshore employment are included by The National Minimum Wage (Offshore Employment) Order 1999.

The Secretary of State has the power to add to those to whom the Act applies.

d) Those excluded from entitlement to the national minimum wage include:

- voluntary workers who are not paid or otherwise remunerated for their work (the Employment Relations Act 1999 also excludes those who are part of a resident religious community);

- prisoners in respect of work done under the prison rules;

- those in the armed forces;

- a person who lives in the employer's household and who is either a member of that household or who is treated as a member of that household is excluded from entitlement to the national minimum wage for:

    - household work, or

    - work in running the family business;

- a worker who is under 26 and who is employed on a contract of apprenticeship, on a modern apprenticeship or under a government training scheme who:

    - is in the first year of employment (including any period of continuous employment), or

    - has not attained the age of 19;

- a worker who is on a government scheme designed to provide him with training, work experience or temporary work which is funded in part or wholly under the European Social Fund;

- a worker who is working as part of a first degree course or initial teacher training;

- a homeless person who is provided with shelter and other benefits for performing work;

- those who are members of residential religious communities (from 25 October 1999).

98.2 Who is liable to pay?

a) Normally the employer is liable to pay the minimum wage.

b) Where a worker is employed by someone who is himself employed by an employer and the worker works on the superior employer's premises, both the worker's immediate employer and the superior employer are considered to be the worker's employer for the purposes of the Act.

98.3 The national minimum wage

a) The national minimum wage is a single hourly rate and is prescribed by the Secretary of State, after consultation with the Low Pay Commission.

b) A lower rate of national minimum wage is set for those who are aged between 18 and 22.

c) A rate between the above two rates is set for those who are:

- over 22;

- in the first six months of continuous employment with their employer; and

- required to take part in accredited training on at least 26 days in the first six months of that contract.

98.4 Items that can and cannot be set off against the employer's liability to pay the national minimum wage

a) The following can be set off against the employer's liability:

- any contractual remuneration;

- any payments made under the Agricultural Wages Act.

b) The following cannot be set off against the employer's liability:

- benefits in kind, other than living accommodation, which can be set off at a very low fixed rate;

- vouchers or stamps which can be exchanged for goods, services or money;

- any loan or advance of wages;

- a pension or compensation for loss of office;

- a redundancy payment;

- any award of a court or payment in settlement of a matter which was or could have been taken to court by the worker;

- any payment made under a suggestion scheme.

98.5 Calculating the worker's entitlement

The worker's entitlement is calculated over a reference period of a month, or a lesser period if the worker is paid more frequently.

There are complex provisions for calculating an employee's entitlement depending on his working regime, contained in the National Minimum Wage Regulations 1999.

98.6 Records

a) Records of payments

The employer must keep records which are sufficient to show that he is remunerating the worker at a rate at least equal to the national minimum wage.

b) The worker's right of access to records

Where the worker believes, on reasonable grounds, that he has been or is being remunerated at less than the national minimum wage, he can serve a 'production' notice on his employer requiring production of any relevant statutory national minimum wage records for the relevant period.

The employer must then give the employee reasonable notice of when and where the records will be produced.

The records must be produced:

- at the worker's place of work,

- at such other place as is reasonable in all the circumstances, or

- at a place agreed between the employer and the employee.

The records must be produced within 14 days of the production notice or such later time as is agreed between the employer and the worker during the 14-day period.

- The worker is entitled to be accompanied at an inspection by 'such other person as the worker may think fit'.

If the employer fails to produce the relevant records or fails to allow the worker to exercise any of his rights, a complaint may be made to an employment tribunal within three months of:

- the end of the 14-day period, or

- the agreed production date if that was to be later; or

- if it is not reasonably practicable for the employee's claim to be presented within these time limits, within such further period as the tribunal considers reasonable.

If the tribunal finds the claim to be valid it will:

- make a declaration to that effect, and

- award 80 times the hourly national minimum wage.

98.7 Officers may be appointed under the Act

a) Officers' powers of inspection

An officer can require a 'relevant person' to allow him to:

- inspect relevant records,

- require an explanation of any relevant records, and

- enter on to premises to carry out the above.

b) A 'relevant person' for these purpose is:

- the worker's employer,

- an employment agent through or for whom the worker is working,

- a person who supplies work to an individual who qualifies for the national minimum wage,

- any employee or agent of any of the above, or

- anyone who qualifies for the national minimum wage.

c) Enforcement and penalty notices

If an officer is of opinion that a worker has been remunerated at a rate that is less than the national minimum wage for any period, he can serve the employer with an enforcement notice requiring the employer to pay the difference.

- The employer can appeal to an employment tribunal against an enforcement notice within four weeks of the notice.

- If an enforcement notice is not complied with, the officer can:
  - sue on behalf of the employee/s covered by the enforcement notice
    - either at an employment tribunal – under the protection of wages provisions; or
    - in the civil court as a breach of contract
  - serve the employer with a penalty notice which states:
    - the amount of the fixed penalty (including the calculation of the fixed penalty) – the amount is currently set at twice the hourly national minimum wage per worker to whom the failure to comply relates per day of non-compliance
    - the time within which the financial penalty is to be paid (which must be not less than four weeks from service of the notice – it should be noted that the fact that an employer has appealed against an enforcement notice does not prevent a penalty notice from being served, although the employer need not comply with it until the appeal has been decided)
    - the period to which the financial penalty relates
    - the respects in which the officer considers that the enforcement notice has not be complied with; and
    - the calculation of the amount of the financial penalty.
  - The employer can appeal against the penalty notice.

98.8 Enforcing the right to national minimum wage

a) A worker can claim any deficiency in pay below the national minimum wage under the protection of wages part of the ERA.

b) Workers who are entitled to the national minimum wage, but who are not generally covered by the protection of the ERA, are given a specific right to be treated as if they were covered by the ERA for purposes of making a claim.

98.9 The right not to suffer a detriment or to be unfairly dismissed

a) A worker is entitled not to be dismissed, or to suffer a detriment by any act or deliberate failure by his employer to act, on grounds:

- that any action was, or was proposed to be, taken by or on behalf of any worker to secure any benefit or right under the legislation;
- of any action taken in prosecuting the employer for an offence under the Act;
- of any action taken because the worker will qualify for the national minimum wage or for a different rate of national minimum wage.

b) There is no qualifying period for the right to bring a claim of unfair dismissal on these grounds.

98.10 Reversal of the burden of proof in civil proceedings

It is presumed

- that the claimant qualifies for the national minimum wage; and

- that the worker was paid at less than the national minimum wage

unless, in either case, the contrary is proved.

98.11 Contracting out

The normal rules against contracting out apply.
   However, a settlement can be reached

- through ACAS, or

- through a compromise agreement.

98.12 Offences under the Act

- refusal or deliberate neglect to pay a worker the national minimum wage

- failure to keep any record required to be kept under the Act

- producing a record with inaccurate information

- delaying or obstructing an officer in the exercise of his duties under the Act

- refusing to answer any question asked by an officer or to produce any document asked for by him.

   It is a defence to any such charge to show that the person charged exercised all due diligence and took all reasonable precautions to secure that the requirements of the legislation were complied with by himself and any person under his control.

   Where an offence is by a body corporate, any director, manager or secretary who has consented to or connived in the offence is made personally liable.

99 National Minimum Wage Regulations 1999 (Amendment) Regulations 2004 (SI 2004 No 1161)

Amend the National Minimum Wage Regulations 1999 (SI 1999 No 584).

   With effect from 1 October 2004, change the method of calculation of the rate of pay of a piece-worker. Under the original Regulations, pay for piece-work was calculated on the basis of a 'fair estimate' of the time taken to do the work. Under the new system the employer has to determine a mean hourly rate for all those who are carrying out piece-work by testing the hourly rate of output of all workers. In effect a time and motion study. The amount of the minimum wage for each piece is then based on the average time taken to produce each piece or to fulfil each task.

   From 6 April 2005 the rate for each piece is increased to 120 per cent of the average time rate to produce each piece.

100 National Minimum Wage Regulations 1999 (Amendment) (No 2) Regulations 2004 (SI 2004 No 1930)

Amend the National Minimum Wage Regulations 1999 (SI 1999 No 584) and National Minimum Wage Regulations 1999 (Amendment) Regulations 2003 (SI 2003 No 1923).

The Regulations provide a new level of national minimum wage for workers above minimum school leaving age but below 18.

The Regulations amend the list of government schemes to be treated as 'apprenticeships'. This excludes those engaged on these schemes from entitlement to national minimum wage rates either completely or for the first 12 months of their contract.

101 Offices, Shops and Railway Premises Act 1963

Amended by Fire Precautions Act 1971, Health and Safety at Work etc Act 1974, Manual Handling Operations Regulations 1992 (SI 1992 No 2793), Provision and Use of Work Equipment Regulations 1992 (SI 1992 No 2932), Workplace (Health, Safety and Welfare) Regulations 1992 (SI 1992 No 3004), and Police Act 1997.

The purpose of this Act was to establish a code of safety and welfare for those places of work not covered by the then existing legislation. It is concerned largely with welfare provisions such as adequate ventilation, light, warmth and washing facilities (much of which is now covered by Regulations). Fire precautions in premises subject to this statute are now covered by the 1971 Act as amended.

102 Part-Time Workers (Prevention of Less Favourable Treatment) Regulations 2000 (SI 2000 No 1551)

Amended by the Part-time Workers (Prevention of Less Favourable Treatment) Regulations 2001 (SI 2001 No 1107) and the Part-time Workers (Prevention of Less Favourable Treatment) Regulations 2000 (Amendment) Regulations 2002 (SI 2002 No 2035).

The Regulations provide that workers who work part-time or who become part-time or who return to work part-time must not be treated less favourably than a comparable full-time worker.

'Part-time' for these purposes means anything less than full-time hours.

a) Different contracts

Workers are considered to be on different contracts if:

- either the claimant or the comparator is employed under a contract of apprenticeship and the other person is not;

- the claimant or the comparator is not employed;

- it is reasonable for the employer to treat a worker of a particular description differently from other workers on the grounds that workers of that description have a different type of contract.

(This amended definition of 'different contracts' was introduced by the Fixed-term Employees (Prevention of Less Favourable Treatment) Regulations 2002 (SI 2002 No 2034); prior to this, various fixed-term arrangements were also to be treated as amounting to 'different contracts' for the purposes of these 2000 Regulations.)

b) Comparable full-time worker:

A full-time worker is a 'comparable' full-time worker if:

- he and the part-time worker are employed by the same employer under the same type of contract;

- they are both engaged on the same or broadly similar work (the level of qualification, skills and experience of each may be taken into account in relation to this assessment where relevant); and

- the full-timer is based at the same establishment as the part-time worker. Only if there is no comparable full-time worker at the establishment where the part-time worker is employed can the part-time worker look to another establishment for a comparator who fulfils the two above comparability conditions.

c) Less favourable treatment

A part-time worker is entitled not to be treated less favourably than a comparable full-time worker either as regards his terms and conditions of employment or by being subjected to any other detriment because he is a part-time worker.

The only exception to this is where a difference in treatment can be objectively justified.

In general the principle is that a part-time worker should be treated pro rata to the comparable full-time worker.

Overtime work is dealt with separately provided that the part-timer is not treated less favourably than the comparable full-time employee would be. So the part-time worker can be paid at basic rates for overtime until he has worked the number of hours that would entitle a full-time employee to receive an overtime premium for extra hours worked.

d) Statement of reasons for less favourable treatment

A worker who claims to have received less favourable treatment is entitled to request a written statement of the reasons for his less favourable treatment.

The employer must provide a statement within 21 days of the request.

An employment tribunal may take into account any deliberate failure by the employer to provide a statement. It may also draw any inferences it considers just and equitable where the employer has given an evasive or equivocal statement.

Where the 'less favourable treatment' amounts to dismissal, the worker is not entitled to ask for a statement under these provisions but is left to ask for written reasons for the dismissal under the normal ERA rules.

e) Automatically unfair dismissal and the right not to suffer a detriment

A worker can complain if he is dismissed or subjected to a detriment because he has brought proceedings under the Regulations, asked for a statement, given evidence or done anything else under or by reference to the Regulations. Dismissal is treated as automatically unfair for purposes of the ERA.

f)   Complaint to an employment tribunal

A complaint may be brought to an employment tribunal within three months of the date of any infringement of the rights conferred by the Regulations. The tribunal can extend the time limit for complaint if it considers it just and equitable to do so.

If the tribunal finds that the complainant is well founded:

- it will make a declaration as to the rights of the worker and of the employer in relation to that complaint, and

- the employer will be ordered to pay such compensation as is 'just and equitable'.

The tribunal can also recommend specific action for the employer to take, within a set time, to obviate or reduce the adverse affect of the discrimination on the employee.

103 Patents Acts 1977 and 2004

Amended by Copyright, Design and Patents Act 1988 and Patents Act 2004.

103.1 Ownership of inventions

The Acts provide a method of determining the ownership, as between employer and employee, of an employee's inventions and also provides for the employee to be given compensation for his invention in certain circumstances.

The invention will belong to the employer if:

- it was made in the course of either the employee's normal duties or special duties that had been assigned to him, and if in either case an invention was, in the circumstances, to be reasonably expected from his carrying out these duties; or

- the employee made the invention in the course of his duties and because of the nature of his duties and the particular responsibilities arising from the nature of those duties he was under a special obligation to further his employer's interests.

In all other cases the invention belongs to the employee.

103.2 Compensation

An application for compensation for an invention may be made to the Comptroller or Patents Court:

- if the invention belongs to the employer under the Act; and it has been patented; and it is of outstanding benefit to the employer; or

- where the patented invention belongs to the employee and has been assigned to the employer or the employer has been granted an exclusive licence to the invention by the employee; and the benefit derived by the employee is inadequate in relation to the benefit derived from the patent by the employer.

The amount of compensation, in either case, is to be a 'fair share' of the benefit that the employer has derived or will derive from the patent.

104 Paternity and Adoption Leave Regulations 2002 (SI 2002 No 2788)

Amended by Paternity and Adoption Leave (Amendment) Regulations 2004 (SI 2004 No 923). Those amendments are taken into account below.

104.1 Paternity leave

To be entitled to paternity leave a male employee must fulfil the following requirements:

- He must have completed 26 weeks' service at the beginning of the 14th week before the expected week of childbirth (EWC). (No account is taken of the baby's being born early in making this calculation.)
- He must be either:
  - the father of the child; or
  - the husband or partner of the mother of the baby, but not the child's father; and
- he must have, or expect to have, parental responsibility for bringing up the child.

  The father can take either one or two weeks' paternity leave. Paternity leave must be taken within the first 56 days after the child's birth.

  The employee must give the employer notice in or before the 15th week before the EWC or, if that is not reasonably practicable, as soon as is reasonably practicable. The notice must specify:

  - the expected week of the child's birth,
  - the length of the period of leave that the employee has chosen to take, and
  - the date on which, in accordance with regulation, the employee has chosen that his period of leave should begin.

  If the employer so requests, the employee must also give the employer a signed declaration that he is going on paternity leave and that he satisfies the conditions of entitlement to paternity leave.

  Where paternity leave is sought by an adoptive parent there are equivalent requirements based on the date of placement of the child rather than the date of birth. Paternity leave must be taken within 56 days of the date on which the child is adopted.

  After paternity leave the employee is entitled to return to the job that he left. If the employee has had other periods of statutory leave in addition to paternity leave and it is not reasonably practicable for him to return to his former position, the employer must provide alternative work that is suitable and appropriate for him to do.

104.2 Adoption leave

An employee is entitled to a period of adoption leave if:

- the employee has completed 26 weeks' service at the date of being matched with the child;
- he or she is the adopter of the child;

- the employee has agreed:
  - that the child should be placed with him or her; and
  - on the date of placement.

Adoption leave begins on a date from 14 days prior to the placement up to the date of placement.

The employee must, within seven days of having been notified of having been matched with a child for purpose of adoption, provide his or her employer with notice which includes:

- the date when the child will be placed with the employee;
- the date when the employee's adoption leave is to begin.

If the employer requests it, the employee must also provide the employer with written evidence from the adoption agency showing:

- the name and address of the agency;
- the name and date of birth of the child;
- the date on which the employee was notified that he had been matched with the child; and
- the date on which the agency expects to place the child with the employee.

Ordinary adoption leave is for 26 weeks and is equivalent to Ordinary Maternity Leave in terms of the conditions that apply to it (**see 95 above**).

An employee who takes Ordinary adoption leave is also entitled to Additional adoption leave unless either:

- the employee took Ordinary adoption leave, but the placement was not made; or
- the employee was dismissed during Ordinary adoption leave.

Additional adoption leave is 26 weeks.

The employee can return at any time during Additional adoption leave on giving 28 days' notice.

The right to return after Ordinary and Additional adoption leave is equivalent to the right of a woman's return after Ordinary and Additional maternity leave.

104.3 Protection from dismissal and detriment in relation to paternity and adoption leave

An employee is entitled not to be subjected to any detrimental act or failure to act or to be dismissed on a number of grounds concerned with paternity and adoption leave including having taken paternity, adoption or parental leave or time off to care for dependants.

105 Paternity and Adoption Leave (Adoption from Overseas) Regulations 2003 (SI 2003 No 921)

Amended by the Statutory Paternity Pay and Statutory Adoption Pay (Amendment) Regulations 2004 (SI 2004 No 488).

a) Adoption leave

The Regulations make provisions for adoption leave where a child is adopted from abroad.

In such cases Ordinary adoption leave must begin within 28 days of the date on which the child arrives in the United Kingdom.

b) Paternity leave in relation to adoption leave

The Regulations provide that the spouse or partner of an adopter of a child from outside the UK is entitled to paternity leave provided the employee has been continuously employed for 26 weeks ('partner' is defined in the 2004 Regulations).

One or two weeks' leave may be taken within 56 days of the child's entry into the United Kingdom.

106 Paternity and Adoption Leave (Amendment) Regulations 2004 (SI 2004 No 923)

Amend the Paternity and Adoption Leave Regulations 2002 (SI 2002 No 2788) – **see 104 above**.

107 Pensions Acts 1995 and 2004

Amend the Equal Pay Act 1970, SDA, EPCA, Companies Acts 1985 and 1989, Insolvency Act 1986, Social Security Act 1989, SSBCA, Pensions Schemes Act 1993, and various other Acts in connection with the equalisation of state pension age.

Amended by ERA and Transfer of Employment (Pension Protection) Regulations 2005 (SI 2005 No 649).

107.1 General regulation of occupational pension schemes

The 1995 Act set up a closer regulatory system to ensure the security of employees' pensions which introduced the Occupational Pensions Regulatory Authority. The OPRA was dissolved in April 2005 and replaced by the Pensions Regulator.

107.2 Employee trustees

The provisions for paid time off and training for employee pension scheme trustees are now contained in the ERA (**see 53.6b above**).

107.3 Equalisation of state pensionable age

Under the 1995 Act state pensionable age was increased for women born after 6 April 1950. There is a gradual increase, over a 10-year period, so that pension age will ultimately be equalised at 65 for all those born after 6 April 1955.

107.4 Equal treatment in relation to occupational pension schemes

Provision for equal treatment in relation to occupational pension schemes was originally introduced by Schedule 5 Social Security Act 1989. These provisions were enacted to give effect to EC Directive 86/378/EEC on the equal treatment of men and women in relation to occupational social security schemes. Following the ECJ's judgment in *Barber v Guardian Royal Exchange Assurance Group* [1990] IRLR 240 it became clear that equal treatment under occupational pension schemes from 17 May 1990, the date of the ECJ's judgment in *Barber*, had to be treated as a matter of equal pay. The provisions of this Act therefore overtook the provisions of the Social Security Act 1989 as far as pensions were concerned. The 1995 Act adopts a framework for equal treatment in relation to occupational pension schemes which closely mirrors the provisions of the Equal Pay Act 1970. These provisions are applicable to pensionable service on or after 17 May 1990.

a) The equal treatment rule

The equal treatment rule relates to the terms on which people become members of the scheme and to the terms on which members of pension schemes are treated. This includes:

- Discretionary matters: trustees or managers of pension schemes are often given discretionary powers under the scheme. The Act provides that where there is any discretionary power that could be exercised in a way that is detrimental to a woman, the effect of the equal treatment rule is to bar the trustees from exercising their discretion in that way.

- Dependants' benefits: where the scheme provides benefits for dependants of members (for example, life assurance cover or survivor's pensions), these too are subject to the requirement of equal treatment between scheme members.

- All occupational pension schemes that do not specifically contain an equal treatment rule are deemed to include one. Where the rules of the scheme do not allow for the scheme to be altered to accommodate the requirements of an equal treatment rule, the trustees are given the power to alter the scheme by resolution to accommodate the equal treatment rule and its effects. Any such alteration can be retrospective.

b) Who can claim?

Those who are on 'like work', 'work rated as equivalent' or engaged on 'work of equal value' to:

- a comparator of the opposite sex, or

- a comparator of the opposite sex and of the same marital status (where benefits differ with marital status)

are entitled to have any term of the scheme which is unfavourable to them modified so as to be as favourable to them as it is to their comparator.

c) Exclusions

- Material difference
  As with equal pay, there is an exclusion where the trustees of the scheme can show that the differences in the terms or effects of the scheme are due to a material difference between the two employees other than the difference in their sex.

- Maternity and family leave
  The equal treatment rule for pensions is subject to the equality provisions in the Social Security Act 1989 relating to maternity and family leave.

■ State pension

A difference in treatment is allowed, in pension schemes, if that difference arises purely out of the difference in entitlement to a state retirement pension between the sexes.

■ Actuarial calculations

A difference in treatment is allowed if it is the result of a difference in actuarial calculations for each sex in respect of:

■ the level of the employer's contributions to the scheme, or

■ the level of benefit from the scheme.

d) Claims

The equal treatment rule is treated as one with the requirement for equal treatment in relation to pay under the Equal Pay Act 1970 and a case may be brought to an employment tribunal in the same way.

To be entitled to claim, the employee must bring a claim within six months of the time when he or she was employed in a category of job to which the pension scheme in question applied.

The SDA is amended to include, within the definition of grounds on which it is unlawful to victimise an employee, the fact that a person has made a claim under these provisions.

107.5 Pension entitlement of transferred employees

Sections 257–258 Pensions Act 2004, together with Transfer of Employment (Pension Protection) Regulations 2005 (SI 2005 No 649), provide rights for employees who are transferred from one employer to another under TUPE.

a) Who is covered?

Employees who prior to the transfer

■ were members of the transferor's occupational pension scheme;

■ were entitled to be members of the transferor's occupational pension scheme, but had not joined; and

■ those who would have been entitled to be members of the transferor's scheme but were not because they did not have sufficient service at the date of transfer to be eligible.

In the case of a money purchase scheme these provisions only apply:

■ where the transferor is required to make contributions to the scheme in respect of the transferred employee; or

■ where the transferor has made one or more contributions.

If the transferred employee is either one who is eligible to join the scheme and has not or is one who has had insufficient service to be eligible to join the scheme, then the rules only apply where the employer is required to contribute under the terms of the scheme.

It should be noted that the statute specifically ignores anything that the transferor has done in anticipation of the transfer to avoid the transferee being liable under these provisions.

b) What must the transferee provide?

Transferees are not required to provide defined benefits (ie final salary) schemes. If they do, however, then:

- they must provide at least 1/60 per year of service of the employee's qualifying earnings for life; and

- there must also be a survivor's pension under the scheme.

Where the scheme the transferee uses is a money purchase scheme:

- if the transferor's scheme was non-contributory, he must contribute at least 6 per cent of the employee's basic pay before tax to the scheme each year;

- if the transferor's scheme was contributory, the transferee must contribute no less than the employee contributes up to a maximum of 6 per cent of the employee's basic pay before tax.

Finally, the transferee can contribute to a stakeholder pension, the basis of contribution being no less than he would be liable to make under a money purchase scheme.

108 Pension Schemes Act 1993

Amends the Social Security Act 1973, Social Security Pensions Act 1975, EPCA, Social Security Act 1979, Social Security Act 1980, Social Security Act 1981, Social Security and Housing Benefits Act 1982, Health and Social Security Act 1984, Insolvency Act 1985, Insolvency Act 1986, Social Security Act 1986, Social Security Act 1988, Social Security Act 1989, Employment Act 1989, Social Security Act 1990, TULRA, Social Security Act 1993.

Amended by the Pensions Act 1995.

This Act was passed to consolidate and amend some of the law relating to pension schemes.

108.1 'Contracted-out pension schemes'

The Act contains the definition of 'contracted-out employment' for pension purposes. Contracted-out pension schemes are those which are contracted out of the earnings-related part of the state scheme. To be contracted out pension schemes must meet the appropriate requirements of the Act.

108.2 Reclaiming unpaid pension deductions

The Act deals with the case where an employer becomes insolvent after an employee has had deductions made from pay for pension scheme contributions. In such cases, if any such contributions have not been paid to the pension scheme, someone acting on behalf of a pension scheme can apply to the Secretary of State for payments to be made equivalent to any such sums. If the Secretary of State fails to pay, a person acting for the pension scheme can apply to an employment tribunal to order those payments to be made. Outstanding contributions to an employer's pension scheme are given priority in the event of the employer's bankruptcy to the extent that those contributions relate to the 12 months prior to insolvency.

108.3 Individuals' rights in respect of pension schemes

a) Preservation of rights under pension schemes – short-term employees

   (i) A 'short-term' member of a pension scheme is one who has had at least two years' pensionable service in an employment with a contracted-out pension scheme. Short-term employees must be provided with a preserved pension unless the accrued pension is transferred to another scheme.

   (ii) The rules of the scheme must not contain any rules that will or could result in a disparity of treatment of a short-term pension scheme member as compared with the way in which a long-term member would be treated in the same circumstances.

   (iii) Short-term members who have a preserved pension in a pension scheme must have their pensions increased to the same extent as those who remain in the scheme.

b) Choice of schemes

   The Act allows employees to opt for personal pension schemes rather than the employer's pension scheme and makes void any contractual provision which purports to make membership of the employer's occupational pension scheme mandatory.

c) Voluntary contributions

   Strict limitations are imposed on a scheme's ability to restrict a member's entitlement to make additional contributions to the scheme.

d) Disclosure of information

   The Secretary of State is empowered to make Regulations to require that certain categories of people are entitled to be given information about pension schemes. (Several sets of Regulations have been made under these provisions.)

   The people who are entitled to this information are:

   - members and, in the case of an occupational pension scheme, prospective members;
   - spouses of the above;
   - those to whom the scheme is applicable or prospectively applicable; and
   - in the case of an occupational pension scheme, an independent trade union that is recognised to any degree for collective bargaining purposes.

   The above categories of people can be required, by Regulations, to be kept informed of:

   - the constitution of the scheme;
   - the scheme's administration and finances;
   - the rights and obligations that arise or may arise under the scheme;
   - any other matters which appear to the Secretary of State to be relevant either to:
     - occupational or personal pension schemes in general; or to

- schemes of a description to which the scheme in question belongs.

The Regulations can specify when the required information is to be given as a matter of course and where it need be given only on application.

Where a person who is entitled to any such information is not given it, that person must serve a default notice on the trustees. If the person still does not get the information within a further 14 days, he or she can apply to the County Court for an Order that the information be provided.

e) Pensions Ombudsman

The Act establishes a Pensions Ombudsman who can deal with disagreements between a member of a pension scheme (or his dependants) and the trustees or managers of the scheme. The Ombudsman is empowered to deal with problems of all types, whether they are matters of fact, of law or of alleged maladministration. The Pensions Ombudsman's powers are amended by the Pensions Act 1995.

109 Personal Protective Equipment at Work Regulations 2002 (SI 2002 No 1144)

These Regulations re-enact, with amendments, Personal Protective Equipment at Work Regulations 1992, which was one of the 'six-pack' of regulations arising from European health and safety Directives. The Regulations amend the Factories Act 1961.

a) Personal protective equipment (PPE)

PPE is industrial body armour. Because it is cumbersome and uncomfortable for the wearer the Regulations, as a whole, encourage PPE to be used only in the last resort where other forms of protection cannot be used or are inadequate. Where PPE is used, a risk assessment must first be carried out to ensure that the PPE proposed is suitable, and it is obviously important that all the PPE supplied to an employee is mutually compatible.

b) Maintenance

Where PPE is provided it must be maintained in an efficient and clean state and in good repair. Proper accommodation must also be made available for its storage.

c) Training

The employee must be given training on the use and purpose of the PPE and on keeping it in a proper condition, and must report any defect in, or loss of, the PPE to his employer. Both the employer and the employee are under a duty to ensure that the PPE is used properly.

d) Guidance

The Regulations contain several pages of guidance to help employers select appropriate PPE for their particular needs.

110 Police (Health and Safety) Act 1997

Amends Health and Safety at Work etc Act 1974 and ERA.

The Act extends the general protection of employees under Part 1 Health and Safety at Work etc Act 1974 to cover police officers. Police officers are also given the right not to be dismissed for health and safety reasons, and as with other employees, any such dismissal is treated as being automatically unfair.

111 Police Act 1997

Amends Offices, Shops and Railway Premises Act 1963, Employers' Liability (Compulsory Insurance) Act 1969, Employers' Liability (Defective Equipment) Act 1969, Employment Agencies Act 1973, SDA, Income and Corporation Taxes Act 1988, ERA.

The provisions of the Police Act 1997 that are relevant for employment purposes are a new system whereby Certificates of Criminal Records can be issued. The Certificates provided under these provisions are issued by the Criminal Records Bureau (CRB).

a) Criminal Conviction Certificate

   (i)   Under the new legislation anyone can apply to the Secretary of State for a Criminal Conviction Certificate provided that:

   ■ the application is made on a prescribed form, and

   ■ the appropriate fee is paid.

   (ii) A Criminal Conviction Certificate gives details of any criminal convictions the person may have, other than any spent convictions (for 'spent convictions' see Rehabilitation of Offenders Act 1974, **121 below**).

b) Criminal Record Certificate

   (i)   Where a person is being considered for employment, or is seeking to join a profession which is exempted from the provisions of the Rehabilitation of Offenders Act 1974 (ie one where questions regarding spent convictions – 'exempted questions' – must be answered fully and truthfully by the applicant), a Criminal Record Certificate (CRC) can be obtained.

   (ii) An application for a CRC must be:

   ■ made in the prescribed form;

   ■ accompanied by the appropriate fee;

   ■ countersigned by a 'registered person'. (A person or body can be registered on application to the Secretary of State if the person or body is likely to ask exempted questions.) The registered person must also certify that the CRC is required for purposes of an exempted question.

   (iii) A CRC will give details of:

   ■ any convictions – whether or not spent; and

   ■ any cautions.

(iv) A copy of the CRC is sent to the registered person who signed the application.

c) Enhanced Criminal Record Certificate

(i) Where an applicant is applying for certain types of employment or licence (see (ii) below), an Enhanced Criminal Record Certificate (ECRC) can be sought.

(ii) The form and method of application is much the same as for a normal CRC (see above), but for an ECRC to be issued, the 'exempted question' must be being asked

■ in the course of considering the applicant for a position whether paid or unpaid which either:

   ■ involves regularly caring for, training, supervising or being in sole charge of persons aged under 18; or

   ■ is of a kind specified in Regulations made by the Secretary of State which involves regularly caring for, training, supervising or being in sole charge of persons aged 18 or over

■ for a purpose relating to any of the following:

   ■ a gaming licence application

   ■ a lotteries and lotteries management licence application

   ■ registration as a child minder

   ■ placing children with foster parents.

(iii) An ECRC will give details of all relevant information relating to the applicant that is recorded in central records. The Secretary of State must also ask all Chief Police Officers in any relevant force to provide any and all information which in that Officer's opinion:

■ might be relevant to the employment or other application which has given rise to the exempted question being asked and which ought to be included in the certificate; and

■ ought not to be included in the certificate in the interests of the prevention of crime but which can be disclosed to a registered person (in a separate document to the ECRC) without harming the interests of the prevention of crime.

(iv) A copy of the ECRC and any accompanying document is sent to the registered person who signed the application.

d) Accuracy

(i) Where an applicant believes that a CCC, CRC or ECRC is inaccurate, he can apply in writing to the Secretary of State for a new certificate. Where the Secretary of State is satisfied that the certificate is inaccurate, a new certificate must be given.

(ii) The Secretary of State may require that an applicant for a certificate under these provisions has fingerprints taken to establish that person's identity. Any Regulations made under this provision may make provision for the destruction of the fingerprints in certain specified circumstances.

e) Unlawful disclosure

   (i) A member, officer or employee of a registered body may disclose information from a certificate only to:

   ■ a fellow member, officer or employee of the registered body in the course of his duties;

   ■ a member, officer or employee of the body which asked the registered person to obtain the information for them.

   Any breach of this is a criminal offence.

   (ii) There are further provisions which make it a criminal offence for a person or body on whose behalf the information has been obtained to further disclose such information, or for a person to whom any such information is disclosed to divulge it to anyone else.

112 Protection from Harassment Act 1997

The Act creates both criminal and civil liability for harassment.

a) Harassment

   (i) A person must not pursue a course of conduct which he knows, or ought to know, amounts to harassment of another.

   (ii) A person 'ought to know' that his conduct amounts to harassment if a reasonable person with the same information would consider that that course of conduct amounted to harassment.

   (iii) A person is not guilty of harassment if in the particular circumstances the course of conduct was reasonable.

   ■ A 'course of conduct' for these purposes must include conduct on two or more occasions; and

   ■ 'conduct' includes speech.

   (iv) Harassment may be dealt with both as a criminal matter, involving a penalty of up to six months' imprisonment, or as a civil matter. In relation to a civil action damages may be awarded for both anxiety caused by the harassment and any financial loss resulting from it. There is no reason, in principle, why an employer cannot be guilty as an accessory to harassment or, more probably in practice, vicariously liable for an employee's harassment.

   (v) Injunctions may also be granted to prevent harassment.

b) Putting another in fear of violence

   ■ A person who puts another in fear that violence will be used against him on at least two occasions is guilty of an offence.

   ■ There is no reason in principle why an employer cannot be guilty as an accessory to harassment or vicariously liable for an employee's conduct.

113 Provision of Work Equipment Regulations 1998 (SI 1998 No 2306)

Revokes and re-enacts with amendments Work Equipment Regulations (SI 1992 No 2932) to give effect to Council Directive 95/63/EC.

a) Maintenance and repair

(i)   There is a duty to ensure that all work equipment is properly maintained and repaired.

(ii) A maintenance log must be kept for each machine.

b) Use, repair and modification of dangerous machinery

Where the use of a machine is likely to involve risks to health and safety,

(i)   only people who are properly trained may use the machine (adequate training for using such machinery is also required); and

(ii) such equipment must be repaired or modified only by those who are properly trained.

This means that employers must make sure that machine operators who are not properly trained do not make their own informal modifications or try to repair such machines.

c) Health and safety information

Any person who uses, or who supervises the use of, work equipment must have adequate health and safety information and where appropriate readily comprehensible written instructions about the use of the equipment. This must include instructions on:

■   the conditions in which, and methods by which, the equipment may be used

■   any foreseeable abnormal situations – and action to be taken if such a situation occurs

■   any conclusions drawn from experience in using the particular equipment.

d) Guarding equipment and employees

(i)   There is a requirement properly to guard machinery and to exclude people from the danger areas surrounding the equipment.

(ii) It is important to ensure that maintenance can be carried out safely – if at all possible with the machine switched off.

(iii) There is a requirement to protect employees against anything coming off or out of any piece of work equipment and giving rise to injury; this includes protection against bits flying off, fire, discharge of any particle, dust or gas, etc.

(iv) Employees must be protected against very high or low temperatures generated by parts of the machine.

e) Mobile work equipment

(i)   Mobile work equipment must not be used to carry an employee unless it is suitable for carrying people and it incorporates features to reduce to a minimum risks to their safety.

(ii) Where there is any risk of mobile work equipment rolling over, it must be minimised, and if there is a danger of the employee being crushed, a suitable restraining system must be provided for the employee.

(iii) Self-propelling equipment must be used only by authorised people. There are also various specific requirements to do with the safe use of self-propelling equipment.

f) Inspection

(i) Where the safety of the equipment depends on installation conditions, the equipment must be inspected after installation or assembly at a new site or location, before being put into service.

(ii) Equipment exposed to deterioration that is likely to cause a dangerous situation must be inspected at suitable intervals or if an event occurs that is liable to jeopardise the safety of the equipment.

g) Working conditions

(i) The stability of the machine when in use must be ensured. This is particularly important in the case of portable machinery.

(ii) The suitability and sufficiency of the lighting for the work that is carried out with the machine must also be ensured.

114 Public Interest Disclosure Act 1998

Came into force on 2 July 1999. The Act takes effect by inserting a series of new sections into the ERA.

a) Protected disclosure

A protected disclosure is a 'qualifying disclosure' which is made to certain specified people or in certain specified circumstances. A contractual duty of confidentiality is void insofar as it purports to prevent a worker from making a protected disclosure.

b) Qualifying disclosure

(i) A qualifying disclosure is the disclosure of information by a worker which in the worker's reasonable belief shows that one or more of the following ('failures') has occurred, is happening or is likely to occur:

■ the commission of a criminal offence;

■ a failure to comply with a legal obligation;

■ the endangerment of anyone's health and safety;

■ environmental damage; or

■ the deliberate concealment of information tending to show any of the above.

(ii) The failure can have occurred anywhere in the world.

(iii) The disclosure is not a qualifying disclosure if:

- the person commits an offence in making it; or
- it is disclosure by a lawyer who has come upon the information while advising a client.

c) To whom the disclosure may be made

(i) A disclosure will be protected only if made in good faith to one of the following:

- the worker's employer or a person authorised to hear such disclosures under a policy or procedure dealing with such disclosures, where the employee reasonably believes that the failure relates solely or mainly to:
    - the conduct of someone other than his employer; or
    - a matter for which a person other than his employer has legal responsibility;
    - the person whose conduct is in question or who is legally responsible for that conduct
- the employee's legal adviser to obtain legal advice
- if the employee is employed by a person who is, or by a body whose members are, appointed by a Minister of the Crown – to a Minister of the Crown
- where the Secretary of State has prescribed someone to whom certain types of disclosure may be made and (then disclosure will be protected if) the employee reasonably believes:
    - that the matter is one in respect of which that person has been prescribed by the Secretary of State; and
    - that the information disclosed and any allegations made are substantially true.

Under the Public Interest Disclosure (Prescribed Persons) Order 1999 a number of people are prescribed to receive information regarding various matters over which there is public control. These range from the Audit Commission – where matters of public business and value for money are concerned – to the Charity Commissioners – where administration of charitable funds is concerned. Further Regulations have prescribed various other people and officers to receive various forms of information.

(ii) There is a series of disclosures which will be protected only if certain prerequisites are first met:

- the worker makes the disclosure in good faith;
- he reasonably believes that the disclosure made and any allegations contained in it are substantially true;
- he does not make the disclosure for personal gain;
- in all the circumstances it is reasonable for him to make the disclosure (see below for further matters to be taken into account in respect of the reasonableness of the disclosure).

Provided the above prerequisites are met, the disclosure will be protected if made in one of the following sets of circumstances:

- At the time of the disclosure the worker reasonably believes that he will be subjected to a detriment by his employer if he makes a disclosure either to his employer or to a person who has been prescribed for that purpose by the Secretary of State.

- There is no one prescribed for the worker to disclose the information to and the worker reasonably believes that the evidence will be concealed or withheld if he makes the disclosure to his employer.

- The worker has made disclosure of substantially the same information either to his employer or to a person who has been prescribed for that purpose by the Secretary of State.

- The relevant failure is of an exceptionally serious nature (what is 'of an exceptionally serious nature' is not defined by the Act).

Matters to be taken into account in deciding whether or not it was reasonable for the employee to make the disclosure:

- In a situation falling under (ii) above, the only matter to which regard is to be had is the person to whom the failure was disclosed.

- In all the other cases under a)–c) regard must also be had to the following:

  - the seriousness of the failure;

  - whether the failure is continuing or likely to re-occur in the future;

  - where there was a previous disclosure to the employer or a prescribed person, what action the person to whom the disclosure was made might reasonably have been expected to take as a result of that previous disclosure;

  - where there was a previous disclosure to the employer, whether the employee followed any procedure laid down by the employer in making that disclosure.

d) Definition of 'worker'

As might be expected, the definition of a worker for these purposes is very wide indeed and includes not only those who work personally for the employer and agency and homeworkers, but also those who are on work experience with the employer.

e) Remedies

(i) The Act provides that a worker can make a claim if he is:

- subjected to any detriment; or

- dismissed

for making any protected disclosure.

(ii) If the employee is dismissed for making a protected disclosure,

- the dismissal is unfair;

- any redundancy on that ground amounts to unfair dismissal.

Qualification for unfair dismissal rights:

- no qualifying service is required;

- the upper age limit for claim does not apply; and

- the exclusion of the right to claim for employees who are taking unofficial strike action does not apply.

The Public Interest Disclosure (Compensation) Regulations 1999 provide that compensation is without limit.

- A worker who is not working under a contract of employment is entitled to the same compensation as an employee for these purposes.

- Interim relief is also available.

115 Race Relations Act 1976

Repeals and replaces the Race Relations Acts 1965 and 1968.

Amended by Employment Act 1989, Further and Higher Education Act 1992, Education Act 1993 and Race Relations (Remedies) Act 1994, Armed Forces Act 1996, Police Act 1997, Employment Rights (Disputes Resolutions) Act 1998, Equal Opportunities (Employment Legislation)(Territorial Limits) Regulations 1999 (SI 1999 No 3163) and Race Relations Act 1976 (Amendment) Regulations 2003 (SI 2003 No 1626).

115.1 Grounds on which discrimination is unlawful

The Act makes discrimination unlawful on the grounds of colour, race, nationality or ethnic or national origin in employment and other fields. It is unlawful to discriminate against a person either directly or indirectly on these grounds.

These provisions apply to employees and all those who are under a contract to provide services personally. It also applies to office holders and contract workers.

115.2 Types of unlawful discrimination

a) Direct discrimination

Direct discrimination occurs where on grounds of race a person treats another less favourably than he treats or would treat other people.

b) Indirect discrimination:

Indirect discrimination occurs where

- the discriminator applies a condition to the other which he would equally apply to those who are not of the same race;

- the proportion of people of the same racial group as that other who can comply with a condition or instruction is considerably smaller than the proportion of persons not of that racial group who can comply with it;

- the discriminator cannot show a condition to be justifiable irrespective of the colour, race, nationality or ethnic or national origins of the person to whom it is applied; and

- it is to the detriment of the person to whom it is applied because he cannot comply with it.

c) Extended definition of indirect discrimination

(This definition was added by the Race Relations Act 1976 (Amendment) Regulations 2003 to comply with the European requirements on race discrimination.)

Indirect discrimination occurs where the discriminator applies a provision, criterion or practice to another which he applies or would apply equally to people not of the same race or ethnic or national origins as that other, but

- it puts or would put persons of the same race or ethnic or national origins as that other at a particular disadvantage when compared with other persons,

- it puts the particular person at a disadvantage because he cannot comply with it; and

- the discriminator cannot show the provision, criterion or practice to be a proportionate means of achieving a legitimate aim.

d) Harassment

(This provision too was added by the 2003 Regulations.)

A person subjects another to harassment where, on grounds of race or ethnic or national origins, he engages in unwanted conduct which has the purpose or effect of:

- violating that other person's dignity, or

- creating an intimidating, hostile, degrading, humiliating or offensive environment for him.

Conduct is to be regarded as having the above effect only if, having regard to all the circumstances, including in particular the perception of that other person, it should reasonably be considered as having that effect.

e) Reversal of burden of proof:

Where a claim is brought either under the extended definition of indirect discrimination or for harassment, the 2003 Regulations provide for a reversal of the burden of proof:

- If, at the hearing the complainant proves facts from which the tribunal could conclude that the respondent has discriminated against or has harassed the complainant, then

  - the tribunal must uphold the complaint unless the respondent is able to satisfy it that he did not commit an act of discrimination.

115.3 The comparison

The comparison of the case of a person of a particular racial group with that of a person not of that group for the purposes or direct and indirect discrimination must be such that the relevant circumstances in the one case are the same, or not materially different, in the other.

115.4 Occasions of unlawful discrimination

It is unlawful for an employer to discriminate on grounds of race either before employment begins, during employment or after employment ends,

pre-employment

- in the arrangements he makes for the purpose of determining who should be offered that employment; or

- the terms on which employment is offered; or

- by refusing or deliberately omitting to offer the individual employment;

during employment

- in the terms of employment which the individual is afforded; or

- in the way the individual is given access to opportunities for promotion, transfer or training, or to any other benefits, facilities or services; or by refusing or deliberately omitting to afford the individual access to those opportunities; or

- by dismissing the individual, or subjecting him to any other detriment;

post employment

- by subjecting him to any detriment; or

- by subjecting him to harassment.

115.5 Genuine occupational qualifications and requirements

Exceptions are made in relation to some of these restrictions where race, etc, is a genuine occupational qualification (GOQ) for a particular job. Being of a particular race, etc, can be a GOQ in the following cases:

- The job involves dramatic performance or other entertainment where a person of a particular racial group is required for reasons of authenticity.

- The job is as a photographic model and a person of a particular racial group is required for reasons of authenticity.

- The job involves serving food or drink to members of the public and a person of a particular racial group is required for reasons of authenticity.

- The holder of the job provides persons of that racial group with personal services promoting their welfare, and those services can most effectively be provided by a person of that racial group.

Unlawful discrimination does *not* occur in a recruitment situation where

- being of a particular race or of particular ethnic or national origins is a genuine and determining occupational requirement;

- it is proportionate to apply that requirement in the particular case; and

- the prospective employee either doesn't meet that requirement or the employer can reasonably conclude that he doesn't meet that requirement.

115.6 Complaint to an employment tribunal

A complaint may be brought to an employment tribunal within three months of the date of discrimination.

> The employment tribunal has jurisdiction to extend time where it is just and equitable to do so.

> Compensation for race discrimination has no upper limit and awards can be made for injury to feelings and personal injuries suffered by reason of discrimination as well as for specific monetary losses.

> Claimants may serve race discrimination questionnaires on employers to obtain answer to questions which will assist them in presenting of pursuing their cases. If a recipient fails, without good cause, to respond to a race discrimination questionnaire within eight weeks of the date on which it was served, the tribunal may draw such inferences as it considers it just and equitable to draw – including an inference that the respondent has discriminated against the claimant.

115.7 The Commission for Racial Equality

The Act established the Commission for Racial Equality (CRE) whose duties are:

- to work towards the elimination of racial discrimination; and

- to promote equality of opportunity and good relations between persons of different racial groups generally; and

- to monitor the working of the Act and to make recommendations to the Secretary of State to amend the Act if and when necessary.

The CRE is given wide powers of investigation and power to draw up codes of practice to eliminate discrimination in employment (see below). An employee or applicant for a job who has been discriminated against may be awarded compensation by an employment tribunal. The address of the CRE is:

Elliot House
10–12 Allington Street
London SW1E 5EH
Telephone: 020-7828 7022

CRE Code of Practice 1984

In April 1984 the CRE Code of Practice for the elimination of racial discrimination and the promotion of equality of opportunity in employment came into force. As with similar codes it is not legally binding but its provisions, and questions of whether or not an employer has complied with those provisions, are admissible in evidence before an employment tribunal. The Code's two most important recommendations on the responsibilities of employers concern:

- the implementation of equal opportunities programmes; and

- the monitoring of such programmes with the aid of analysis of the ethnic origins of the workforce and of job applicants.

Specifically, the Code recommends that:

(a) Employers should adopt, implement and monitor an equal opportunities policy.

(b) The policy should be clearly communicated to all employees.

(c) Overall responsibility for the policy should be allocated to a member of senior management.

(d) Where appropriate, the policy should be discussed and agreed with trade unions or employee representatives.

(e) Training and guidance should be provided for supervisory staff and other relevant decision-makers to ensure that they understand their position in law and under company policy.

(f) Employers should monitor the effects of selection decisions and of personnel practices/procedures to assess whether equal opportunity is being achieved. The information needed for effective monitoring may be obtained in a number of ways but, says the Code, will best be achieved by records showing the ethnic origins of existing employees and job applicants. (Abstracted from *IPM Digest*, No 229, August 1984, pp.9–10.)

116 Race Relations Amendment Act 2000

Amends the RRA.

The Act makes chief police officers vicariously liable for the actions or inactions of their officers. Because police officers are 'office holders' rather than 'employees', chief police officers were not previously covered by its provisions.

117 Race Relations Act 1976 (Amendment) Regulations 2003 (SI 2003 No 1626)

Amend the RRA (**see 115 above**).

118 Race Relations (Remedies) Act 1994

Amends the RRA.

The Act abolished the upper limit on compensation for race discrimination with effect from 3 July 1994.

119 Redundancy Payments (Continuity of Employment in Local Government etc) (Modification) Order 1999

Revokes the Redundancy Payments (Local Government)(Modification) Order 1983 and consolidates it and later amendments to it into a single Order with some further modification. The Order came into effect on 1 September 1999. Amended by the Redundancy Payments (Continuity of Employment in Local

Government etc) (Modification) (Amendment) Order 2001 (SI 2001 No 866) and the Redundancy Payments (Continuity of Employment in Local Government etc) (Modification) (Amendment) Order 2002 (SI 2002 No 532) which both add certain bodies to those specified by the 1999 Order.

The Order provides that employment with certain designated local government employers is to be treated as continuous with employment with other designated local government employers. The effect is to treat the designated employers as if they were 'associated employers' for the purposes of continuity of employment.

120 Regulation of Investigatory Powers Act 2000

Amended by Telecommunications (Lawful Business Practice) (Interception of Communications) Regulations 2000 (SI 2000 No 2699).

The Regulations make it an offence to intercept either the public postal communications or public or private telecommunications without lawful authority. If a person consents to his or her communications' being intercepted, for example as a term of employment, those interceptions will not be unlawful.

Telecommunications (Lawful Business Practice) (Interception of Communications) Regulations 2000 (SI 2000 No 2699) authorise the interception of some telecommunications which would otherwise be prohibited by the Act.

Interceptions are allowed by these Regulations if they are made by a business in its own internal communications system.

For the purposes of the Regulations 'business' includes government departments and public authorities. Businesses may intercept communications under these Regulations for purposes including:

- quality control and training

- the detection of crime and national security

- the investigation of unauthorised use of the telecommunication systems and the monitoring of received communications to determine whether they are business or personal communications.

For interceptions to be authorised, the controller of the telecommunications system must first make all reasonable efforts to inform potential users that interceptions may be made.

121 Rehabilitation of Offenders Act 1974

Amended by Armed Forces Act 1996.

The Act provides that a convicted offender, other than one given a sentence of more than 30 months' imprisonment, may become rehabilitated if he commits no further serious offences during the rehabilitation period. The rehabilitation periods vary with the sentences imposed and the age of the offender is also taken into account. Where a conviction has expired, under the terms of the Act it is unlawful for the offender to be refused employment or to be dismissed from employment on the grounds of that conviction. Certain professions and occupations are excluded from the provisions of the Act; these include the legal profession, accountants and teachers.

122 Reserve Forces Act 1980

Amended by Reserve Forces (Safeguard of Employment) Act 1985, and greatly amended and replaced by the Reserve Forces Act 1996.

Amends Trade Union and Labour Relations Act 1974, EPCA.

The provision for reserve forces and Territorial Army to be called up are now contained in Part VI Reserve Forces Act 1996. They were previously made under s 10 of the 1980 Act. Orders authorising the calling out of reserve forces/TA are made by the Queen, under the hand of the Secretary of State, under s 10 of the Act.

123 Reserve Forces Act 1996

Amends Reserve Forces (Safeguard of Employment) Act 1985.

Repeals and replaces much of the Reserve Forces Act 1980 and the whole of the Reserve Forces Act 1982.

123.1 Definition

Reserve forces are: the Royal Fleet Reserve, Royal Naval Reserve, Royal Marine Reserve, Army Reserve, Territorial Army, Air Force Reserve and the Royal Auxiliary Air Force.

123.2 Calling up reserve forces

The statutory provisions allowing for reserve forces to be called up are now contained in Part VI Reserve Forces Act 1996.

a) Reserve forces may be called up

  ■ when the nation appears to be in imminent danger

  ■ when a great emergency has arisen or there is an actual or apprehended attack on the UK

  ■ when warlike operations are in preparation or progress

  ■ when the Secretary of State considers it desirable to use armed forces for:

   ■ the protection of life or property outside the United Kingdom; or

   ■ in operations anywhere in the world to save lives or property in time of disaster or apprehended disaster.

b) In cases where an Order calling out reserve forces is made, the employment of those who are called up is protected under the Reserve Forces (Safeguard of Employment) Act 1985. In the Gulf War an Order was made calling up reservists who had volunteered for service with the forces as well as those who were actually called up. This had the effect of ensuring that the employment of volunteers was protected under Reserve Forces (Safeguard of Employment) Act 1985.

123.3 Special agreements/Employee agreements

a) Special agreements

An employee who is employed to work for more than 14 hours per week may, with the consent of his employer, enter into an agreement that will make him liable:

- to be called out for permanent service anywhere in the world; and

- to fulfil any training obligations specified in the agreement for a period of up to nine months.

b) Employee agreements

(i) Employee agreements are agreements primarily between the employer and Secretary of State for employees to enter into agreements to become special members of the reserve forces.

(ii) An employee can enter into an agreement to become a special member of the reserve forces in such circumstances with his employer's consent.

c) A person who is called up under either of these schemes can seek a deferral or exemption from call-up.

d) Employees who are called up under these schemes have their employment protected under the Reserve Forces (Safeguard of Employment) Act 1985.

123.4 Former members of the forces

a) Former members of the regular forces are liable to be recalled unless they are 55 or over, or if they were discharged or transferred to the reserve forces 18 or more years previously. (Former members of the Royal Navy or Royal Marines remain liable to be recalled for only six years after discharge or transfer to the Reserves.)

b) Employees who are recalled under these provisions have their employment protected under the Reserve Forces (Safeguard of Employment) Act 1985.

124 Reserve Forces (Safeguard of Employment) Act 1985

Amends Reserve Forces Act 1980, EPCA, Tribunals and Enquiries Act 1971.
Repeals National Service Act 1948, Reinstatement in Civil Employment Act 1950.
Amended by Reserve Forces Act 1996.

124.1 When is protection given?

The Act provides safeguards, in relation to employment, for: reservists and those who have entered into special or employee agreements who are called up into full-time service in the forces and those who are recalled to full-time service in the forces.

(NB: Those who volunteer for service without being called up are generally outside this statutory protection, but in the Gulf War an Order was made calling up volunteers so that their employment would be protected – see Reserve Forces Act 1996, **123 above**.)

124.2 The rights provided for by the Act

a) The right to return

The Act provides for an employee who was employed within four weeks before being called up to be offered a job by his last employer, at the first reasonable opportunity after his release from full-time service, and to be kept in that job for no less than the minimum statutory period.

b) Minimum statutory period

The minimum statutory period for which the employee must be employed after returning from the forces depends on the employee's length of service before being called up.

If the employee had less than 13 or more than 26 or 52 weeks' employment before call-up, he will be entitled to be kept on for at least 13, 26 or 52 weeks respectively, following his reinstatement. The only restriction on this right is that it must be reasonable and practicable for the employer to keep the employee on (or to keep him on the terms and conditions on which he was reinstated) throughout that period.

c) The right to return to what?

The employee's right is primarily a right to be offered employment in the occupation in which he was engaged before his full-time service with the forces began, on terms and conditions no less favourable than those that would have applied had he not been away. If it is not reasonable and practicable for the employee to be taken back into his former occupation on those terms and conditions, then he is entitled to be offered a job in the most favourable occupation and on the most favourable terms and conditions that are reasonable and practicable in his case.

d) The right to return when?

The employee must be offered employment to begin at the first opportunity (if any) at which it is reasonable and practicable for it to begin after the date that he has notified to the employer as the date on which he will be available for work (**see 124.3 below**).

The right to be offered a job is also limited to the first six months after the ex-employee's service with the forces ends. After this the former employer has no duty to take the employee back (unless he is required to take the employee back following any order to that effect made by a Reinstatement Committee).

e) The effect of refusing employer's offer

Once the employer has offered the employee a job, his obligation to take the employee back is *prima facie* discharged. However, it will not be discharged if the applicant believes that he has reasonable cause for not taking the job that is offered and he, or someone acting on his behalf, notifies the employer in writing of his reasons for not taking the job 'as soon as may be' after the job is offered.

124.3 Enforcement of these statutory rights

Either the applicant or someone acting on the applicant's behalf must apply in writing to the applicant's former employer asking that the applicant be taken back into employment. The application must be made within the first two weeks after the applicant's release from full-time service with the forces. If the applicant is sick, or if because of some other reasonable cause the applicant cannot apply within the prescribed time, the application will still be valid provided it is made as soon as it reasonably can be.

The applicant must also provide his former employer with a date when he will be available to take up work if it is offered. That date must be within 21 days of the latest date on which the application can be validly made (this is, again, extended where the applicant is sick or where it is otherwise reasonable for him not to comply).

> An application to be taken back into employment ceases to have effect 13 weeks after it was made, unless it has been renewed during the 13-week period. It is also preserved during any period while there are any proceedings pending regarding the application.

> An applicant can apply to a Reinstatement Committee if he considers that any of his rights under the Act (including his right to be taken back and to be kept on for the minimum statutory period) are being or have been denied to him.

124.4 Statutory presumptions as to whether or not it is reasonable and practicable to take an employee back

The Act provides that the fact that taking the applicant back will involve dismissing someone else does not, of itself, make taking the applicant back either unreasonable or impracticable. The only exception to this is where taking the employee back would involve dismissing another employee who had been employed for longer than the applicant by the date when the applicant left employment to join the forces. Where both the applicant and the other employee were called up, the comparison is between the length of service given by each before the first of them left to join the forces.

124.5 Continuity of employment

Employees who are entitled to apply to be employed by their former employer, and who are taken back within six months of the termination of their full-time service with the forces, have their employment before they were called up treated as continuous with their employment after their return to work. The actual period of absence does not itself count as a period of continuous employment.

125 Road Vehicles (Construction and Use) (Amendment) (No 4) Regulations 2003 (SI 2003 No 2695)

It is an offence to drive a motor vehicle or to cause or permit another person to drive a motor vehicle while using a hand-held mobile phone.

- A mobile phone is 'hand-held' if it is, or must be, held at some point during the course of making or receiving a call.

  There is an exception where the phone is used to call emergency services in a genuine emergency, where it is impracticable to stop driving.

126 Safety Representatives and Safety Committees Regulations 1977 (SI 1977 No 500)

The Regulations were amended by the Management of Health and Safety at Work Regulations 1999 and by Health and Safety (Consultation with Employees) Regulations 1996 (SI 1996 No 1513).

These Regulations were made under the Health and Safety at Work etc Act 1974 and provide for consultation where trade unions are recognised. Where trade unions are not recognised, employers are required to consult either the employees themselves or representatives of employee safety, under the Health and Safety (Consultation with Employees) Regulations 1996 (SI 1996 No 1513)(**see 79 above**).

a) The appointment of safety representatives

(i) Where an independent trade union is recognised by an employer, the union can appoint safety representatives. The union must inform the employer in writing who they have appointed.

(ii) Employees appointed as safety representatives should normally have had two years in that employment or in similar employment so that they have experience of the type of workplace.

b) The functions of safety representatives

(i) The employer must consult safety representatives with a view to:

- establishing and maintaining arrangements for effective co-operation between the employer and his employees; to ensure the health and safety at work of employees; and

- checking the effectiveness of those arrangements,

    - particularly on the introduction of

        - any measures that may substantially affect employees' health and safety; and

        - new technology;

    - and making arrangements for

        - appointing people to be responsible for statutory health and safety duties;

        - nominating people to deal with serious and imminent dangers at work and danger areas;

- furnishing the health and safety information he is required by statute to provide;

- the planning of health and safety training he is required by statute to provide.

(ii) Inspections of the workplace must be carried out

- once every three months after giving written notice to the employer; or

- more often:

    - with the employer's consent;

    - where there has been a substantial change in the conditions of work, such as the introduction of new machinery, since the last inspection;

    - where relevant advice from the Health and Safety Executive (HSE) has been given since the last inspection;

- where there has been a notifiable accident or dangerous occurrence or where a notifiable disease has been contracted. In such cases safety representatives may inspect the area affected and any other areas that it is necessary to inspect to determine the cause.

The employer may accompany the safety representative on any such inspection.

(iii) Investigating

- potential hazards at the workplace

- dangerous occurrences at the workplace

- causes of accidents at the workplace

- complaints by employees relating to their health and safety at work.

(iv) Making representations to the employer

- on matters arising out of the above investigations; and

- on general matters affecting the health, safety and welfare of the employees at the workplace.

(v) Representing employees in consultations with the Health and Safety inspectorate.

(vi) Attending Safety Committee meetings as a safety representative.

c) The requirement to provide information and documentation

(i) The employer must provide information for safety representatives so that they have all the relevant information that the employer has available which will allow them to carry out their duties. Certain types of confidential information are excluded from this requirement.

(ii) The employer must allow safety representatives to inspect and take copies of all health and safety documentation that the employer is obliged by statute to keep – other than documentation relating to an identifiable individual.

d) Facilities

(i) Safety representatives are entitled to paid time off:

- to carry out their duties as safety representatives; and

- to undergo training.

(ii) If a safety representative is refused paid time off, he can complain to an employment tribunal within three months of the time off being refused (or where that is not reasonably practicable within such further time as is reasonably practicable).

(iii) The employer must provide safety representatives with such facilities and assistance as they may reasonably require to carry out their duties.

e) Safety committees

(i) An employer must establish a safety committee if two or more safety representatives request him to do so in writing.

(ii)   When safety representatives request the establishment of a safety committee, the employer must:

- consult with those representatives and trade union representatives in the areas that will be covered by the safety committee;

- post a notice, giving the composition of the safety committee, where all relevant employees will be able to see it; and

- establish the safety committee within three months of the request being made.

127 Sex Discrimination Act 1975 (SDA)

Amended by Employment Act 1989, Further and Higher Education Act 1992 and Education Act 1993 and Sex Discrimination and Equal Pay (Remedies) Regulations 1993 (SI 1993 No 2798), Pensions Act 1995, Armed Forces Act 1996, Police Act 1997, Employment Rights (Disputes Resolutions) Act 1998, Sex Discrimination (Gender Reassignment) Regulations 1999, Equal Opportunities (Employment Legislation)(Territorial Limits) Regulations 1999 (SI 1999 No 3163), Sex Discrimination (Gender Reassignment) Regulations 1999 (SI 1999 No 1153), Sex Discrimination (Indirect Discrimination and Burden of Proof) Regulations 2001 (SI 2001 No 2660), SDA (Amendment) Regulations 2003 (SI 2003 No 1657) and Gender Recognition Act 2004. (Amendments to the SDA from the Gender Recognition Act 2004 are noted under Sex Discrimination (Gender Reassignment) Regulations 1999, **131 below**.)

The Act makes discrimination on grounds of sex or marital status unlawful. Its provisions are similar in extent and effect to those of the Race Relations Act 1976. The main differences are:

a)   The Sex Discrimination Act (SDA) does not cover discrimination in pay – this is dealt with by the Equal Pay Act 1970 as amended.

b)   The SDA makes special provision to deal with discrimination in matters relating to death or retirement (amended by SDA 1986, Employment Act 1989 and prospectively by the Pensions Act 1995 – see commentary under Sex Discrimination Act 1986, **128 below**). The SDA excludes special, more beneficial, provisions relating to pregnancy from being treated as discrimination.

c)   The Equal Opportunities Commission (EOC) is established by the Act and has an equivalent function to the Commission for Racial Equality (CRE) in matters related to sex discrimination, including the power to draw up codes of practice (see below). The EOC also has jurisdiction to monitor and review the working of the Equal Pay Act 1970.

d)   The reversal of the burden of proof, brought into effect by the 2001 Sex Discrimination (Indirect Discrimination and Burden of Proof) Regulations provides that

- where a claim is brought for any type of discrimination, and

- where at the hearing the complainant proves facts from which the tribunal could conclude that the respondent has discriminated against or has harassed the complainant,

the tribunal must uphold the complaint unless the respondent is able to satisfy the tribunal that he did not discriminate against the claimant.

e) It deals, by various amendments, with the protection of those who are undergoing or have undergone gender reassignment. (See mainly Sex Discrimination (Gender Reassignment) Regulations 1999 (SI 1999 No 1102), **131 below**, and Gender Recognition Act 2004, as detailed also in **131 below**).

128 Sex Discrimination Act 1986

Amended by Employment Act 1989 and ERA. Its provisions are also amended by the Pensions Act 1995.

Amends SDA, EPCA, Equal Pay Act 1970, Employment Protection Act 1975, Hours of Work Convention Act 1936, Factories Act 1961, Health and Safety at Work etc Act 1974.

128.1 Employment in private households

The Act removes the right to discriminate, on grounds of sex, where employment is for a private household, except in a case where the amount of intimate contact with a person living in the home or the knowledge of intimate details of a person's life which the employee might come upon means that the householder might reasonably object to having a man/woman do that work.

128.2 Death and retirement

The exclusion of matters related to 'death or retirement' from the sex discrimination legislation under the 1975 Act is largely removed. Whereas in the normal case it is unlawful for an employer to discriminate by dismissing an employee or subjecting her to any other detriment, in cases where the discrimination is concerned with retirement it is unlawful to discriminate by 'dismissing or subjecting [the individual] to any detriment which results in her dismissal or consists in or involves her demotion'. This still allows some scope for discrimination in relation to pension matters. There is an equivalent provision inserted into the Equal Pay Act 1970. The provisions regarding discrimination in relation to pensions are, however, prospectively modified by the Pensions Act 1995 to allow for unequal treatment of men and women in a pension scheme where that treatment would not offend against the 'equal treatment' requirements under the Pension Act 1995.

128.3 Normal retirement age

The 1986 Act amended the exclusion, from claiming unfair dismissal, for those over normal retirement age or statutory pension age so that an employee's claim is excluded only if he has reached either:

- 'normal retirement age' for a person holding that position in the organisation (provided that that retirement age is the same for both men and women); or

- in any other case, 65.

This provision is now contained in s 109 ERA.

128.4 Terms in collective agreements

The Act invalidates any terms in collective agreements, in an employer's rule and in the rules of qualifying bodies, which are unlawfully discriminatory or which give rise to unlawful discrimination.

128.5 Women's hours of work

The erstwhile restrictions on women's hours of work, under various statutes, are removed.

The address of the EOC is:

Overseas House
Quay Street
Manchester M3 3HN
   Tel. 0161-833 9244

129 Sex Discrimination and Equal Pay (Remedies) Regulations 1993 (SI 1993 No 2798)

Amend the SDA.

These Regulations removed the upper limit of compensation in sex discrimination cases from 22 November 1993.

EOC Code of Practice 1985

The EOC launched its Code of Practice for the elimination of discrimination on grounds of sex or marital status in employment on 30 April 1985. The Code is divided into two main parts. The first deals with the role of good employment practices in eliminating sex and marital-status discrimination and the second with the role of good employment practices in promoting equality of opportunity. The Code does not carry the force of law but both parts may be taken into account by employment tribunals in proceedings under the Sex Discrimination Acts. As with the CRE Code of Practice that has been in force since April 1984, one of the key recommendations is the formulation and implementation of an equal opportunities policy which, says the EOC, 'will ensure the effective use of human resources in the best interests of both the organisation and its employees'. In summary, the Code's main suggestions for successfully implementing an equal opportunities policy are:

1 The policy must be seen to have the active support of top management.

2 The policy should be clearly stated and, where appropriate, should be included in a collective agreement.

3 Overall responsibility for implementing the policy should rest with senior management.

4 The policy should be made known to all employees and, where reasonably practicable, to all job applicants.

5 Trade unions have an important part to play in implementing genuine equality of opportunity and will obviously be involved in the review of established procedures to ensure that they are consistent with the law.

6 The policy should be monitored regularly to ensure that it is working in practice.

7 In a small firm it may be quite adequate to assess the distribution and payment of employees from personal knowledge.

8 In a large, complex organisation a more formal analysis will be necessary – for example, by sex, grade and payment in each unit. This may have to be introduced by stages as resources permit.

9   Sensible monitoring will show, for example, whether members of one sex:

- do not apply for employment or promotion, or whether fewer apply than might be expected

- are not recruited, promoted or selected for training development or are appointed/selected in a significantly lower proportion than their rate of application

- are concentrated in certain jobs, sections or departments.

Other aspects covered by the Code include job advertising, selection methods – with particular reference to the avoidance of certain discriminatory questions at interviews – promotion, transfer and training, terms of employment, grievance and disciplinary procedures, and victimisation.

130 Sex Discrimination Act 1975 (Amendment) Regulations 2003 (SI 2003 No 1657)

Amend the SDA.

The Regulations provide for police officers to be treated as being in the employment of the Chief Constable to enable them to bring sex discrimination claims arising from their employment

The Regulations make it unlawful to subject a person to a detriment after employment has finished.

131 Sex Discrimination (Gender Reassignment) Regulations 1999 (SI 1999 No 1102)

Amend the SDA to give effect to the ECJ's judgment in *P v S and Cornwall County Council* [1996] IRLR 347, where it was held that discrimination on grounds of gender reassignment is unlawful under Council Directive 76/207/EC. Amendments to the SDA from the Gender Recognition Act 2004 are also noted below.

a) Gender reassignment is defined as 'a process which is undertaken under medical supervision for the purpose of reassigning a person's sex by changing physiological or other characteristics of sex and includes any part of such a process'.

b) A person discriminates unlawfully if he treats a person who intends to undergo, is undergoing or has undergone gender reassignment less favourably on those grounds than he treats or would treat others in relation to employment or vocational training.

c) Exceptions

(i)   where sex is a genuine occupational qualification (within the existing terms of the SDA); and the employer can show that the treatment is reasonable in view of:

- the particular genuine occupational qualification; and

- any other relevant circumstances.

(ii)   Supplementary genuine occupational qualifications are also added for cases of gender reassignment:

- where the job-holder is likely to be called upon to perform intimate physical searches pursuant to statutory powers;

- where the job-holder is working or living in a private home and objection might reasonably be taken to allowing a person who is or who has undergone gender reassignment the degree of physical or social contact with a person living in the home or the knowledge of intimate details of his life.

Where the person intends to undergo or is undergoing gender reassignment there are two further supplementary genuine occupational qualifications:

- where the person undertaking the job has to live on the premises and reasonable objection could be taken for the purposes of decency or privacy to sharing accommodation while undergoing gender reassignment and it is not reasonable to expect the employer to equip the premises with suitable accommodation or to make alternative arrangements; or

- where the job-holder provides vulnerable individuals with services promoting their welfare or similar services and in the employer's reasonable view those services cannot be effectively provided by a person while undergoing gender reassignment.

(iii) The Gender Recognition Act 2004 provides that these GOQs do not apply once the individual has had the new sex recognised under the terms of the Gender Recognition Act 2004.

d) A specific provision is put in to deal with absence from work due to gender reassignment. A person is deemed to be treated less favourably if, in relation to any arrangements for absence due to gender reassignment:

- he is treated less favourably than he would be if the absence was due to sickness or injury; or

- he is treated less favourably than he would be if the absence was due to some other cause and, having regard to the circumstances of the case, it is reasonable for him to be treated no less favourably.

e) Discrimination in relation to pay on grounds of gender reassignment is dealt with under the terms of the SDA, as amended, rather than under the Equal Pay Act 1970.

132 Sex Discrimination (Indirect Discrimination and Burden of Proof) Regulations 2001 (SI 2001 No 2660)

Amend the SDA; the amendments are in the text under that Act – **see 127 above**.

133 Sex Disqualification (Removal) Act 1919

This Act provides that no person shall by reason of sex or marriage be excluded from any public function, any judicial or civil office or post 'or from entering or assuming or carrying on any civil profession or vocation, or for the admission of any incorporated society (whether incorporated by Royal Charter or otherwise) . . .'.

134 Shops Acts 1950–1965

Amended by Employment Act 1989 and Deregulation and Contracting Out Act 1994; the relevant provisions of the latter were consolidated into the ERA.

The Acts were designed to ensure that shop assistants do not have to work excessive hours and that they are allowed adequate rest periods. (See also Offices, Shops and Railway Premises Act 1963, **101 above**.) Certain restrictions on shop workers' working on Sundays were removed by the Deregulation and Contracting Out Act 1994, the relevant provisions of which have been consolidated into the ERA.

135 Social Security Act 1989

Amended by Employment Act 1990, Social Security Act 1990, Pension Schemes Act 1993 and Pensions Act 1995.

Amends Social Security Acts 1986 and 1988.

Section 23 and Schedule 5 of the Act were enacted to give effect to EC Directive 86/378/EEC on equal treatment for men and women in relation to occupational social security schemes. The main area in which these provisions were intended to operate was in relation to pension schemes. But this changed dramatically following the ECJ's judgment in *Barber v Guardian Royal Exchange Assurance Group* [1990] IRLR 240 and a number of later cases, which further explained the European equal treatment requirements in relation to pension schemes. Equal treatment under occupational pension schemes from 17 May 1990, the date of the ECJ's judgment in *Barber*, had to be treated as a matter of equal pay, which meant that it had to be dealt with rather more stringently than was envisaged by the 1989 provisions. The provisions of this Act, insofar as they relate to pension schemes, were therefore overtaken by the Pensions Act 1995. The only areas in which the 1989 provisions have been brought into effect are unfair maternity and family leave provisions. It should be borne in mind that these are social security measures and, as such, apply to social security as well as employment benefits.

a) Entitlement to equal treatment

A woman during a period of paid maternity leave and a person during a period of paid family leave (ie a period throughout which the employee is on leave for family reasons) are entitled not to be treated less favourably in relation to any employment-related benefit schemes than they would be if they were at work. This means that:

- any continuing rights they may have under the scheme must be equivalent to those that would have applied if they had not been on leave; and

- where their overall entitlement under a scheme takes into account a period of maternity or family leave, they must again be in an equivalent position to that which would have applied if they had not been on leave.

Schemes are, however, specifically permitted to provide more favourable treatment for women who are on maternity leave.

Where the employee pays into the scheme, the amount that she is required to pay during her maternity leave or family leave must be based on the amount that she is actually being paid during that period.

Where these requirements are not complied with, and less favourable treatment is given to a woman on maternity leave or to a person on family leave, she can claim entitlement to the more beneficial treatment afforded to other equivalent members of the scheme:

- in the case of a woman on maternity leave, her treatment must be no less favourable than other women members of the scheme;

- in the case of those on family leave, they are to be treated no less favourably than they would be if they were working normally but being paid only what they are actually paid during their family leave.

b) Schemes to which the requirements apply

These requirements apply to any of the following types of scheme which are employment-related and which provide different levels of benefit dependent on service. They apply even if the scheme is a discretionary one, provided only that the benefits under the scheme are payable in money or in money's worth. Relevant schemes are those providing benefit in respect of:

- termination of service;

- retirement, old age or death;

- time off because of sickness or invalidity;

- accidents, injuries or diseases connected with employment;

- unemployment; or

- expenses incurred in connection with children or other dependants;

and in the case of an employee, include any such benefits which are payable as a result of that person's employment.

The following types of scheme are, however, excluded from these provisions:

- any personal scheme for employees to which the employer does not contribute;

- any insurance scheme which is for the benefit of employees and to which the employer is not a party.

136 Social Security Administration Act 1992 (SSAA)

Amended by Statutory Sick Pay Act 1994 and Jobseekers Act 1995.

Together with the Social Security Contributions and Benefits Act (SSCBA) 1992, the Act consolidates most social security law. The SSCBA deals with the substantive law and the SSAA deals with the administrative parts.

136.1 Investigation, inspection and disclosure of documents

These provisions were originally in the Social Security Act 1986. The Act provides for the appointment of inspectors who are given certain powers.

a) Power to enter premises

An inspector has power under this provision to enter premises where he has reasonable grounds for supposing:

- that there are people employed; or

- that any type of employment agency or 'employment business' is being carried on; or

- that an occupational health scheme is being run or administered from those premises.

Private dwellings that are not used for business purposes by the occupier (or with his permission) are excluded from this provision.

If requested to do so, the inspector must produce a certificate of his appointment when seeking to enter any premises.

b) Extent of powers

An inspector's powers extend to:

- entering premises liable to inspection at all reasonable times;

- making such examination and enquiry as may be necessary for estimating whether the provisions of the various benefits acts are being complied with;

- making such examination and enquiry as may be necessary for investigating any circumstances giving rise to any industrial injuries benefit claim;

- examining anyone whom he reasonably believes might be liable to pay Social Security contributions of any sort;

- requiring the production of information in accordance with c) below.

c) Disclosure of information to an inspector

During an inspection those asked are required to provide the inspector with all the information and documentation he may reasonably require, for the purposes of ascertaining:

(i) whether or not any Social Security contributions are payable in respect of any person, and if they are, whether or not those contributions have been duly paid; or

(ii) whether benefit under any of the benefits acts is or was payable in respect of any person. (This is a potentially far-reaching provision which provides a facility for ensuring that the employees are not also receiving Jobseekers' Allowance or other undeclared social security benefits.)

In practice, requests for disclosure of information are usually made by post.

136.2 Employer's and employee's notification requirements in respect of SSP and SMP

a) This Act now contains the requirements for employees to provide their employers with proper medical information of

- any time off for sickness; and

- the expected date of confinement in maternity cases.

b) The Act also requires an employer, if requested to do so by an employee, to provide a statement specifying:

(i) any days within a period in the case of SSP (or of any weeks within a period, in the case of SMP) in which he considers he is liable to pay the employee SSP or SMP;

(ii) the reason he considers he is not liable to pay the employee SSP or SMP for the other days/weeks in that period; and

(iii) the amount of SSP/SMP that he considers himself liable to pay in respect of each of the days or weeks in question.

137 Social Security (Consequential Amendments) Act 1992

This Act was used to repeal the various provisions that had to be repealed as a consequence of the two social security consolidating statutes: the Social Security Contributions and Benefits Act 1992 and the Social Security Administration Act 1992.

138 Social Security Contributions and Benefits Act 1992 (SSCBA)

Amended by Statutory Sick Pay Act 1994, Social Security (Incapacity for Work) Act 1994, Jobseekers Act 1995, Statutory Maternity Pay (General) (Modification and Amendment) Regulations 2000 (SI 2000 No 2883), Employment Act 2002 and Social Security, Statutory Maternity Pay and Statutory Sick Pay (Miscellaneous Amendments) Regulations 2002 (SI 2002 No 2690).

Together with the Social Security Administration Act 1992 (SSAA), this Act consolidated a great deal of social security law, the SSCBA dealing with the substantive law and the SSAA with the administrative parts. Most important for employment purposes is the consolidation of the law relating to SSP and SMP.

138.1 Statutory Sick Pay (SSP)

a) The benefit

(i) Statutory Sick Pay (SSP) is payable by the employer to an employee for any day of incapacity for work in respect of which the employee meets the statutory qualifications.

(ii) SSP is a flat-rate benefit. An employee's maximum entitlement in any one Period of Entitlement (**see c)(iii) below**) is 28 times the weekly SSP rate.

(iii) SSP is subject to income tax and National Insurance.

(iv) The daily rate for payment where the employee is entitled for part weeks is:

SSP weekly rate x number of Q days for which payment is due ÷ agreed number of Q days per week (**see c)(iv) below** for the definition of 'Q day')

(v) Any contractual sick pay goes towards discharging the employer's liability to pay SSP and vice versa.

(vi) Employers were originally able to recoup the costs of SSP. This facility has now been removed except in very restricted cases – for the current position see Statutory Sick Pay Act 1994, **147 below**.

(vii) Any agreement between an employer and employee for the employer not to pay the employee the SSP to which he is entitled is void. This does not, however, prevent an employer from making deductions from SSP to the same extent as could be made from the employee's normal pay. So where there is a pre-existing arrangement – for example, where deductions are being made in respect of the repayment of a loan – those deductions can continue to be made from any SSP that would otherwise be payable.

b) Who is covered?

(i) All employees over 16 and who are employed in Great Britain and who pay Class 1 National Insurance contributions (including married women and widows who pay at a lower rate).

(ii) Part-timers, provided their earnings are above the Lower Earnings Limit for NI contributions.

(iii) Those with two jobs can claim from both employers.

c) Qualification for entitlement

There are five qualifications for entitlement.

(i) The day must be a day of incapacity for work.

A 'day of incapacity for work' means a day when the employee is, because of a disease or physical or mental disablement, incapable of doing work which he could reasonably be expected to do under his contract of employment.

- Under the Statutory Sick Pay (General) Regulations 1982 (SI 1982 No 894) an employee who is sick at the beginning of the day or during the working day is deemed to be incapable of work for the whole day if he does no work during that day.

(ii) The day in question must form part of the Period of Incapacity for Work (PIW).

A PIW is a period of four or more consecutive days during which the employee is incapable of work due to sickness.

- For the purposes of a PIW all days of incapacity for work count – regardless of whether or not the employee would normally be working on that day. This also applies to days of incapacity for work which occur before the contract begins and after it ends.

- Any two PIWs that are separated by not more than eight weeks form a single PIW. This means that the employee will not have to be without SSP during the 'waiting days' which would otherwise apply to the later, linked, PIW (for 'waiting days', see below).

(iii) The day must be part of the Period of Entitlement (PE).

A PE begins at the beginning of the PIW and ends when:

- the employee's PIW ends;

- the employee's entitlement to SSP from that employer is exhausted;

- his employment has ended; or

- a pregnant employee reaches the 'disqualifying period' (ie 18 weeks beginning with the 11th week before the expected week of confinement).

A PE does not arise where, at the date when a PE would otherwise begin:

- the employee is over the age of 65 (the age was increased from 60 for women by the Statutory Sick Pay Act 1994);

- the employee is under a fixed-term contract of three months or less (unless the employee has actually been employed for more than three months – either under the contract in question, or under one or more contracts each separated by eight weeks or less);

- the employee is earning less than the lower earnings limit for NI contributions;

- during the 57 days prior to the day in question the employee had at least one day where he was entitled to:

  - incapacity benefit,

  - maternity allowance, or

  - severe disablement allowance;

- the employee has done no work under his contract of employment (NB: where the employee was employed by the same employer less than eight weeks before the start date of the contract in question, the two contracts are treated as one);

- on the day in question there is a trade dispute at the employee's place of work, unless the employee can show that he had no interest in that dispute at any time either on or before the day in question;

- the employee is or has been pregnant and the day falls within the disqualifying period unless her pregnancy ended (otherwise than by confinement) before the disqualifying period began.

Where an employee in an excluded category is off sick for four or more consecutive days the employer must complete and send to the employee an exclusion form within 11 days of the employee's first day off sick.

(iv) The day must be a qualifying day (Q day).

Q days are those days which, subject to Regulations, the employer and the employee have agreed as being either:

- the days on which the employee would normally be required to work under his contract; or

- days which are chosen to reflect the employee's normal working pattern.

The agreement as to Q days is left largely to the employer and employee but:

- there must be at least one Q day per week;

- the Q days can vary from week to week;

- Q days must be specified;

- if no Q days are agreed, Q days will normally be those days on which the employee would be required to work.

Alternatively, if these cannot be agreed, Q days will be those days which are not specifically agreed to be rest days.

NB: A restriction on the ability of employers and employees to agree Q days was introduced by the Statutory Sick (General) Amendment Regulations 1985 (SI 1985 No 126). This prevents 'maximising' SSP by setting Q days as being those days when the employee is off sick.

The employee is not entitled to be paid for the first three Q days in any PIW – these are known as 'waiting days'.

(v)   The absence is duly notified and certified.

The notification requirements are left to the employer but:

- he cannot require notification before the first Q day;

- he cannot require notification by a specific time of day (ie notification can be insisted on only by the end of the first Q day);

- the employer must specify whether notification should be oral or written or both (if written and posted it is the day of posting which is the day of notification);

- the employer cannot demand notification by the employee in person;

- the employer cannot demand notification in the form of medical evidence of sickness or on a printed form;

- the employer cannot demand notification more than once every seven days during a PE.

Where notification is late, the employer has discretion to treat the days before notification is given as not being Q days (ie he can withhold SSP and treat the first three Q days after notification as waiting days).

The Act requires that the employer must obtain suitable evidence of incapacity. This will usually take the form of medical certificates. (See also Social Security (Medical Evidence, Claims and Payments) Amendment Regulations 1982, **140 below**.)

138.2 Statutory Maternity Pay (SMP)

The Statutory Maternity Pay provisions came into effect for women whose expected date of confinement was after 21 June 1987. They were brought in by the Social Security Act 1986. The following outline of the Statutory Maternity Pay scheme deals with the provisions of both the Act and various Regulations made under the Act.

Amended by Statutory Maternity Pay (General) (Modification and Amendment) Regulations 2000 (SI 2000 No 2883).

a)   Qualifications for SMP

To qualify for entitlement to SMP a woman must (subject to very limited exceptions that are not dealt with here) fulfil all of the following requirements:

(i)   She must be over the age of 16.

(ii)   She must be employed under a contract of employment (ie be an employee rather than self-employed).

(iii) She must have completed not less than 26 weeks' continuous service by some time during the 15th week before the Expected Week of Confinement (EWC).

It is noteworthy that the woman need only work during the 15th week before the EWC – she need not work out the whole of that week. (A 'week' for SMP purposes starts from midnight on Saturday night.)

(iv)   She must have had normal weekly earnings that were not lower than the Lower Earnings Limit for NI contributions for the eight weeks of employment ending with the 15th week before the EWC (NB: Normal weekly earnings are the employee's average earnings over this eight-week period. This means that she would not necessarily have to earn more than the Lower Earnings Limit in each of these weeks.)

(v)   She must have given her employer notice at least 21 days in advance of her absence, stating that she is going to be absent from work wholly or partly because of pregnancy or confinement. This notice must be given in writing if the employer so requests. (NB: If the woman also intends to return to work – and has a statutory right to return – after extended maternity leave, she will have to give written notice both of the fact that she is leaving to go on maternity leave and that she intends to return to work. A woman who is entitled only to the statutory minimum of 14 weeks' maternity leave need not give notice of her intention to return.)

(vi)   She must provide her employer with evidence of her EWC (or, if she is receiving SMP because she has already been confined, of her actual week of confinement) by the end of the third week of the Maternity Pay Period (MPP). If there is a good reason stopping her from producing evidence within this time limit, the evidence can be submitted at any time up until the end of the 13th week of the MPP.

b) The Maternity Pay Period (MPP)

SMP is not payable before the 11th week before the EWC unless the woman has been confined earlier, in which case it is paid in the week following confinement. It is paid on the employee's normal pay days or, if there are no 'normal pay days', on the last day of the month.

The MPP is a flexible period which starts not earlier than the 11th week before EWC or later than the sixth week before EWC. It lasts for 26 weeks. The MPP may start at any time up to the sixth week before EWC if the woman continues in employment up to the end of the seventh week before EWC, without affecting her overall 26-week entitlement. (The entitlement to SMP was extended from 18 to 26 weeks by the Social Security, Statutory Maternity Pay and Statutory Sick Pay (Miscellaneous Amendments) Regulations 2002 (SI 2002 No 2690).)

An employee can continue working up until the EWC without losing her entitlement to SMP, and similarly there is no regulation that prevents the payment of the SMP beyond the 11th week after the EWC. No SMP can be paid earlier than the 11th week before the EWC.

c) Rates of SMP

There are two rates of SMP, the Lower Rate and the Higher Rate:

- Higher-rate SMP is $\frac{9}{10}$ of the woman's 'normal weekly earnings' for the last eight weeks into the qualifying week. Higher-rate SMP is payable for the first six weeks of the Maternity Pay Period. Prior to 1994, higher-rate SMP was payable only to women who had completed two years' service by the 11th week before the EWC. The additional service requirement was removed by the Maternity Allowance and Statutory Maternity Pay Regulations 1994 (SI 1994 No 1230).

- Lower-rate SMP is fixed by the Secretary of State for Employment. Once a woman's entitlement to higher-rate SMP is exhausted, the balance of her SMP entitlement is paid at the lower rate.

(i) Originally, as with SSP, the whole of the employer's liability to pay SMP could be reclaimed from the state. Now employers can reclaim:

- in the case of a small employer (ie one whose total annual primary and secondary NI contributions do not exceed £20,000), all SMP plus an additional 5.5 per cent towards the cost of his NI contributions on the payments (see Statutory Maternity Pay (Compensation of Employers) and Miscellaneous Amendment Regulations 1994 (SI 1994 No 1882));

- in the case of any other employer, 92 per cent of the cost of any SMP paid.

(ii) The amount of SMP that is reclaimable is reclaimed by deduction from the NI and income tax payments which would otherwise be payable for the period.

d) Normal weekly earnings

A woman's normal weekly earnings are used for two purposes:

- First, to calculate whether or not her earnings are above the NI Lower Earnings Limit (and hence whether or not she is entitled to receive SMP at all).

- Second, to calculate the woman's Higher-rate SMP entitlement. Normal weekly earnings are calculated as the woman's average weekly earnings over the eight weeks immediately preceding the 14th week before EWC.

Where a woman is paid monthly, her normal weekly earnings for this period are calculated as the sums that she has been paid in the relevant eight-week period divided by the number of months in respect of which she has been paid during that period multiplied by $\frac{12}{52}$.

There is also a special definition of 'earnings' for SMP purposes. 'Earnings' are a woman's gross earnings and include any remuneration or profit derived from a woman's employment. Specifically, 'earnings' are taken to include and to exclude the following main items:

Inclusions

- SSP, contractual sick pay (except for any amount that the woman has contributed towards her own sick pay) and any contractual payment made because of pregnancy or confinement

- certain sums paid under employment tribunal orders relating to unfair dismissal and redundancy claims

- where a woman is paid an annual bonus or some other such lump sum during the relevant eight-week period then this will generally form part of her 'earnings' for that period, and a payment of this type may greatly enhance her normal weekly earnings for SMP purposes.

  The Statutory Maternity Pay (General)(Amendment) Regulations 2005 provide that where an employee would be entitled to a pay rise at time during her statutory maternity leave, the amount of that pay rise must be taken into account in deciding her earnings for SMP purposes.

Exclusions

- any holiday pay where it is paid from a fund contributed to by more than one employer;

- any payment in respect of a gratuity or offering which is not made by the employer;

- any payment in kind or provision of board, lodgings or other services;

- any pension payment;

- any payment towards expenses incurred by a woman in travelling to her place of employment or training under the Disabled Persons (Employment) Act 1944;

- a payment by way of, or derived from, shares apportioned under a statutorily approved profit-sharing scheme;

- any VAT paid on goods or services supplied by the woman;

- any redundancy payment;

- any payment of, or contribution to, expenses incurred by the woman in carrying out her employment (where an 'allowance' is paid in respect of expenses, if part of that allowance represents a profit in the woman's hands, that profit will be a part of her 'earnings').

e) Who is liable to pay?

A woman's employer is liable to pay SMP, provided the woman meets all the conditions. An employer, for these purposes, is a person who is liable to pay Secondary Class 1 NI contributions in respect of the woman.

A woman cannot be asked to contribute to her own SMP except that SMP may be set off against any contractual maternity pay that is paid to her. Neither can any agreement be made to modify or exclude any terms of the SMP scheme. There is also provision for any employer who has dismissed an employee solely or mainly to avoid SMP liability to be made liable to pay the woman's SMP.

f) Exclusion and disqualification from SMP entitlement

It should be noted that unlike SSP, which deals with payments and disqualifications in units of 'days', SMP is dealt with in units of 'weeks'. A woman may lose her entitlement to SMP, or to a part of it, in any of the following circumstances:

(i) Working during the MPP

SMP is not payable for any week during which the employee works for her employer under a contract of employment.

If the woman works for another employer after her confinement during her MPP she ceases to be entitled to SMP for the remainder of the MPP. The woman is obliged to notify her 'liable' employer of any such employment within seven days of its starting. (Since most women are unlikely to know that they are under a duty to inform you if they work for someone else during the MPP, your Staff Handbook should make this clear.)

(ii)   In legal custody

There is no liability to pay SMP for any week during which a woman is in legal custody or sentenced to a term of imprisonment (unless the sentence is suspended).

(iii)   Death

If the woman dies during the MPP the employer's liability ends in the week following the week of her death.

g)   The nature of SMP

SMP, like SSP, is subject to income tax and NI deductions. There is also a right to make deductions from SMP in the same way and to the same extent as such deductions could be made from the woman's ordinary pay.

h)   Records

Employers must retain the following records for three years following the tax year in which the MPP ends:

(i)   the first notified day of absence in the MPP and the first day of the MPP if different (eg because of early confinement);

(ii)   the weeks of the tax year in which SMP was paid and the amount paid in each week;

(iii)   any week in the tax year during an employee's MPP for which no payment was made to her, together with the reason why no payment was made;

(iv)   any medical evidence presented to the employer of the EWC or of the actual week of confinement. If the employer has returned this evidence to the woman for her to make any social security claims, it is sufficient if he keeps a copy. If the medical evidence is of the actual week of confinement, the employer must keep a note of this. If the employee gives her employer the birth certificate, it must be returned to her.

i)   Disputes

Disputes about SMP liability are generally dealt with through the social security scheme rather than at employment tribunal, although the inclusion of SMP in the definition of 'wages' under the protection of wages provisions of the ERA means that an employer's failure to pay could be treated as an unlawful deduction and thus be amenable to litigation before an employment tribunal. If the employer fails to pay the woman, or fails to pay the correct amount, or fails to pay it at the right time, he can be prosecuted under the social security legislation.

j) Special cases

There are special rules that deal with cases where the employer has dismissed the employee to avoid SMP liability. In such cases the employee may, nonetheless, be able to claim SMP from him provided that she has been continuously employed for at least eight weeks.

If the woman is confined before the 14th week before EWC, she will be entitled to SMP if she would otherwise have qualified for SMP. The position as it would otherwise have been at the 14th week before EWC may be difficult to judge, however, since form MAT-B 1, which specifies EWC, is not usually available until the 14th week before EWC.

138.3 Industrial injuries benefit

a) Entitlement

An employee who is injured by an accident arising out of and in the course of his employment will be entitled to industrial injuries benefit.

- Where an accident occurs in the course of employment then there is a presumption that the accident also arose out of that employment unless the contrary is proven.

- An injury caused by an accident to an employee who is, with the employer's permission, travelling to or from work as a passenger in a vehicle provided by or under an arrangement with his employer, is taken to be an industrial injury.

- An injury caused by an accident to an employee in an emergency or supposed emergency, while the employee is on any premises where he is employed to work, is taken to be an industrial injury if he is trying to help people or save property.

- An injury to an employee that was not caused or contributed to by the employee's own misconduct is treated as an industrial injury if it:

  - arises out of another person's misconduct, skylarking or negligence;

  - arises out of any steps taken in consequence of another person's misconduct, skylarking or negligence;

  - arises out of the behaviour or presence of an animal (including a bird, fish or insect);

  - is caused by or consists of an employee being struck by an object or lightning.

Employees who suffer from prescribed industrial diseases or prescribed personal injuries (which are not caused by accidents arising out of and in the course of their employment) can also claim industrial injuries benefit.

b) The benefit

Industrial injuries benefit consists of:

(i) Disablement benefit

Where the loss of mental or physical faculties arising out of the disablement is not less than 14 per cent (20 per cent where the claim was made before 1 October 1986), the employee will be entitled to a disablement pension. In assessing the employee's disability level any pre-existing disability is taken into account as adding to the overall percentage of disability.

A higher disability pension is payable where the level of disability is 100 per cent and constant attendance is needed.

(ii)   Reduced earnings allowance

A reduced earnings allowance can be claimed in respect of an accident which happened before 1 October 1990 and which resulted in the employee being permanently disabled from following his normal occupation. Where the accident results in a diminution in the employee's earning capacity, a reduced earnings allowance may be available to supplement the employee's earnings.

(iii)   Retirement allowance

When a person who was entitled to a reduced earnings allowance retires, he may also be entitled to a retirement allowance that will top up his normal pension to take into account his reduced earning capacity.

(iv)   Industrial death benefit

The Act provides for a widow's benefit where a person dies who was entitled, or who but for his death would have been entitled, to claim in respect of an industrial injury.

138.4 Notional strike pay

Where an employee is on strike or has an interest in a trade dispute, a set amount of notional strike pay is to be taken into account in assessing any entitlement that he may have to social security benefits. This notional sum is taken into account in assessing the employee's entitlement to benefit whether or not he actually receives it.

139 Social Security (Incapacity for Work) Act 1994

Amends the Social Security Contributions and Benefits Act 1992 (SSCBA) and the Social Security Administration Act 1992 (SSAA).

The major thrust of this Act is to bring in a new way of assessing a person's ability or inability to work. This method of assessment is relevant only for benefits under the SSCBA itself and even then is expressly not applicable to assessment of inability for industrial injuries or SSP purposes. From an employment point of view it therefore has very little effect. Other employment-related provisions in the Act amend existing legislation and are dealt with in the relevant statutes.

140 Social Security (Medical Evidence, Claims and Payments) Amendment Regulations 1982

These Regulations provide that medical practitioners need not give National Health insurance certificates to cover the first seven calendar days when a person is ill.

141 Social Security, Statutory Maternity Pay and Statutory Sick Pay (Miscellaneous Amendments) Regulations 2002 (SI 2002 No 2690)

Amend the SSCBA.

The Regulations extend the period for which SMP is paid from 18 to 26 weeks.

142 Social Security (Welfare to Work) Regulations 1998 (SI 1998 No 2231)

These Regulations provide that where Welfare to Work beneficiaries have two periods of incapacity for work that are separated by less than 52 weeks, the two are to be treated as a single period of incapacity for work. The effect of this is that where Welfare to Work beneficiaries are taken into employment the state, rather than the employer, picks up the sick pay liability for such employees.

143 Statute Law (Repeal) Act 2004

Repeals Apprentices Act 1814, Job Release Act 1977, Employment Subsidies Act 1978, Employment Act 1982 and various sections in a number of other employment-related statutes.

144 Statutory Maternity Pay (General) (Modification and Amendment) Regulations 2000 (SI 2000 No 2883)

Amend the SSCBA as it relates to the conditions of entitlement to statutory maternity pay.

The Regulations make provision to deal with pregnant women who are dismissed after the 11th week before the expected week of confinement, and make provision to entitle them to SMP.

145 Statutory Paternity Pay and Statutory Adoption Pay (Amendment) Regulations 2004 (SI 2004 No 488)

Amend the Statutory Paternity Pay and Statutory Adoption Pay (General) Regulations 2002 (SI 2002 No 2822). The amendments are dealt with under the main Regulations.

146 Statutory Paternity Pay and Statutory Adoption Pay (General) Regulations 2002 (SI 2002 No 2822)

The Regulations provide for those on statutory paternity and statutory adoption leave to be paid.

147 Statutory Sick Pay Act 1994

Amends the Social Security Contributions and Benefits Act 1992 and the Social Security Administration Act 1992.

a) The removal of the right to recoup SSP

Under the original SSP scheme the employer was able to recoup 100 per cent of the SSP paid out to employees. Indeed, under the Social Security Act 1985, the principle of reimbursement was extended to allow the employer to reclaim a further amount in respect of the secondary Class 1 National Insurance contributions he was liable to pay on SSP payments.

From 6 April 1991, the Statutory Sick Pay Act 1991 provided that an employer could recoup only 80 per cent of the amount of SSP which he paid out, and removed the provision for reclaiming the allowance for secondary National Insurance contributions.

The Statutory Sick Pay Act 1994 removes the general right for employers to reclaim any SSP paid to employees after April 1995.

b) 'Small employer's' relief (SER)

SER was introduced by the Statutory Sick Pay Act 1991, to allow small employers to reclaim at least part of the amount they expended on SSP. The original scheme is replaced by a scheme made under the 1994 Act together with the Statutory Sick Pay Percentage Threshold Order 1995 (SI 1995 No 512), which came into effect in April 1995. The scheme allows employers to recoup SSP payments from the state to the extent that those payments exceed 13 per cent of the employer's NI contributions for the month in question. The level of 13 per cent was set to equate to the cost of the original SER.

148 Sunday Working (Scotland) Act 2003

Amends the ERA to extend the Sunday working provisions of the ERA to Scotland.

149 Tax Credits Act 1999

Amends the ERA.

From 5 October 1999 this Act gives employees a right not to be dismissed/have action short of dismissal taken against them because they are claiming tax credits. Neither the one-year service qualification nor the upper age limit restrict the right of an employee to claim unfair dismissal for claiming tax credits. There is an equivalent provision protecting employees who are made redundant because they are claiming tax credits.

150 Tax Credits Act 2002

Amends the ERA.

Schedule 1 of the Act amends the ERA to enable an employee who suffers a detriment because he is claiming tax credits to complain to an employment tribunal. Dismissal for claiming tax credits is made automatically unfair.

151 Teaching and Higher Education Act 1998

Amends the ERA and provides a right to paid time off for young people to study or train.

a) The right

An employee who is:

- aged 16 or 17 (18 if the employee started the course before reaching 18)
- is not receiving full-time education; and
- has not attained certain specified standards of educational achievement

is entitled to have paid time off to undertake study or training leading to a relevant qualification.

b) Time off can be taken whether the employee works directly for an employer or through an agency.

c) The standards of educational achievement below which the employee can take time off for study under this provision are set down by the Right to Time Off for Study or Training Regulations 1999 (SI 1999 No 986). Broadly the standards are:

- GCSEs: five at grades A* to C
- SQA Standard Grades: five at grades 1 to 3
- one intermediate GNVQ or one GSVQ at level 2
- one NVQ or one SVQ at level 2
- one BTEC First Diploma awarded by the Edexel Foundation
- one BTEC First Certificate awarded by the Edexel Foundation
- City and Guilds of London Institute Diploma of Vocational Education at Intermediate Level; or
- 16 SQA unit or assessment credits at least eight of which are at Intermediate 2 or above and the remainder at Intermediate 1.

There are various provisions for lower-qualification levels to be treated as part-qualifications for these purposes.

d) The amount of time off to which an employee is entitled under these provisions and the occasions on which time off may be taken and any conditions subject to which it may be taken are those that are reasonable in all the circumstances having regard to:

- the requirements of the employee's study or training;
- the circumstances of the employer's business (or the principal's business where the employee works through an employment agency); and
- the effect of the employee's time off on the running of that business.

e) The employee can apply to an employment tribunal if he is refused time off or payment for time off. There is a three-month time limit for claiming, with the usual provision to extend time if it is not reasonably practicable for the claim to be brought within that time.

152 Telecommunications (Lawful Business Practice) (Interception of Communications) Regulations 2000 (SI 2000 No 2699)

These Regulations amend Regulation of Investigatory Powers Act 2000 – **see 120 above**.

153 Trade Union and Labour Relations (Consolidation) Act 1992 (TULRA)

Consolidates the law relating to trade unions from the following statutes: Conspiracy and Protection of Property Act 1875, Trade Union Act 1913, Industrial Courts Act 1919, Trade Union (Amalgamations, etc) Act 1964, Industrial Relations Act 1971, Trade Union and Labour Relations Act 1974, Trade Union and Labour Relations (Amendment) Act 1976, Employment Protection Act 1975, EPCA, Interpretation Act 1978, Reserve Forces Act 1980, Employment Acts 1980–1990, Trade Union Act 1984, Companies Consolidation (Consequential Provisions) Act 1985, Public Order Act 1986.

Amended by TURERA, Collective Redundancies and Transfer of Undertakings (Protection of Employment) (Amendment) Regulations (SI 1995 No 2587), ERA, Employment Rights (Disputes Resolutions) Act 1998, Deregulation (Deduction from Pay of Union Subscriptions) Order 1998, Transfer of Undertakings (Protection of Employment) (Amendment) Regulations 1999, Employment Relations Act 1999 and Employment Relations Act 2004.

153.1 The meaning of 'trade union', list of unions and certification of independence

Originally ss 2, 8 and 30 Trade Union and Labour Relations Act 1974 and s 8 Employment Protection Act 1975.

a) The definition of 'trade union'

A union is defined as:

- an organisation consisting of workers of one or more types whose main purposes include the regulation of relations between workers of that type and employers or employers' associations; or

- an organisation whose members are trade unions (such as the TUC).

b) List of trade unions

(i) The Certification Officer keeps a list of trade unions. Organisations wishing to be registered as trade unions can apply to the Certification Officer. They must provide him with:

- a copy of the rules of the organisation;

- a list of its officers;

- the address of its head or main office;

- the name by which it is, or is to be, known; and

- the prescribed fee.

(ii) If the Certification Officer is satisfied that the organisation is a trade union, that it fulfils the above requirements and is not using a name which belongs to, or which has been used by, another registered trade union, he must enter it on to the list of trade unions.

(iii) The Certification Officer also has certain powers to strike unions off the list he holds.

c) Independent trade unions

(i) The majority of employment law rights conferred on trade unions have been restricted to those unions that are independent. A trade union is defined as independent if:

- it is not under the domination or control of one or more employers or employers' associations; and

- it is not liable to interference by any employer/s or employers' associations (through the provision of financial or material support or other means tending towards such control).

(ii) A trade union that is on the list of trade unions can apply to the Certification Officer for a certificate of independence.

(iii) The Certification Officer can withdraw a union's certificate of independence if he is of the opinion that the union is no longer independent. If he does this, however, the union can appeal against his decision.

153.2 The status and property of trade unions

a) The status of trade unions

Although trade unions are not corporate bodies they have power to make contracts and to sue and to be sued in their own right. Their objects, which might otherwise be considered to be void as being in restraint of trade (since, for example, their objects might include preventing people from working), are specifically declared by statute not to offend against the general common law principles outlawing agreements that are in restraint of trade.

b) The property of trade unions

(i) The property of trade unions must be vested in trustees. The trustees can be personally liable, and can be sued by individual members of the union, if they misuse union property.

(ii) It is unlawful for a trade union to use any of its property to pay for any penalty imposed on a union member by a court. If a union does make any such payment, it is under an obligation to recoup it and an individual member is entitled to force the union to pursue recoupment.

(iii) Death benefits

- Unions may pay sums of up to £5,000 on the death of a member.

- Members can nominate their beneficiaries under these provisions.

c) Liability in tort

The liability of unions in tort is dealt with under Industrial action (**see 153.13 below**).

153.3 Trade union administration

a) Register of members

Unions are required to keep an up-to-date register of their members, including their home or work addresses. Where the names on the register are required to be given to an outsider, such as a scrutineer in relation to elections for certain union offices, the union is required to impose a duty of confidentiality on that person as regards the information on the register. This requirement was brought in by TURERA.

b) Duty to supply rules

Unions are required to supply any person with a copy of its rules either free of charge or on payment of a reasonable fee.

c) Accounting records

(i) Unions are required to prepare accounts and to keep them available for inspection for six years. Union members can inspect any such accounts, with their accountants if desired, for the time for which they have been members of the union.

(ii) Unions are required to appoint auditors and to send annual returns to the Certification Officer. At the same time as sending an annual return to the Certification Officer unions are required to send an annual statement to members – broadly similar to a company's annual return. This latter amendment was introduced by TURERA.

153.4 Elections for trade union officers

a) Who must be elected

The president, general secretary and members of the executive of a union must be re-elected every five years. This does not apply to long-serving members of the executive who are within five years of retirement and who would otherwise be allowed by the union rules to stay on until retirement without being re-elected.

b) The election process

(i) No union member may be unreasonably excluded from standing for election.

(ii) Each candidate is allowed to prepare an election address in his own words. The candidates' election addresses must be distributed by the union.

(iii) The union must appoint an independent scrutineer to oversee the election.

(iv) Generally, each union member must be given the same right to vote, but the union is entitled to exclude certain categories, such as those who are unemployed or in arrears with their subscriptions, or to limit the vote to certain classes of member within the union (eg to those within a particular geographical location or to members of a particular trade).

(v) Each eligible member has a right to vote in a secret postal ballot. The votes must be counted by an independent person (this is a TURERA amendment) and there must be a scrutineer's report produced saying that the scrutineer is satisfied with the way in which the election has been conducted. The results of the election cannot be published until the scrutineer's report has approved the election. The union must send a copy or inform all members of the terms of the scrutineer's report within three months of receiving it. By amendments added by TURERA, the scrutineer is also required to examine the union's register of members and to satisfy himself that it is accurate and up to date.

153.5 The use of funds for political objectives

a) Political fund resolution

A union's funds cannot be used for political purposes, as defined by the Act, unless the union has adopted a political resolution. Such a resolution must be approved by a majority of those voting in a ballot and the political resolution must be reballoted every 10 years.

- The union must make payments for political objectives out of a separate fund, from which members can be exempted from contributing.

- The union's rules regarding the use of funds for political purposes must be approved by the Certification Officer.

b) Members' contributions to political funds

(i)   When a union adopts a political resolution it must tell its members of that fact. It must also tell them that they are entitled to be exempted from contributing to the political fund. They must be told that they can obtain an exemption notice, exempting them from political fund contributions from the union's Head Office or from the Certification Officer. Section 84 sets out a statutory form of exemption notice that can be used by members not wishing to contribute to the political fund.

(ii) If an employee who has union subscriptions deducted from his pay under the check-off system is exempt from making political fund contributions and notifies his employer of this in writing:

- the employer must not deduct political fund contributions from that employee's pay; and

- the employer must not refuse to make deductions under the check-off system in respect of the employee while he continues to make check-off deductions for other employees (unless his refusal has nothing to do with the fact that the employee is exempt from making political fund contributions).

(iii) Where the employer either:

- makes deductions despite the employee's being exempt from contributing to the political fund, or

- refuses to continue to make deductions of the employee's union subscriptions after being notified that the employee is exempt from contributing to the union's political fund,

the employee can apply to the county court (sheriff's court in Scotland) which can make a declaration if it finds for the employee.

(iv) If the employee's complaint is that the employer has made unlawful deductions from his pay – by making deductions in respect of the political fund contribution when the employee was exempt – the time for bringing a claim under the s 23 ERA (claim for unlawful deductions from wages) runs from the date of the declaration by the court of the employee's right not to have had that amount deducted.

153.6 Funding and the use of the employer's premises for ballots

TULRA originally provided that public funding would be available for certain trade union ballots, including those for elections of the executive committee, political fund ballots and industrial action ballots. These provisions were repealed by TURERA with effect from 1 April 1996. The provisions allowing for the unions to use the employer's premises to hold such ballots where the employer recognised the union and had more than 20 employees were also repealed by TURERA with effect from 1 April 1996. To a large extent using the employer's premises would be of no assistance now since most types of ballot require a postal rather than a workplace ballot.

153.7 Employers' Associations

The Act defines Employers' Associations, provides for the Certification Officer to keep a list of them, and deals with the status and property of Employers' Associations and their administration, ability to apply funds for political objectives and for amalgamations and similar matters.

153.8 The rights of trade union members against the union

a) Rights on unballoted union action

TULRA allows a trade union member to bring an action against the union where the union has authorised or endorsed any industrial action that has not been approved by a secret ballot. A member can bring an action only if members of the union (including the complainant himself) have been or are likely to be induced to take part in, or to continue, the 'unapproved' industrial action.

This provision gives individual union members the right to complain that the trade union has failed to hold a proper ballot or to obtain a vote in favour of the industrial action as a result of that ballot (see Industrial action, **153.13 below**). Originally only employers were in a position to complain about a union's failure to obtain the sanction of a ballot before taking industrial action. This extension, to allow individual trade union members to complain of unballoted strike action, was originally brought into effect by the Employment Act 1988.

b) Access to the courts for members

Where a trade union member has applied for any matter to be determined in accordance with the trade union's rules and that matter has not been dealt with within six months, then, regardless of anything in the union rules, the member can take his grievance to court. There are provisions which allow this six-month period to be extended where the reason for the union failing to deal with the issue was the member's own fault.

If the individual's application to the union to deal with any matter is invalid, the union must inform him, within 28 days of the application, of the ways in which the application is invalid. If the union fails to do this, the member is entitled to treat his application as validly made.

c) The right not to be unjustifiably disciplined

A trade union member/former member is given the right not to be unjustifiably disciplined by the union. It is unjustifiable for a union to discipline someone because he is or is believed to be guilty of any of the following:

- not supporting, or indicating opposition to, or lack of support for, a strike or other industrial action;

- not breaching an agreement between himself and his employer to support a strike or other industrial action (NB: the wording of this makes it clear that this is not limited to employees who are trade union members);

- asserting, or vindicating someone else's assertion, that the union or any official or representative of the union or a trustee of any union property has contravened or proposes to contravene any agreement, union rule or rule of law, or consulting the Certification Officer in respect of any such matter – unless the member is acting in bad faith in making or vindicating an assertion which he believes to be false;

- encouraging or helping someone else not to breach his agreement with his employer;

- failing to agree to, or withdrawing agreement from, deductions being made from his wages in respect of union dues;

- resigning, or proposing to resign, from a union, becoming, or proposing to become, a member of another union or refusing to become a member of another union;

- working with, or proposing to work with, non-union members;

- working for, or proposing to work for, an employer who employs or who has employed non-union members, whether of the particular union or of another union; or

- requiring the union to do anything that the union is required by TULRA to do if asked by a member.

Unjustifiable discipline in this context includes:

- expulsion, from the union or from a branch of it;

- a fine of any sort;

- withdrawal of any of the services or benefits of membership;

- any other detriment.

Complaints under these provisions must be presented to an employment tribunal within three months of the decision which gave rise to the complaint.

If the tribunal finds the complaint well founded it will make a declaration to that effect. The claimant can then apply to the tribunal if the union's decision has been withdrawn and it has done all it can to ensure a reversal of the effects of that decision or to the Employment Appeals Tribunal (EAT) if those steps have not been taken.

Any such application cannot be made earlier than four weeks after the tribunal's declaration. In these, later, proceedings the tribunal or EAT can:

- order repayment of any sums the member has paid out under the union's decision; and

- award such compensation as it considers 'just and equitable in all the circumstances of the case', subject to the total not exceeding the maximum basic award plus the maximum compensatory award that could be obtained in an unfair dismissal case (see ERA – unfair dismissal remedies).

d) The right to terminate union membership

Every union member has the right to terminate his union membership on giving reasonable notice and complying with any reasonable conditions.

e) The right not to be excluded or expelled from the union

The Employment Act 1980 provided a right for employees who were in 'closed shop' employment not to be unreasonably expelled or excluded from the trade unions that were party to the closed shop agreement. (A 'closed shop' meant that only members of the appropriate unions could be employed in that employment.) TURERA has extended this protection, in modified form, to protect all trade union members and would-be trade union members from being excluded from or expelled by a trade union other than on certain specific grounds. The Employment Relations Act 2004 amended this protection. The amendments are inserted below.

(i) The right

The grounds on which a person can be excluded or expelled from a trade union are:

- if the person no longer meets an 'enforceable membership requirement'. An 'enforceable membership requirement' is one that restricts membership by reference purely to:

  - employment in a specified trade, industry or profession;

  - occupational description (including grade, level or category of appointment); or

  - possession of specific trade, industrial or professional qualifications or work experience;

- if the person is not within the geographical area in which the union operates;

- where the union operates within a single company or within a group of associated companies, if the person ceases to be employed by the company/group;

- where the exclusion or expulsion is solely because of the individual's conduct. But there are certain types of conduct for which it is not permissible to expel or exclude an individual. These are:

  - the individual being or ceasing to be

    - a member of another trade union

    - employed by a particular employer or at a particular place, or

  - conduct in relation to any trade union for which, under the Act (see c) above), an individual may not be disciplined by a trade union.

Conduct which consists of an individual's being or ceasing to be a member of a political party is 'protected conduct', and it is not permissible to exclude or expel a member because of such conduct. However conduct which consists of activities undertaken by the individual while a member of a political party is not granted this protected status.

(ii) Remedies

A complaint may be made to a tribunal within six months of the date of expulsion or exclusion from the union or, if that is not reasonably practicable, within such further time as is reasonably practicable.

Where the tribunal finds the claim to be substantiated it must make a declaration to that effect. Where the tribunal finds that the primary reason for exclusion or expulsion was a 'protected conduct' it must also make a second declaration to that effect. In such cases the tribunal must also go on to consider whether any other conduct for which the individual was expelled or excluded from the union was wholly or mainly conduct which was contrary to a rule or objective of the union. If it considers that it was such conduct, the tribunal must make a third declaration to that effect.

Compensation

If the employee has not been admitted/readmitted by the union on the date when his application was made, there is a minimum award of £5,900 unless the tribunal has made a third declaration in the case (see above).

The claim, in either case, must be made within four weeks of the tribunal's declaration.

Subject to the cases where the statutory minimum applies, the amount of compensation awarded is such as is considered just and equitable, and a reduction can be made for any contributory conduct on the part of the claimant.

The maximum award that can be made is:

- 30 weeks' pay (subject to the statutory upper limit for a 'week's pay'); plus

- the maximum compensatory award for unfair dismissal.

f) Commissioner for the Rights of Trade Union Members

The Employment Relations Act 1999 abolished this post and moved some of its functions to the Certification Officer.

153.9 The rights of trade union members in relation to employment

a) The right to require the employer to stop deductions of union subscriptions

A more extensive right was substituted by TURERA. The original requirement (in the 1992 Act) was that if an employee informed his employer that he had left the union with effect from a particular date, the employer must stop checking off union dues from that date or as soon thereafter as is reasonably practicable. TURERA introduced a rather more onerous set of requirements for employers and employees to comply with if check-off was to apply. This included a requirement that the employee's authorisation for the employer to continue the check-off arrangement in his case should be renewed every three years. The Deregulation (Deduction from Pay of Union Subscriptions) Order 1998 allows employers to send a notice to employees (in a form laid down in the Order). These notices ask employees to write back and make a positive election if they wish to limit to the original three-year period their authorisation for their union dues to be checked off. If they do not write back to the employer within 14 days, the original authorisation is to be treated as continuing until it is specifically withdrawn by the employee. The requirement for employers to give employees a month's notice of any change in subscription levels is also removed. Apart from these amendments:

(i) The right requires an employer:

- not to make any union subscription deduction which is not authorised; and

- to ensure that any subscription deduction that is made is not more than the authorised amount.

(ii) To be authorised, permission to make the subscription deduction must be authorised in a written document which is:

- signed and dated by the worker;

- subject to what is said above, no more than three years old at the date when the deduction is made.

 Where the authorisation has been withdrawn, no deductions may be made after the withdrawal has been received by the employer (subject to there being enough time after the date of the withdrawal for it to be reasonably practicable to stop the deductions being made from the payment in question).

(iii) An employee can complain to an employment tribunal that an employer has made unauthorised or excessive deductions, within three months of the deduction in question or, where that is not reasonably practicable, within such further time as is reasonably practicable.

(iv) Nothing in these arrangements, however, requires an employer to deduct union subscriptions from an employee's pay for the union if he does not wish to do so.

(v) (For the right of union members not to have unauthorised political fund contributions deducted from their pay and for their right to continue to have the remainder of their union subscriptions deducted by the employer after they have elected not to contribute to the political fund see Use of funds for political objectives, **153.5 above**.)

b) Discriminatory recruitment on 'trade union grounds'

(i) Refusing employment

The Act provides that it is unlawful for a person to be refused employment on 'trade union grounds'. This makes it unlawful for an employer to refuse to employ a person because:

- he is or is not a member of a trade union;

- he is unwilling to accept a requirement to remain, or to become, or to cease to be, a union member; or

- he refuses to have money deducted from his pay as an alternative to being a union member, etc.

Where there is an arrangement whereby employment is offered only to people put forward by a trade union, an applicant who applies for and is refused employment because of this practice is deemed to have been refused employment on trade union grounds.

The Act contains an extended definition of 'refusing employment', which includes:

- failing to entertain the applicant's application or enquiry, or causing him to withdraw it;
- refusing to offer the applicant employment;
- offering the job on terms which no one who wanted to fill the post would offer;
- offering it on condition that the employee must meet the 'trade union' requirement (eg by joining or leaving the union); or
- offering the job and then withdrawing that offer.

(ii) Discriminatory advertising

Where an advertisement is published which indicates, or which might reasonably be understood as indicating, that the employer will require the successful applicant to be or to become a trade union member or to cease to be one, then an employee who applies for and is refused employment is conclusively presumed to have been refused employment on trade union grounds if:

- he either does not meet that requirement; or
- he is unwilling to accept that requirement.

  This is particularly stringent since it imposes strict liability on an employer in such cases.

(iii) Discrimination by an employment agency

There are provisions equivalent to items (i) and (ii) above relating to employment agencies. These make it unlawful for an employment agency either to refuse to offer its services on trade union grounds, or to publish a discriminatory advertisement.

  For these purposes a trade union is not to be considered an employment agency in relation to services provided for its members.

(iv) Union membership requirements in contracts for supply of goods or services

Any term or condition in a contract for the supply of goods or services which requires the work to be carried out by union members is declared void. Similarly, any term which requires an employer to recognise, consult with or negotiate with a trade union is also void.

  It is unlawful to refuse to deal with any supplier of goods or services on grounds relating to the trade union status of any of that supplier's employees. It is also unlawful to refuse to deal with a supplier on the grounds that they recognise, consult or negotiate with a trade union (or because they do not do so).

(v) Remedy

Time limit

A complaint may be made to an employment tribunal within three months of the discrimination in question. The type of case where problems can immediately be envisaged, in terms of trying to determine when the discrimination actually occurred, is where an employer has simply omitted to offer employment. In such a case the Act provides that time for application is to run from 'the end of the period within which it was reasonable to expect the employer to act'. This may lead to some interesting case law.

Remedies

The employment tribunal can order the employer to pay compensation, which is to be assessed in the same way as compensation for breach of statutory duty (and which can include compensation for injury to feelings). The maximum amount of compensation that can be awarded is the same as the maximum unfair dismissal compensatory award (set at £50,000 by the Redundant Relations Act 1999 with effect from 25 October 1999 and index-linked thereafter).

> In addition to a monetary award, the tribunal can recommend that the respondent take specific action to obviate or reduce the adverse effect on the claimant of the conduct complained of. If the respondent fails to take the recommended action the tribunal can award compensation, or greater compensation to reflect that failure. The total award, however, is still subject to the same overall maximum as the maximum unfair dismissal compensation.

Joinder of third parties

Where the employer's conduct was to any extent caused by a third party exercising pressure by threatening to call a strike or to take other industrial action, that third party (which will usually be a trade union) can be joined to the proceedings. In such cases the tribunal can make a compensatory award against either or both parties and in such proportions as it sees fit. Where the case could be brought against an employer or an employment agency and the union member takes action against only one, then the other can be joined at the instance of either party and any compensation can again be awarded against either or both in such proportions as the tribunal considers just in the circumstances.

c) Subjection to a detriment for trade union reasons

The original terms of the Act that protected employees against 'action short of dismissal' on union grounds were changed by the Employment Relations Act 1999 to a prohibition against subjecting an individual to detriment on union grounds. This protection has been further extended and replaced by the Employment Relations Act 2004.

(i) The prohibition

An employer is not allowed to subject the worker to a detriment by any act or failure to act:

- to prevent or deter him from, or to penalise him for:
  - being a member of an independent trade union; or
  - taking part, at an appropriate time, in the activities of an independent trade union (An 'appropriate time' for taking part in trade union activities is either outside working hours or at a time agreed or arranged with the employer during working hours.);

- to compel him to be a member of a trade union;

- to enforce a requirement to pay an amount in lieu of union dues for non-union members;

- to prevent or deter him from making use of trade union services at an appropriate time (Trade union services are services provided for a worker by an independent trade union by virtue of the worker's trade union membership.);

- because an independent trade union of which the worker is a member raises a matter on the worker's behalf;

- because the worker has declined an inducement relating to trade union membership or collective bargaining.

(ii) Remedy

An employee can bring a claim at any time within three months of the action in question (with a provision to extend this time limit if it cannot reasonably be met). Where there is a series of actions giving rise to the complaint, it is from the last that the three-month time limit runs.

No account is to be taken of any pressure placed on the employer to take the action complained of. Any third party can be joined to the proceedings, and the tribunal can make an award against the third party to the extent that is just and equitable.

d) Dismissal for trade union reasons

(i) The prohibition

The dismissal or selection for redundancy of an employee on grounds of trade union membership or taking part in trade union activities is to be regarded as unfair. Such dismissals are considered to be for an inadmissible reason. The Employment Relations Act 2004 extended the categories of inadmissible reasons for dismissal and removed the upper age limit and qualifying period for entitlement to make a claim to an employment tribunal for dismissals for an inadmissible reason. Inadmissible reasons for dismissal are:

- because the employee was, or proposed to become, a member of an independent trade union;

- because the employee had taken part, or proposed to take part, in the activities of an independent trade union at an appropriate time (An 'appropriate time' for taking part in trade union activities is either outside working hours or at a time agreed or arranged with the employer during working hours.);

- because he was not a member of a union or of a particular trade union;

- because he refused to agree to allow his employer to deduct an amount in lieu of union dues from his pay;

- because he refused an inducement relating to union membership, activities or collective bargaining.

(ii) Remedies

The remedies in a case of unfair dismissal, or unfair selection for redundancy on grounds of trade union membership or activities, are the same as those for 'special cases' of unfair dismissal under ERA; both were modified by Employment Relations Act 1999. There is also a facility to join third parties to proceedings and a provision for interim relief to be provided to allow for the contract of employment to be continued pending the outcome of the tribunal case (see also ERA: Protection for health and safety representatives, trustees of pension schemes and employee representatives, **53.6 above**, where these remedies are dealt with in more detail).

e) Time off for trade union duties

(i) The right

An employee who is an official of a recognised independent trade union is entitled not to be unreasonably refused paid time off during working hours for:

- negotiations with the employer about:

  - things falling within the statutory definition of collective bargaining (see Industrial relations, collective bargaining below)

    - in respect of which the union is recognised by the employer;

- the performance of functions which the employer has agreed may be performed by the union related to:

  - things falling within the statutory definition of collective bargaining (see Industrial relations, collective bargaining below)

    - in respect of which the union is recognised by the employer;

- training to enable the official to carry out the above duties, provided that the training is approved by the TUC or by the independent trade union of which he is an official.

  The amount of time off which is to be permitted and the reasons for it are subject to what is reasonable and to the terms of an ACAS Code of Practice.

(ii) Remedy

A trade union official who is unreasonably refused paid time off or who is not paid for it can complain to an employment tribunal within three months of the incident, or within such further time as is reasonably practicable if it is not reasonably practicable to meet the three-month time limit. Where the tribunal finds that the official has not been paid where he should have been, it must award payment for time off which should have been given; it may also award compensation for the failure to give time off.

f) Time off for trade union activities

(i) The right

An employee who is a member of a recognised independent trade union is entitled to reasonable time off during working hours to take part in:

- any activities of the union; and

- any activities of the union in relation to which he is an official or representative of the union.

  The amount of time off that is to be permitted and the reasons for it are subject to what is reasonable and to the terms of an ACAS Code of Practice.

(ii)   Remedy

A trade union member who is unreasonably refused time off for trade union activities can complain to an employment tribunal within three months of the incident, or within such further time as is reasonably practicable if it is not reasonably practicable to meet the three-month time limit. On an application the tribunal may make an award of compensation for time off which should have been given.

g)   Time off for learning representatives

(i)   The right

An employee who is a member of a recognised independent trade union and who is a learning representative is entitled to reasonable paid time off during working hours for any of the following purposes:

- to analyse training needs;

- to provide information and advice about learning or training matters;

- to arrange learning or training; and

- to promote the value of learning or training for the members of a recognised trade union in respect of which the employee is their learning representative; or

- to undergo training which is relevant to his functions as a learning representative.

Before the learning representative is entitled to time off the trade union must give the employer written notice that:

- the employee is a learning representative; and

- that he has met one of the following training conditions:

  - He has undergone sufficient training to enable him to undertake the purposes for which he is entitled to time off. The union must give the employer notice that this is the case.

  - The union has given the employer notice in the previous six months that the employee will be undergoing such training. (Only one such notice may be given by the union in respect of any employee.)

  A learning representative is a person who has been appointed or elected to be a learning representative in accordance with the union's rules.

(ii)   ACAS Code

ACAS is required to produce a Code on time off for learning representatives. Time off for learning representatives is included in the revised ACAS Code of Practice on 'Time off for union duties and activities' published by ACAS in April 2004.

(iii) Time off to consult the learning representative

Employees who are members of a recognised independent trade union are entitled to time off to have access to the services provided by their learning representative.

h) Inducements relating to union membership or activities and relating to collective bargaining

(i) Inducements relating to union membership or activities – the right

A worker has a right not to be offered an inducement by his employer to induce the worker:

- not to be or become a member of:
    - an independent trade union;
    - a particular trade union; or
    - one of a number of trade unions;
- at an appropriate time
    - not to take part in trade union activities;
    - not to make use of trade union services.

    An 'appropriate time' is either outside working hours or at a time during working hours which has been agreed with his employer.

    'Trade union services' are services provided for the worker because of his membership of an independent trade union.

(ii) Inducements relating to collective bargaining – the right

A worker who is a member of an independent trade union which is recognised or seeking recognition has a right not to have an offer made to him by his employer if:

- the offer is made to the worker and other members of the union;
- acceptance by him and other workers would result in the workers' terms and conditions no longer being negotiated collectively by the union; and
- the employer's main purpose in making the offer is to achieve this result.

(iii) Complaint to a tribunal

A worker may present a complaint to an employment tribunal within three months of the date of the offer or, where the offer was one of a series of offers made to workers, within three months of the last of those offers. (There is a usual facility for time to be extended where it is not reasonably practicable to present the claim within the three-month time limit.)

It is for the employer to show his reason for making the offer or offers in question. In looking at this question the tribunal must take into account any evidence of:

- attempts by the employer to change collective bargaining arrangements;
- the employer's wish not to use agreed collective bargaining arrangements or to enter into arrangements proposed by the union;

- offers that were made only to particular workers and were made primarily to reward them for high performance or to retain them because they were of special value to the employer.

No account is to be taken of any pressure put on the employer by third parties.

(iv) Remedy

If the tribunal finds in favour of the worker, then, subject to any deduction that falls to be made for any failure to follow the statutory disputes resolution procedures, the tribunal award is set at £2,500.

Although the only remedy for infringement of these rights is by way of complaint to an employment tribunal under the above provisions, the right to complain under these provisions does not prevent the worker from complaining that that he has suffered a detriment in relation to trade union matters in an appropriate case.

153.10 The procedure for handling redundancies

Until 1995 the right to have representatives consulted in relation to redundancies would have been seen as a right accorded to trade union members. TURERA and the Collective Redundancies and Transfer of Undertakings (Protection of Employment) (Amendment) Regulations 1995 (SI 1995 No 2587), which were brought in to give effect to requirements under Council Directive 92/56/EEC and to deal with the shortfall in the way in which the UK had dealt with its original obligations in respect of collective redundancies under Council Directive 75/129/EEC (the Collective Redundancies Directives), have had the effect of extending these provisions both in relation to when and how consultation must occur and in terms of requiring consultation where unions are not recognised.

a) The extended meaning of 'redundancy' for consultation purposes and presumption of redundancy

For the purposes of the consultation requirements, 'dismissal for redundancy' is widely defined as meaning dismissal for a reason or reasons not related to the individual concerned. It is presumed that any proposal to dismiss an employee is because of redundancy in this extended sense, unless the employer shows the dismissal to be for some other reason.

b) Consultation

(This section has been considerably amended by the Collective Redundancies and Transfer of Undertakings (Protection of Employment) (Amendment) Regulations 1999 (SI 1999 No 1925) – **see 10a above**).

(i) Circumstances in which consultation is required, and the timing

Where an employer is proposing to dismiss 20 or more employees at one establishment within a period of 90 days or less, he must consult with the appropriate representative of all employees affected by the proposed redundancies or who may be affected by measures taken in connection with those dismissals at least 30 days before the first dismissal takes effect. (This provision was amended by the Collective Redundancies and Transfer of Undertakings (Protection of Employment) (Amendment) Regulations 1999 (SI 1999 No 1925) – **see 10a above**.)

Where the employer is proposing to dismiss more than 100 employees at one establishment within a period of 90 days, then he must start consultations at least 90 days before the first dismissal takes effect.

In considering the numbers of employees being dismissed, no account is to be taken of employees in respect of whom consultation has already begun.

These provisions do not apply to those who are employed:

- under a contract for a fixed term of three months or less, or

- under a contract to perform a specific task which is not expected to last for more than three months, provided that the employee/s in question have not been continuously employed for more than three months.

  Where there are special circumstances that make it not reasonably practicable for the employer to start consultations with employee representatives on time, he must do what he can towards meeting these requirements. (It is no excuse if the employer's decision to make redundancies has been taken by someone who controls the employer (such as a holding company) and that person has not given the employer information that he needs to start consultations.)

(ii) Employee representatives

The provisions relating to election of employee representatives were fundamentally changed by the Collective Redundancies and Transfer of Undertakings (Protection of Employment) (Amendment) Regulations 1999 (SI 1999 No 1925) – **see 10a above**.

An employer must allow employee representatives:

- access to the employees who are affected by the redundancy; and

- accommodation and such other facilities as may be appropriate.

(iii) Starting consultation

To begin consultation, the employer must disclose the following matters in writing to the appropriate representatives:

- the reasons for his proposals;

- the numbers and descriptions of employees whom it is proposed to dismiss as redundant;

- the total number of employees of any such description employed by the employer at the establishment in question;

- the proposed method of selecting the employees who may be dismissed;

- the proposed method of carrying out the dismissals, with due regard to any agreed procedure, including the period over which the dismissals are to take effect; and

- the proposed method of calculating the amount of any redundancy payments in excess of the statutory which are to be made to those who are made redundant.

The above information must be given to appropriate representatives directly or sent by post.

The employer must also provide employee representatives with a copy of any notice that the employer is required to give to the Secretary of State regarding the redundancies (see d) below).

Where there are special circumstances that make it not reasonably practicable for the employer to give the employee representatives this information, or to give it to them on time, he must do what he can towards meeting these requirements. (It is no excuse if the employer's decision to make redundancies has been taken by someone who controls the employer (such as a holding company) and that person has not given the employer any of the information he needs for these purposes.)

(iv)   What consultation involves

Consultation must be undertaken by the employer with a view to reaching agreement with the appropriate representatives on matters including ways of:

■   avoiding the dismissals;

■   reducing the numbers of employees to be dismissed; and

■   mitigating the consequences of the dismissals.

Where there are special circumstances that make it not reasonably practicable to fulfil these requirements, the employer must do what he can towards meeting them. (It is no excuse if the employer's decision to make redundancies has been taken by someone who controls the employer (such as a holding company) and that person has failed to provide the employer with any information he may require.)

c)   Protective award

(i)   Protective award

A protective award is made in respect of:

■   employees who have been dismissed, or whom it is proposed to dismiss, as redundant; and

■   in respect of whom the consultation requirements have not been fully complied with.

The order requires the employer to pay the employees their remuneration during the protected period. (Employees who are employed during the protective period are entitled to remuneration only if they are entitled to it under their contracts or if they are entitled to it as payment for their statutory notice period under the ERA.)

The protected period begins with the earlier of:

■   the date on which the first of the dismissals takes effect; or

■   the date of the award.

The protected period continues for such time as the tribunal considers just and equitable having regard to the seriousness of the employer's default, but can be no longer than 90 days. (The erstwhile lower limit of 30 days for cases where between 30 and 100 employees were made redundant has been removed by the Collective Redundancies and Transfer of Undertakings (Protection of Employment) (Amendment) Regulations 1999 (SI 1999 No 1925).)

Where an employee is entitled to be paid under a protective award and the employer fails to pay, the employee can bring a claim to an employment tribunal within three months of that failure, or such longer time as is reasonably practicable where it is not reasonably practicable to meet the three-month limit.

(ii) Who may claim a protective award and when?

(This area has been significantly altered by the Collective Redundancies and Transfer of Undertakings (Protection of Employment) (Amendment) Regulations 1999 (SI 1999 No 1925).)

The appropriate claimant where an employer has not fulfilled the consultation requirements depends on the employer's particular failure, and will be:

- in the case of any failure relating to election of employee representatives, any of the affected employees or any of the employees who have been dismissed as redundant;

- in the case of any other failure relating to employee representatives, the employee representatives to whom the failure relates;

- in the case of any failure to fulfil any requirement relating to a trade union representative, the trade union;

- in any other case, an affected employee or one who has been or may be dismissed as redundant.

The burden of proof is put on the employer in two cases:

- If the question arises as to whether or not the employee representative was appropriate, the employer must prove that the employee representative had authority to represent the affected employees; and

- it is for the employer to prove that the requirements concerning the election of employee representatives have been complied with.

A claim must be brought either:

- before the last dismissal to which the claim relates; or

- within three months of the last dismissal (or if that is not reasonably practicable, within such further period as is reasonably practicable).

If the tribunal finds the claim to be well founded, it must make a declaration to that effect. It may also make a protective award.

(iii) Termination of employment during the protected period

If the employee is fairly dismissed (other than for redundancy) or unreasonably terminates his employment during the protective period, his right to be paid under the protective award ceases when his employment ends.

Where an employee is offered suitable alternative employment while still employed, he will lose his right to be paid under the protective award if he unreasonably refuses the offer. His entitlement to be paid under the protective award will cease from the time when the alternative employment would have started and he is, instead, dismissed or leaves.

An employee who takes alternative employment on a trial basis and unreasonably terminates his employment during the trial period will lose his right to be paid under the protective award from the time his employment ends.

d) Notifying the Secretary of State of redundancies

Where the employer is proposing to dismiss more than 100 employees at one establishment within a period of 90 days, he must notify the Secretary of State of his proposals at least 90 days before the first dismissal takes effect.

Where an employer is proposing to dismiss between 20 and 100 employees at one establishment within a period of 90 days then he must notify the Secretary of State of his proposals at least 30 days before the first dismissal takes effect.

In considering the numbers of employees being dismissed, no account is taken of employees in respect of whom a notice has already been given to the Secretary of State.

A notice under this requirement must be in a form specified by the Secretary of State, and after receiving it the Secretary of State can ask for such further information as he may require.

Where there are special circumstances that make it not reasonably practicable for the employer to notify the Secretary of State on time, he must do what he can towards meeting these requirements. (It is no excuse if the employer's decision to make redundancies has been taken by someone who controls the employer (such as a holding company) and that person has not given the employer information which he needs to notify the Secretary of State.)

It is an offence to fail to notify the Secretary of State, or to fail to notify him on time. The company and any manager, officer or secretary responsible can be convicted of the failure.

e) Collective agreements

Where there is a collective agreement in force which establishes

■ agreements for providing alternative employment for employees if they are dismissed as redundant, or

■ arrangements for handling the dismissal of employees as redundant,

if the terms of the agreement are at least as beneficial to employees as the statutory consultation provisions, the parties can apply to the Secretary of State to be exempted from the statutory consultation requirements.

153.11 Collective bargaining

a) Collective agreements

(i) Definitions

A 'collective agreement' is an agreement about any matter that can be the subject of collective bargaining (see below). To be a collective agreement, the agreement must be reached between trade union/s and employer/s or employers' associations.

'Collective bargaining' means negotiations relating to or connected with one or more of the following:

- terms and conditions of employment;

- physical conditions in which any workers are required to work;

- engagement/non-engagement, termination or suspension

  - of employment, or

  - of the duties of employment of one or more workers;

- allocation of work or the duties of employment between workers or groups of workers;

- matters of discipline;

- a worker's membership or non-membership of a trade union;

- facilities for officials of trade unions;

- machinery for negotiation or consultation;

- other procedures, relating to any of the above matters, including recognition by an employer of the right of a trade union to represent workers in such negotiations or consultation or in the carrying out of such procedures.

'Recognition' means recognition to any extent for collective bargaining purposes.

'Trade dispute' has two separate meanings – one for the purposes of collective bargaining and the duties of ACAS, which is considerably wider than the second, which is used for the purposes of deciding whether or not a trade union is immune from action in tort in respect of industrial action taken by its members. Both of these definitions are dealt with below, the first under Arbitration, mediation and conciliation, and the second under Industrial action.

(ii) Legal enforceability

A collective agreement is conclusively presumed not to be legally binding unless:

- it contains a provision, however expressed, saying that the parties intend it to be legally enforceable; and

- it is in writing.

A term in a collective agreement which prohibits or restricts the right of workers to take strike or other industrial action cannot form part of the worker's contract of employment unless the following conditions are met:

The collective agreement must:

- be in writing;

- expressly say that those terms can be incorporated into the worker's contract;

- be reasonably accessible at the worker's place of work for him to consult during working hours; and

- be one where each trade union that is a party to the agreement is an independent trade union; and

- the worker's contract must expressly or impliedly incorporate those terms of the collective agreement.

Where the above criteria are met, the 'no strike' provisions take effect, notwithstanding:

- the general proposition that collective agreements are unenforceable; and

- despite any provision to the contrary in any agreement (including a collective agreement or a contract with any worker).

 NB: Even if a 'no-strike' agreement is enforceable, an employee still cannot be forced by a court either to work or to attend at any place to do any work. The employer's only remedy against the employee will be in damages or to dismiss the employee.

b) Disclosure of information for collective bargaining

(i) General requirement

An employer who recognises an independent trade union must disclose information to that union's representatives, if they ask for it. The trade union representatives can request information for the purposes of collective bargaining about matters for which the union is recognised by the employer. Subject to this, the types of information that may be requested are:

- information without which the trade union representatives would be materially hampered in their collective bargaining with the employer, and

- information which it would be good industrial relations practice for the employer to disclose to them for collective bargaining purposes.

When considering what it is 'good industrial relations practice to disclose', the provisions of the ACAS Code of Practice on Disclosure of Information must be taken into account, but not to the exclusion of any other evidence of what is good practice.

 The employer can ask for the union's request for disclosure to be in writing, or to be confirmed in writing, and the union can ask for the information to be in writing, or to be confirmed in writing.

(ii) Limitations on duty of disclosure

An employer is not required to disclose information for collective bargaining purposes:

- where disclosure would be against the interests of national security;

- which he could not disclose without contravening a statutory prohibition;

- which has been communicated to him in confidence, or obtained as a result of a confidence being entrusted to him by another person;

- which relates specifically to an individual (unless that individual has consented to its being disclosed);

- where disclosure would cause substantial injury to the employer's undertaking for reasons other than its effect on collective bargaining;

- where the information was obtained by the employer for the purpose of bringing, prosecuting or defending any legal proceedings.

Nor is an employer required:

- to produce, make copies, or allow inspection of any document (other than a document prepared for the purpose of conveying or confirming the information);

- to compile or assemble any information where the cost or work involved in compiling or assembling that information would be out of reasonable proportion to the value of the information in collective bargaining terms.

(iii) Complaints of failure to disclose

A trade union can complain to the Central Arbitration Committee (CAC) that:

- an employer has failed to disclose collective bargaining information; or

- has failed to confirm that information in writing.

The CAC refers such cases to ACAS for conciliation where possible, or, if conciliation is not possible or has failed, the CAC hears the case. Where the CAC determines the case in favour of the union, it must make a declaration and give the employer a date not less than a week later by which the employer must disclose the information or in which to confirm the disclosed information in writing.

If the employer fails to comply with the CAC's decision, the union can put in a further claim and can ask the CAC to make an award modifying the terms and conditions of relevant employees. The CAC can, on hearing the matter, award the terms and conditions claimed, or such other terms and conditions as it considers appropriate.

c) Codes of practice

ACAS can issue Codes of Practice containing practical guidance aimed at improving industrial relations.

The Secretary of State may issue Codes of Practice containing practical guidance aimed at:

- improving industrial relations, or

- promoting good practice in relation to the way in which trade unions conduct ballots and elections.

Any failure to follow any of these Codes of Practice does not give rise to any liability in itself, but may be taken into account by a tribunal, a court or the CAC as evidence in any case.

d) Arbitration, mediation and conciliation

(i) ACAS

Under an amendment made by TURERA, ACAS can offer advice to workers, employers and trade unions, or may publish advice on industrial relations issues. ACAS, under the TURERA amendments, is now also able to charge for its advice. ACAS's erstwhile 'general duty' to promote the improvement of industrial relations, particularly by helping to settle trade disputes, was removed by Employment Relations Act 1999.

Where there is a trade dispute, ACAS can at the request of either party offer conciliation or mediation by an independent third party.

Where there is a trade dispute, ACAS can at the request of one of the parties and with the consent of all of the parties, refer the matter to arbitration by arbitrators appointed by ACAS or by the CAC. Arbitration should not normally be used unless it is felt that conciliation will not work.

ACAS can also involve itself in inquiries into industrial relations generally, or in relation to any particular industry where it sees fit to do so.

(ii)   Courts of inquiry

Where a trade dispute exists or is expected, a Court of Inquiry can be set up by the Secretary of State to look into it.

(iii) Trade dispute

A 'trade dispute' is defined more widely for purposes of the duties of ACAS in relation to trade disputes than it is for the part of the Act that deals with industrial action (**see 153.12b below**). For the purposes of the duties of ACAS the definition of 'trade dispute' includes:

- a dispute between different sets of workers;

- a dispute between workers and any employer;

- disputes arising solely outside the UK which have no impact on those taking action in the UK;

- disputes involving unions and employers' associations;

but does not include the mere threat of industrial action which is given in to by the party who or which was threatened.

153.12 Collective bargaining recognition

These provisions were brought into being by the Employment Relations Act 1999 with effect from 6 June 2000 (see Employment Relations Act 1999 (Commencement no 6) Order 2000 (SI 2000 No 1338)). A new schedule A1 was inserted into the 1992 Act. This schedule was amended by the Employment Relations Act 2004.

a) Request for recognition

(i)   General

Where a trade union wishes to be recognised to conduct collective bargaining on behalf of a group of workers it must first make a request for recognition to the employer of the workers it is seeking to represent.

Under these provisions 'collective bargaining' generally means negotiations about pay, hours and holidays (the 'core topics'), but if the trade union and the employer agree the matters about which the union is to be entitled to negotiate, then that agreement takes precedence.

(ii) The recognition request – validity

For a recognition request to be validly made, the request must:

- be made by an independent trade union and must be in writing;

- identify the union or unions and the bargaining unit; and

- say that it is made under schedule A1 TULRA.

The request must be received by the employer, who, taken together with any associated employer:

- must employ at least 21 employees on the date of the request; or

- must have employed an average of 21 employees over the 13 weeks preceding the recognition request.

    In calculating whether or not the employer has employed an average of 21 or more employees over the preceding 13 weeks:

    - the number of employees, including part-timers, who were employed in each of the last 13 weeks is added together; and

    - the total is divided by 13.

The request must comply with any requirements laid down by the Secretary of State as the appropriate form in which to make any such requests.

A request for recognition may only be made by a union which is already recognised for collective bargaining if the matters in respect of which the union is entitled to conduct collective bargaining do not include all the core topics (see a)(i) above).

b) Response to the recognition request

(i)   Definitions

The 'first period' is a period of 10 working days starting the day after the recognition request is received by the employer.

The 'second period' is a period of 20 working days (or such longer period as the parties may from time to time agree) starting the day after the end of the first period. (The reference to the parties 'from time to time' agreeing presumably means that they can extend the period as they go along.)

(ii) The first period

If the employer agrees the bargaining unit and agrees to recognise the union/s as entitled to conduct collective bargaining for that unit, nothing further happens under part 1 of schedule A1.

If, before the end of the first period, the employer fails to respond to the union/s' request or says that he is not prepared to accept that request (without suggesting that he is prepared to negotiate), the union/s may apply to the CAC to determine:

- the appropriate bargaining unit (which may either be the one proposed or a different one);

- whether the proposed bargaining unit is appropriate; and

- whether the union/s has/have the support of the majority of the workers constituting the appropriate bargaining unit.

    The parties may ask ACAS to assist them in conducting their negotiations

(iii) The second period

If, during the first period, the employer informs the union that he is not prepared to accept the recognition request, but is prepared to negotiate with them, the parties may negotiate the appropriate bargaining unit and the appropriate union/s with which to conduct negotiations.

    The parties may ask ACAS to assist them in conducting their negotiations.

If a bargaining unit and the appropriate union are agreed before the end of the second period, then again, no further action falls to be taken under part 1 of schedule A1.

If the negotiations fail, the union/s may apply to the CAC to determine:

- whether the proposed beginning unit is appropriate;

- the appropriate bargaining unit (which may either be the one proposed or a different one); and

- whether the union/s has/have the support of the majority of the workers constituting the appropriate bargaining unit.

If the employer and the union have already agreed the appropriate bargaining unit, the CAC will only be asked to decide whether the union/s has/have the support of the majority of the workers in that bargaining unit.

If the employer at some time during the first period proposes to the union/s that ACAS assist them in their negotiations and the union/s either reject that proposal or fail to accept that proposal within 10 days of its being made, it/they cannot apply to the CAC under this provision until 10 days after the proposal to involve ACAS was made.

(iv) Acceptance or non-acceptance of the application by the CAC

Where two or more applications are made to the CAC, if:

- one or more workers fall into more than one of the proposed or agreed bargaining groups; and

- no application has been accepted by the CAC; then

    the CAC must decide if the 10 per cent rule is satisfied within the 10 days immediately following the date of the application (or such longer period as the CAC may specify).

The 10 per cent rule is that at least 10 per cent of the workers in the proposed or agreed bargaining unit must be members of the union/s in question.

- If the 10 per cent rule is satisfied with regard to more than one or to none of the applications, the CAC must not accept any of the applications.

- If the 10 per cent rule is satisfied with regard to only one application, the CAC must proceed with that application and reject all other applications.

- If the CAC rejects an application under this provision, no further steps are to be taken on that application under this part of the schedule.

Where an application is made to the CAC which the CAC is not excluded from proceeding with under the above provisions, the CAC must decide:

- whether all the stages prior to an application being made to the CAC have been properly fulfilled;

- whether the application has been properly made; and

- whether the application is admissible.

To be admissible all the following requirements must be fulfilled:

- the application must be made in the form approved by the CAC;

- it must be accompanied by any documents required by the CAC; and

- notice of the application, together with a copy of it and the accompanying documents must be given to the employer.

An application is only admissible if the CAC decides that:

- at least 10 per cent of the proposed or agreed bargaining unit are members of the applicant union/s; and

- a majority of the workers in the proposed or agreed bargaining unit would be likely to favour union recognition.

    The CAC must give its reasons for making its decision under this heading.

When an application is made jointly by more than one union, the application will only be admissible if the unions can show that:

- they will co-operate in a manner that will secure stable and effective collective bargaining arrangements; and

- they will enter into joint arrangements to conduct collective bargaining on behalf of the employees in the proposed or agreed bargaining unit if the employer so wishes.

An application cannot be made if there is a recognised trade union for any of the workers within the proposed or agreed bargaining group *except in two situations*:

either:

- the union making the application is the one that is already recognised for collective bargaining; and

- the matters about which they are entitled to bargain under the collective agreement do not include pay hours, or holidays (ie: the 'core topics');

or:

- the union that is recognised is not an independent one;

- it had previously been recognised to conduct collective bargaining on behalf of substantially the same group of employees and the previous agreement ceased to have effect within the three years prior to the current agreement taking effect.

   (It is for the CAC to decide whether the group of employees in respect of which the union was recognised under the previous agreement is substantially the same as the group for which it is currently recognised.)

If the CAC decides that the application is admissible and has been validly made:

- it must accept the application; and
- it must give notice to the parties that it has accepted the application.

If the CAC decides that the application is inadmissible or has been invalidly made:

- it must not accept the application; and
- it must give notice to the parties of its decision.

   (In such cases no further steps are taken under this part of the schedule.)

The acceptance period is 10 days starting with the day after the application was received by the CAC or such longer period as the CAC may specify.

(v)   Acceptance of the application by the CAC

If the CAC accepts an application, it must try to help the parties to reach agreement on the appropriate bargaining unit within 20 days after it accepts the application. (If it appears to the CAC or to the parties that there is no hope of the parties' reaching agreement within that period, the CAC can, on its own initiative or on the application of the parties, cut the 20-day period short.)

Within five days of acceptance of the application the employer must provide the union/s and the CAC with:

- a list of the categories of workers in the proposed bargaining unit;
- a list of the workplaces in which those workers work; and
- the number of workers in each category at each workplace.

If the employer is in breach of this requirement, and an application is made by the union, the CAC must decide, within the 20-day period, what the appropriate bargaining unit is. The matters to be taken into account by the CAC in determining what the appropriate bargaining unit is are the same as those set out below.

If the parties are unable to reach a decision as to the appropriate bargaining unit within the initial period, the CAC must decide in the ensuing 10 days what the appropriate bargaining unit should be, taking into account primarily the need for the unit to be compatible with effective management. Subject to this overriding requirement they must also take into account such of the following as are compatible with this overriding requirement:

- the views of the employer and the union/s;

- existing national and local bargaining arrangements;

- the desirability of avoiding small fragmented bargaining units in an organisation;

- the characteristics of the workers covered by the bargaining unit and any other employees which the CAC considers relevant; and

- the location of the workers.

The CAC must give notice of its decision to the parties.

(vi)   The decision on recognition

Where the bargaining group agreed on or decided upon by the CAC as being the appropriate bargaining unit is different from the proposed bargaining group:

- if the CAC decides that the application is invalid, it must give notice to the parties of this and proceed no further with the application;

- if the CAC decides the application is not invalid, it must proceed with it.

If the appropriate bargaining unit is the same as the proposed bargaining unit, the CAC must proceed with the application.

If the CAC proceeds with the application and the majority of workers who make up the bargaining unit are members of the union, the CAC must declare that the union is recognised to conduct collective bargaining on behalf of the bargaining unit unless any of the 'qualifying conditions' apply: The 'qualifying conditions' are:

- The CAC is satisfied that a ballot should be held in the interests of good industrial relations.

- A significant number of union members within the bargaining unit inform the CAC that they do not want the union to conduct collective bargaining on their behalf.

- The CAC has credible evidence from a significant number of union members within the bargaining unit that they do not want the union to conduct collective bargaining on their behalf.

- Membership evidence is produced to the CAC to conclude that there are doubts whether a significant number of the union members within the bargaining unit want the union to conduct collective bargaining on their behalf.

   'Membership evidence' is relevant evidence of:

   - the circumstances in which workers became members of the union; and

   - the time for which those workers have been members of the union.

Where any of the qualifying conditions apply, a workplace ballot must be held to determine whether or not the union is to be recognised for collective bargaining purposes.

The union will be recognised for collective bargaining purposes if it is supported in the ballot by:

- a majority of the workers who vote; and

- at least 40 per cent of the workers constituting the bargaining group.

(vii) The appointment of an independent person

Under the 2004 amendments the CAC may appoint someone (an independent person) to handle communications between the union and the workers until the ballot is set up or the application is withdrawn or declared to be invalid.

Where an independent person is appointed, the employer is obliged to provide information regarding the workers which form part of the bargaining unit or the proposed bargaining unit.

The costs of the independent person are to be borne by the union which asked for the appointment to be made.

(viii) The consequences of recognition

Where the CAC issues a declaration that a union is entitled to conduct collective bargaining on behalf of a bargaining unit, the parties are given a 30-day negotiation period during which to agree the method by which they will conduct collective bargaining. The CAC is under a duty to try to help the parties to reach this agreement.

> If the parties are unable to agree, the CAC will specify the method of collective bargaining. If this happens, then, unless the parties agree otherwise, the CAC's method takes effect as a binding contract between the parties. This 'binding contract' can, however, be excluded or changed by a written agreement between the parties. If the binding contract collective bargaining method is put in place, the statute provides that the *only* remedy for breach is to be specific performance – ie the courts will enforce the requirement for the parties to go through the collective bargaining processes.

(ix) Termination of the agreement

An agreement for recognition cannot be terminated by the employer for three years. After this period has expired the employer can terminate the agreement with or without the consent of the union/s.

The union/s can terminate the agreement at any time without the employer's consent.

(x) Further applications

Where an application has been refused by the CAC, no further application can be made for three years.

c) Changes affecting collective bargaining

(i) Where either party considers that the bargaining unit is no longer appropriate

Where either party considers that the bargaining unit is no longer appropriate, the party in question may apply to the CAC to make a decision as to what is an appropriate bargaining unit.

For an application to be admissible there must have been:

- a change in the organisation or structure of the employer's business;

- a change in the employer's business activities; or

- a substantial change in the number of workers employed in the original bargaining unit.

(ii)   Where the employer believes that the bargaining unit has ceased to exist

If the employer believes that the original bargaining unit has ceased to exist and wants the bargaining arrangements to cease, he must give a notice to the union and the CAC.

The notice must identify the unit and the bargaining arrangements and declare that the unit has ceased to exist. It must also give 35 working days' notice that bargaining arrangements are to cease to have effect.

Where such notice is given, the bargaining arrangements will cease if the union does not raise a question with the CAC as to whether the original bargaining unit continues or as to whether for any of the reasons in (i) above a different bargaining unit is appropriate.

d)   Derecognition

The employer may give notice to the union and the CAC for bargaining arrangements to cease where, after the third anniversary of the bargaining arrangements being put in place:

- the number of workers employed by the employer (taken together with those of any associated employers) is fewer than 21;

- the employer requests the union to agree to end bargaining arrangements; or

- one or more workers apply to the CAC to have the bargaining arrangements ended.

Where the employer or workers request that the bargaining arrangements be ended, and the union objects, a derecognition ballot must be held. If the ballot results in a majority of those voting voting in favour of discontinuing the bargaining arrangements in a ballot in which at least 40 per cent of the workers constituting the bargaining unit voted, the CAC must issue a declaration terminating the bargaining arrangements.

e)   Protection from unfair dismissal and detriment in connection with recognition

An employee's dismissal for anything to do with either supporting or not supporting or taking part in collective bargaining recognition is made automatically unfair.

Employees are also protected against being subjected to a detriment for any such involvement.

Workers are also given protection against unfair practices by either the union or the employer in relation to the conduct of ballots.

f)   Time off for training

Where a trade union is recognised under these provisions and the method for collective bargaining is specified by the CAC rather than being agreed between the employer and the unions, the employer must invite union representatives to a meeting to:

- consult about the employer's policy on training for workers within the bargaining unit;

- consult about his plans for training those workers in the six months immediately following the meeting; and

- report on the training provided for those workers since the previous meeting.

The first of these meetings must be held within six months of the union's being granted rights to conduct collective bargaining, and must then be held at intervals of no more than six months thereafter.

At least two weeks prior to each meeting the employer must provide the union with any information:

- without which the union representatives would be materially impeded in participating in the meeting; and

- disclosure of which would be good industrial relations practice. (The restriction on the general duty of disclosure of information for collective bargaining purposes applies equally to disclosure under these provisions.)

The employer must take into account any written representations about matters raised at the meeting which he receives from the union within four weeks of the meeting.

> If the employer fails to comply with these requirements a claim can be brought by the union to an employment tribunal. If the tribunal finds the complaint well founded it can award up to two weeks' pay to each employee who is a member of the bargaining unit.

153.13 Industrial action

a) Liability of trade unions in tort

(i) General

A trade union can be liable in tort only if the action in question is one that is taken to have been authorised or endorsed by the trade union.

An act is taken to have been authorised or endorsed by a trade union if it was done, authorised or endorsed:

- by a person who is empowered by the union's rules to do, authorise or endorse acts of that kind, or

- by the principal executive committee, the president or general secretary, or

- by any other committee of the union, or

- by any other official of the union who is part of a group whose duties or functions involve organising or co-ordinating industrial action.

> In relation to the last two groups above, an act is not to be taken as having been authorised or endorsed by virtue of these provisions if it is repudiated by the president, general secretary or executive committee of the union as soon as is reasonably practicable after it comes to the knowledge of any of them.

(ii) Repudiating an action

To repudiate an act:

- written notice must be given to the offending committee or official without delay; and

- the union must give a written notice to all those whom they believe are taking part, or might otherwise take part in industrial action because of the act being repudiated. The notice must contain:

  - the fact of repudiation

  - the date of the repudiation; and

  - the following statement:

    Your union has repudiated the call (or calls) for industrial action to which this notice relates and will give no support to unofficial industrial action taken in response to it (or them). If you are dismissed while taking unofficial industrial action, you will have no right to complain of unfair dismissal.

  Employers of those to whom the above notice is required to be given must also be given written notice of the fact and the date of the repudiation.

An act is not, however, to be treated as having been repudiated if, at any time after the purported repudiation, the president, general secretary or executive committee do anything inconsistent with that repudiation. A person who has a commercial contract (including a contract of employment) which was, or was liable to be, interfered with by the repudiated act is given certain rights. Such a person, if he has not already had notice that the act in question has been repudiated, can, within three months of the date of the repudiation, ask the union to confirm the repudiation in writing. If the union fails to provide written confirmation of the repudiation 'forthwith', this is to be treated as doing something inconsistent with the repudiation and thus will undermine the effect of the repudiation.

(iii) Limit of trade union liability in tort

Other than in relation to claims for:

- personal injury arising out of negligence, nuisance or breach of duty,

- breach of duty in connection with the ownership, occupation, possession, control or use of property, and

- product liability claims,

the amount of damages awarded against a trade union in any action is limited by the size of the membership of the union.

The limits are:

Number of members in union	Maximum damages
Fewer than 5,000	£10,000
5,000–25,000	£50,000

| 25,000–100,000 | £125,000 |
| 100,000 or more | £250,000 |

Amounts awarded by way of damages cost and expenses against

- a trade union, or

- trustees of union property, all the members of a trade union or the officials of a trade union when acting as such

cannot be recovered from 'protected property'.

Protected property is:

- property belonging to the trustees other than in their capacity as such;

- property belonging to any member of the union otherwise than jointly or in common with the other members;

- property belonging to an official of the union who is neither a member nor a trustee;

- property comprised in the union's political fund provided that at the time of the action complained of, the fund was not allowed to be used for financing strikes or other industrial action;

- property comprised in a separate provident fund, including funds to provide benefits:

    - for members during sickness, incapacity from personal injury or accident;

    - for members while out of work;

    - by way of superannuation for aged members;

    - for members who have lost their tools by fire or theft;

    - for help with funeral expenses on the death of a member or the wife of a member;

    - for making provision for the children of a deceased member.

b) Action taken in contemplation or furtherance of a trade dispute

(i)   The meaning of a trade dispute

The definition of a 'trade dispute' for the purposes of immunity from liability in tort in relation to industrial action is defined more strictly than it is defined in relation to the duties of ACAS (**see 153.11d(i) above**). In relation to industrial action and a union's immunity from action in tort, 'trade dispute' means a dispute between workers and their employer which relates wholly or mainly to one or more of the items that can be the subject of collective bargaining between a union and an employer (see Collective bargaining, **153.11a(i) above**).

A dispute between a Minister of the Crown and any workers is to be treated as a trade dispute if it relates to matters that:

- have been referred for consideration by a joint body on which the Minister is represented, or

- cannot be settled without his exercising a statutory power.

A trade dispute can relate to matters occurring outside the United Kingdom, so long as the people taking action in the United Kingdom are likely to be affected by the outcome of the dispute in respect of one or more of the matters on which a union can collectively bargain with the employer.

(ii) Protection of action taken in contemplation or furtherance of a trade dispute

One of the most important provisions of the Act is that, subject to certain limits, it provides that an act done by a person in contemplation of a trade dispute is not actionable in tort only on the grounds that it:

- induces another person to break his contract; or

- induces another person to interfere with the performance of a contract; or

- threatens to do either of the above.

This provision is important because it allows for industrial action to be called by a union and taken by employees without exposing them to the possibility of being sued for the torts of inducement to breach of contract, or interference with the performance of a contract.

> An *ex parte* injunction/interdict ('ex parte' means that the person against whom the claim is brought is not present or represented at the hearing) must not generally be granted where a person has claimed or is likely to claim that the action that it is sought to restrain is being taken in contemplation or furtherance of a trade dispute. The only exception is where the judge is satisfied that all reasonable steps have been taken to try to ensure that the defendant has had an opportunity of being heard before the application is decided.

> Where a court is asked to grant an interlocutory injunction in a case where a person claims, or is likely to claim, that the action was being taken in contemplation or furtherance of a trade dispute, the court must consider the likelihood of that claim's succeeding at the full trial before granting an injunction to restrain picketing or inducement to breach or interference with a contract. This does not extend to Scotland.

(iii) Peaceful picketing

It is lawful for a person in contemplation or furtherance of a trade dispute:

- to attend (a picket) at or near his own place of work;

- where a person works at more than one place or if picketing at his place of work is impracticable, to attend at any of his employer's premises from which he works or from which his work is administered;

- if a worker has been dismissed in connection with a trade dispute or if the termination of his employment gave rise to a trade dispute, to attend at his former place of work; or

- if he is a trade union official, to attend at or near the place of work of a member of the union whom:

    - he is accompanying, and

- whom he represents,
    - for the purpose of peacefully:
    - obtaining or communicating information, or
    - persuading any person to work or abstain from working.

The ACAS Code of Practice on picketing suggests that there should be a maximum of six pickets outside any place of work – although this requirement is advisory only.

If picketing goes beyond what is allowed, the immunity from tortious liability is lost, and pickets (and if the action is official, the unions) can be sued.

(iv)   Actions specifically excluded from protection

Action to enforce trade union membership

Any action that is taken

- to enforce a trade union membership requirement for any employees or for people used on contracts, or
- because an employer has used non-union people,

cannot be protected even if taken in contemplation or furtherance of a trade dispute.

Action taken because of dismissal for taking unofficial action

An action loses its immunity if it relates, in whole or in part, to people being dismissed for taking unofficial industrial action.

Secondary action

Secondary action occurs where a person

- induces another to break a contract of employment;
- interferes with the performance of a contract of employment;
- induces another to interfere with its performance;
- threatens that a contract of employment under which he or another is employed will be broken or its performance be interfered with; or
- threatens that he will induce another to break a contract of employment or to interfere with its performance;

where the employer under the contract of employment is not party to the dispute. Where there are a number of employers in dispute with their workers, each dispute between an employer and his workers is treated as a separate dispute.

> Where action is primary action in one dispute (ie where the action is taken by workers against their own employer), it cannot be outlawed as unlawful secondary action in relation to another dispute.

Secondary action (other than that which occurs in the course of lawful picketing) is not immune from action in tort.

Action to impose union recognition

Action is not immune from suit in tort if it:

- is taken to make those supplying goods or services use only union labour;

- is taken to try to stop someone obtaining a contract for goods or services because they use or will use non-union labour;

- interferes with the supply or goods or services and is taken by employees not employed by the supplier who believe that the supplier does not or might not recognise a union or consult or negotiate with a union.

(v)   No order to compel work

It should be noted that even if unlawful action is taken by an employee, no order for specific performance or injunction can be made by any court that would compel a person to work or to go anywhere to do work.

c)   Ballot requirements before industrial action

These provisions were extended considerably and amended by TURERA.

(i)   General

- A trade union is not protected against liability for tort in relation to any industrial action unless that action has the support of a ballot; and

- a trade union is not protected in relation to any particular employer, in respect of industrial action, unless all proper notices and sample voting papers have been given to that employer.

In the case of a workplace ballot, however, the action will be protected for that workplace if it has the support of a ballot and the proper notices and sample voting papers have been given to that employer which are valid for employees who work in the place of work in which the ballot is held.

For an act to have the support of a ballot, all the requirements for a valid ballot and proper scrutiny of the ballot must be complied with.

(ii)   Scrutiny of the ballot

A scrutineer must be appointed to oversee an industrial action ballot unless

- there are 50 or fewer employees who are being balloted; or

- there are separate workplace ballots, the average number voting in each workplace ballot is 50 or fewer.

In all other cases the trade union must:

- appoint a scrutineer who is competent and of a type or from a list approved by the Secretary of State and who the union has no reason to believe will be biased;

- ensure that the scrutineer carries out his duties in relation to the ballot fully, and that he is not subjected to any interference from any official, employee or member of the union in carrying out those functions;

- comply with all reasonable requests made by the scrutineer in carrying out his functions;

- where, within six months of the ballot, a person who was entitled to vote in the ballot or an employer of any such person requests a copy of the scrutineer's report, provide one as soon as is practicable. (The union can make a reasonable charge for this.)

The scrutineer's terms of appointment must require him:

- to take such steps as appear to him to be appropriate for the purpose of enabling him to make a scrutineer's report to the union; and

- to make the report as soon as is reasonably practicable after the date of the ballot, and in any event within four weeks of the ballot.

The scrutineer must make a report to the union, following the ballot, which states:

- that there are no grounds for believing that there has been any breach of statute in relation to the ballot;

- that the arrangements for producing, storing and handling the voting papers used in the ballot, and the arrangements for the counting of the votes, were sufficiently secure to minimise any risk of unfairness or malpractice; and

- that he has been able to carry out his functions without any interference from the union or any of its members, officials or employees.

  If he is not satisfied as to any of the above, the report must say with what he is dissatisfied.

(iii) Notice of ballot

The union must ensure that the employers of those entitled to vote in the ballot receive:

- not later than the seventh day before a voting paper is sent to anyone entitled to vote in the ballot (ie the 'opening day of the ballot'), a notice:

    - stating that the union intends to hold the ballot;

    - stating the opening day of the ballot; and

    - describing (so the employer can readily identify them) the employees whom the union reasonably believes will be entitled to vote in the ballot;

- not later than the third day before the 'opening day of the ballot' a sample voting paper which must be:

    - a sample of the form of voting paper that is to be sent to the employees who are entitled to vote in the ballot, or

    - where different employees are to be given different voting papers, a sample of each.

(iv) Entitlement to vote in a ballot

Entitlement to vote in the ballot must be given to all the union's members whom the union believes will be induced to take part or continue to take part in the industrial action in question, and no one else.

> The above requirement is to be taken not to have been satisfied if a person who was a union member at the date of the ballot and who was not given a vote is called upon to take industrial action.

Where members of a union have different places of work, separate workplace ballots must normally be held to ballot the members of the union working in each separate place of work, but

- separate workplace ballots are not used where those who are given the right to vote in the ballot have some factor in common with other union members who are given the right to vote (although the factor they have in common need not be the same factor in each case – so, for example, all the staff employees or blue-collar employees over a number of sites could be balloted together).

- The factor referred to above must be one that relates to the terms and conditions of those members' employment; or to the occupational description applicable to those members in their employment.

- The factor must not be one that other employees who are not given a right to vote also have; or which individuals employed by that employer have in common because of their place of work.

Where a trade union has overseas members, it can decide whether or not to ballot them. If it does, the scrutiny requirements and many of the other ballot requirements do not apply.

(v) The ballot

Voting must be by the voter marking a voting paper.

Each voting paper must:

- state the name of the independent scrutineer (where one is required);

- specify *the date* by which and *the address* to which the voting paper is to be returned;

- specify who is authorised to call upon members to take the industrial action if the vote is in favour of industrial action;

- be marked with a unique number that is part of a consecutive series of numbers used for the ballot;

- contain at least one of the following:

  - a question which requires the voter, by answering 'Yes' or 'No', to say whether he is prepared to take part or in a strike;

  - a question which requires the voter, by answering 'Yes' or 'No', to say whether he is prepared to take part or in industrial action short of a strike;

- contain the following statement (without qualification or comment):

    If you take part in a strike or other industrial action, you may be in breach of your contract of employment.

Each person entitled to vote must

- have a voting paper sent to him at his home or other mailing address;
- be given an opportunity to vote by post;
- be allowed to vote without interference from the union or any of its members, officials or employees; and
- so far as is practicable be able to vote without incurring any cost to himself.

A ballot must be conducted so that

- so far as is practicable the voter can vote in secret; and
- the votes in the ballot are fairly and accurately counted.

As soon as is reasonably practicable, the union must ensure that those who were entitled to vote and their employers are informed of the numbers of:

- votes cast;
- individuals answering 'Yes' to the question or to each question;
- individuals answering 'No' to the question or to each question;
- spoiled voting papers.

(vi) Calling industrial action

For industrial action to have the support of a ballot:

- it must be called by the person specified on the voting paper as having authority to call it;
- there must not have been any call to take the action before the date of the ballot; and
- the industrial action must take place within four weeks beginning with the date of the ballot. Where a court prohibits or suspends the taking of industrial action for any time, the union can apply to the court to extend the period so it has a full, unconstrained, four weeks in which to take industrial action.

For industrial action to be protected, the union must also ensure that the employer of anyone who will be called upon to take industrial action receives a notice of the action. This notice must not be given before the results of the ballot have been sent to voting members, and must be received by the employer in question at least seven days before the industrial action referred to in the notice begins.

The notice must:

- identify the employees who are going to be called to take industrial action;

- state whether the action is intended to be continuous or discontinuous (ie whether once it starts it will take place on all the employees' working days or not); and

  - if continuous, state the intended date when any employees will start to take part;

  - if discontinuous, state the dates when any employees will partake in the action;

- state that the notice is given for purposes of s 234A TULRA.

d) Action by an individual where goods or services are disrupted

This provision was a major amendment to the law brought into effect by TURERA

(i) The right

Where, because of unlawful industrial action, whether actual or threatened, the supply of goods or services to an individual will or could be delayed or prevented, or an individual would not be able to get the same standard of goods or services, that individual may apply to a court. This applies whether or not the individual has a right to be supplied with those goods or services. Unlawful industrial action for these purposes is action that is actionable in tort by one or more persons, or that would entitle an individual trade union member to take action against the trade union in question (see Rights of trade union members against the union, **153.8 above**). Where a court finds an action well founded it can grant an injunction/interdict to restrain further action being taken.

e) Dismissal of an employee while taking part in industrial action

These provisions were amended slightly by TURERA and were amended again by the Employment Relations Act 1999.

(i) Dismissal of those taking part in unofficial industrial action

An employee has no right to claim unfair dismissal if at the time of dismissal he was taking part in unofficial industrial action.

By various statutory amendments this exclusion does not apply if the reason, or primary reason, for dismissal or for selection for redundancy was:

- to do with maternity or family leave;

- to do with being a health and safety representative or safety committee member or with taking action in a health and safety case; or

- to do with being an employee representative;

- to do with a protected disclosure or with flexible working hours.

A strike will not be unofficial for these purposes if:

- the person concerned is a trade union member and the action has been endorsed by his union;

- the person concerned is not a trade union member, but some of the people taking action are trade union members and the action has been endorsed by their union; or

- none of the people taking part in the strike is a trade union member.

Note that for these purposes:

- if an employee is a member of a trade union that is not connected to his employment, this is to be disregarded; conversely if he was a member of a union when the action began, but thereafter ceased to be one, he is then deemed to have continued to be a union member;

- where an employee is dismissed with notice, the date of dismissal is the date when notice of dismissal is given;

- where the union repudiates any industrial action, that repudiation does not take effect to make the strike unofficial until the end of the next working day after the repudiation.

(ii)   Dismissal of those taking part in official industrial action

An employment tribunal cannot determine the fairness or unfairness of an employee's dismissal if, at the date of dismissal:

- the employer was conducting or instituting a lock-out; or

- the complainant was taking part in strike or other industrial action;

unless one or more of the employees who were also involved in the industrial action or strike or were directly interested in the dispute giving rise to the lock-out ('relevant employees'):

- have not been dismissed; or

- have been offered re-engagement within three months of their dismissal, when the complainant has not.

By an amendment brought in by TURERA this restriction does not apply if the reason, or primary reason for dismissal or for selection for redundancy was:

- to do with maternity;

- to do with being a health and safety representative or safety committee member or taking action in a health and safety case; or

- to do with being an employee representative.

A complaint under this heading must be brought within six months from the date of the complainant's dismissal, or if that is not reasonably practicable, within such further time as is reasonably practicable.

> Where the complaint is of discriminatory re-engagement, the principal reason for dismissal for the purposes of the ERA unfair dismissal/unfair selection for redundancy provisions and for the purposes of dismissal/selection for redundancy for trade union reasons under TULRA is the reason for which the complainant was not offered re-engagement.

By a further amendment brought in by Employment Relations Act 1999, and extended by the Employment Relations Act 2004, an employment tribunal is not precluded from considering whether an employee's dismissal was fair (even if all the relevant employees have been dismissed or have not been offered re-engagement) if:

- the employee is dismissed because he took part in protected industrial action (ie official industrial action supported by a ballot); and

- one or more of the following conditions applies to the dismissal:

  - The employee is dismissed within the protected period (the 'protected period' is a period of 12 weeks from the day on which protected industrial action began to which is added any period during which the employee is locked out by his employer).

  - The employee is dismissed after the protected period where the employee had stopped taking industrial action before the end of the protected period.

  - The employee is dismissed after the protected period

    - where the employee had not stopped taking industrial action during the protected period; and

    - where the employer had not taken reasonable procedural steps for the purposes of resolving the dispute which gave rise to the protected industrial action.

In deciding whether an employer has taken reasonable procedural steps to try and resolve the dispute, the tribunal should take into account:

- whether the employer or the union followed agreed procedures;

- whether either party offered or agreed to negotiate after the start of the protected action;

- whether, after the protected industrial action began, either party unreasonably refused the services of ACAS either to conciliate or to mediate.

Where there was an agreement to use either conciliation or mediation, the tribunal must also take into account:

- whether at any meetings which had been arranged, the employer and the union were represented by an 'appropriate person' – ie either a person with the authority to settle the matter or someone who was authorised by such a person to make recommendations regarding settlement;

- whether the employer and the union co-operated in arrangements for meetings;

- whether the employer and the union fulfilled any commitments either had given in relation to the mediation or conciliation process – including compliance with any agreed timetable; and

- whether the employer's and the union's representatives answered any reasonable questions regarding the subject matter of the mediation or conciliation.

In deciding whether the employer has taken the relevant steps no account is to be taken of the merits of the dispute.

f) Criminal charges arising out of industrial action

(i) Breach of contract involving injury to persons or property

A person commits a criminal offence, punishable by a fine, if he wilfully breaches his employment contract knowing or believing that the probable result of doing so (whether alone or with others) will be:

- to endanger life

- to cause serious bodily injury; or

- to expose real or personal property to destruction or serious injury.

(ii) Intimidation or annoyance by violence or otherwise

A person (the intimidator) commits a criminal offence, punishable by a fine, if to make another do or abstain from doing something which that person is legally entitled to choose to do or not to do (as he wishes), the intimidator

- uses violence to, or intimidates, that person or his wife or children, or injures his property;

- persistently follows that person about from place to place;

- hides any tools, clothes or other property owned or used by that person, or deprives him of or hinders him in the use thereof;

- watches or besets the house or other place where that person resides, works, carries on business or happens to be, or the approach to any such house or place; or

- follows that person with two or more persons in a disorderly manner in or through any street or road.

(iii) Restrictions on the offence of conspiracy

In England and Wales

Where an act that amounts to a criminal conspiracy which:

- is carried out in contemplation or the furtherance of a trade dispute, and

- is a summary offence, not punishable with imprisonment,

it is not to be treated as a criminal conspiracy for the purposes of prosecuting it as such.

In Scotland

An agreement or combination by two or more persons to do, or procure to be done, an act in contemplation or the furtherance of a trade dispute is not indictable as a conspiracy if that act committed by one person would not be punishable by imprisonment.

Where a person is found guilty of an offence that is punishable only on summary conviction, the maximum sentence is to be no more than three months or the statutory maximum that would apply if the offence had been committed by one person.

154 Trade Union Reform and Employment Rights Act 1993 (TURERA)

Amended the EPCA, TUPE, Employment Acts 1980, 1982 and 1989 and TULRA. The amendments have now, largely, been consolidated into the Employment Tribunals Act 1996 and the ERA. The provisions of this Act are examined under the statutes into which they have been consolidated or which they amend.

Amended by Employment Rights (Disputes Resolutions) Act 1998.

155 Transfer of Employment (Pension Protection) Regulations 2005 (SI 2005 No 649)

These Regulations supplement the provisions concerning pensions on transfers of undertakings under Pensions Act 2004. Their effect is noted under that Act – **see 107 above**.

156 Transfer of Undertakings (Protection of Employment) Regulations 1981

Amended by TURERA, Collective Redundancies and Transfer of Undertakings (Protection of Employment) (Amendment) Regulations (SI 1995 No 2587) and Transfer of Undertakings (Protection of Employment) (Amendment) Regulations 1999.

The Regulations were originally restricted to dealing with cases where a business, or part of a business, that was in the nature of a commercial venture was transferred from one person to another. This restriction, limiting the application of the Regulations to cases where the undertaking transferred was in the nature of a commercial venture, was removed by TURERA to bring the Regulations into line with the EC Directive which they were introduced to implement. This means that the transfer of any undertaking is now covered by the Regulations, provided only that the undertaking was situated in the United Kingdom before the transfer and that the subject matter of the transfer is an 'undertaking' within this wider definition. TURERA further widens the ambit of what can amount to an undertaking by providing that no property need be passed from the transferor to the transferee for there to be a transfer under the Regulations. This makes it clear that the Regulations can cover the contracting-out of services by both commercial and non-commercial bodies – including government departments and local authorities – as well as the types of transaction which might more traditionally be viewed as the transfer of an undertaking. The major provisions of these Regulations are as follows.

156.1 Before the transfer

a) Consultation

Originally the Regulations required employers to consult only where they recognised independent trade unions. The Collective Redundancies and Transfer of Undertakings (Protection of Employment) (Amendment) Regulations (SI 1995 No 2587) now require consultation whether or not an independent trade union is recognised. Consultation is required in respect of all those employees who will be affected by the transfer. NB: 'employees affected' by the transfer are any employees in either the transferor undertaking (ie the seller) or the transferee undertaking (ie the buyer) who will be affected by the transfer. This does not apply merely to employees who will actually be transferred with the business.

b) Representatives for consultation

These provisions have been significantly changed by the Collective Redundancies and Transfer of Undertakings (Protection of Employment) (Amendment Regulations) 1999 (SI 1999 No 1925).

An employer must allow employee representatives:

- access to the employees whom it is proposed to make redundant;

- accommodation and such other facilities as may be appropriate; and

- time off for training, taking part in elections, receiving information regarding the transfer and consulting about it.

c) Information to be given to employee representatives

Long enough before the transfer for consultations to take place, the employer must inform the employee representatives of:

- the fact of the transfer and the reasons for it;

- the legal, economic and social implications of the transfer for the affected employees;

- the measures that he envisages taking with regard to those employees in connection with the transfer; and

- if he is the transferor, any measures the transferee envisages taking (a duty is placed on the transferee to provide the necessary information in this respect).

Where an employer envisages that he will be taking measures in connection with the transfer, he must consult with employee representatives about these. TURERA modified the consultation required about measures to be taken in connection with a transfer, so that the employer must now seek in these consultations to obtain agreement to the measures to be taken.

d) Compensation for failure to consult

If an employer fails to consult or to ensure that employee representatives are properly elected, an award can be made against him by an employment tribunal. The amount of the award will depend on the seriousness of the employer's failure and is subject to a maximum of 13 weeks' pay for each employee in respect of whom consultation should have taken place and did not. (TURERA raised the original level of two weeks' to four weeks'; the Collective Redundancies and Transfer of Undertakings (Protection of Employment) (Amendment) Regulations 1999 (SI 1999 No 1925) have raised it further.)

The appropriate claimant where an employer has not fulfilled the consultation requirements depends on the employer's particular failure. These have been amended by the Collective Redundancies and Transfer of Undertakings (Protection of Employment) (Amendment) Regulations 1999 (SI 1999 No 1925). Where an employer has failed, the claim is made:

- in the case of any failure relating to election of employee representatives, by any of the affected employees or by any of the employees who have been dismissed as redundant;

- in the case of any other failure relating to employee representatives, by any of the employee representatives to whom the failure relates;

- in the case of any failure to fulfil any requirement relating to a trade union representative, by the trade union;

- in any other case, by an affected employee or one who has been or may be dismissed as redundant.

A claim must be brought within three months of the completion of the transfer (or if that is not reasonably practicable within such further period as is reasonably practicable).

The Collective Redundancies and Transfer of Undertakings (Protection of Employment) (Amendment) Regulations 1999 (SI 1999 No 1925) changed the burden of proof in relation to two situations. In both, the burden is put on to the employer:

- in relation to the question of whether or not the employee representative was 'appropriate', the employer must prove that the employee representative had authority to represent the affected employees; and

- it is for the employer to prove that the requirements concerning the election of employee representatives have been complied with.

If the transferor claims that he has failed to provide information about the measures the transferee intended to take after the transfer because the transferee failed to provide him with that information,

- he must notify the transferee of this claim; and

- the transferee will then automatically be joined to the proceedings.

156.2 On transfer

a) Transfer of contracts

The transferred employees' contracts are transferred with them and take effect as if they had been entered into with the transferee employer from the outset. An employee cannot leave and claim constructive dismissal unless either:

- the change of ownership is a significant, detrimental, change for that employee; or

- the employee's conditions of work are substantially changed to his detriment.

By a TURERA amendment, however, an employee can leave when the undertaking is transferred simply because he objects to becoming an employee of the transferee's. But if he does this he will not be treated as having been dismissed by either the transferor or the transferee.

b) Occupational pension schemes

Occupational pension schemes are expressly excluded from transfer under these provisions. TURERA has amended this provision to make it clear that this restriction is confined strictly to pensions *per se*. If there are benefits within the pension scheme that are not themselves to do with 'old age, invalidity or survivors', then they are not to be treated as part of the pension scheme and would have to be preserved by the transferee. The effect of the Pensions Act 2004 together with the Transfer of Employment (Pension Protection) Regulations 2005 (SI 2005 No 649) is that employees who transfer after 6 April 2005 will have pension rights with the transferor. (**See 107.5 above**.)

c) Transfer of liability

All the transferor's civil liability to, or in connection with, the transferred employees is also transferred to the transferee, except in a case where the employee elects, 'on a whim', not to be transferred to the transferee (see a) above).

Criminal liability is specifically excluded from being transferred, but this would not prevent the transferee from becoming criminally liable immediately after the transfer for any offences that are continuing – such as continuing breaches of health and safety requirements.

d) Trade unions and collective agreements

Where an independent trade union was recognised before the transfer, and the part of the business transferred maintains a separate identity, union recognition is transferred for that part of the business.

Any collective agreement pertaining to a transferred employee is also transferred.

156.3 Unfair dismissal and redundancy

a) It is *prima facie* automatically unfair to dismiss an employee because of a transfer unless there are economic, technical or organisational reasons entailing a change in the workforce in either transferor or transferee workforce. If there is such a reason, and that reason entails a change in the workforce, the employer is treated as having a substantial reason for dismissal. The tribunal is then required, in terms of s 98(4) ERA, to decide whether or not the dismissal was fair. If the dismissal was fair, the employee will usually be entitled to a redundancy payment.

b) If the employee leaves voluntarily upon transfer, then, unless he can show that there has been a substantial change in his terms and conditions of employment which is to his detriment, he will not be entitled to a redundancy payment because he will not have been dismissed.

157 Unfair Contract Terms Act 1977

The Act has relevance for employers who want to limit their liability to employees. Section 2 of the Act states that:

- a person cannot, by reference to any contract terms or to a notice given to persons generally or to particular persons, exclude or restrict his liability for death or personal injury resulting from negligence;

- in the case of other loss or damage a person cannot so exclude or restrict his liability for negligence except insofar as the term or notice satisfies the requirement of reasonableness;

- where a term of a contract or a notice purports to exclude or restrict liability for negligence, a person's awareness of the term or notice is not of itself to be taken as indicating his voluntary acceptance of any risk.

158 Unfair Dismissal and Statement of Reasons for Dismissal (Variation of Qualifying Period) Order 1999 (SI 1999 No 1436)

Amends the ERA.

These Regulations reduce the qualifying period for claiming unfair dismissal and entitlement to written reasons for dismissal from two years to one year with effect from 1 June 1999.

159 Welfare Reform and Pensions Act 1999

The Act lays down the basis for stakeholder pensions with the Stakeholder Pension Scheme Regulations 2000 (SI 2000 No 1403).

160 Working Time Regulations 1998 (SI 1998 No 1833)

Amend the ERA. These Regulations implement the Working Time Directive 93/104/EC and provisions concerning working time in the Protection of Young People at Work Directive 94/33/EC. The provisions of this Protection of Young People at Work Directive covered by the Regulations relate only to young people (ie those who are over compulsory school age and under 18). The provisions dealing with children's working hours are contained in the Children (Protection at Work) Regulations 1998 (SI 1998 No 276) **(see 9 above)**.

Amended by Working Time Regulations 1999 (SI 1999 No 3372), Working Time (Amendment) Regulations 2001 (SI 2001 No 3256), Working Time (Amendment) Regulations 2002 (SI 2002 No 3128) and Working Time (Amendment) Regulations 2003 (SI 2003 No 1684).

160.1 Who is covered

a) The Regulations cover 'workers', who include:

- all employees;

- all those who are under a contract to provide services personally other than in a case where the relationship is such that the 'employer' is the client or customer of the worker's business;

- 'agency workers';

- non-employed trainees;

- the police and armed forces – but in relation to these sectors the Regulations are disapplied where the characteristics particular to these services inevitably conflict with these Regulations.

    A 'young worker' for the purposes of the Regulations **(see particularly 160.1e, 160.3e and 160.4a(iii) and 4c(ii) below)** is one who is above compulsory school age, but below the age of 18.

b) Excluded sectors

The Regulations do not apply to workers in:

- sea, inland waterway and lake transport;

- sea fishing or any other work at sea which is subject to the European Agreement on the organisation of working time of seafarers.

Most of the Regulations are excluded for workers:

- where the characteristics particular to certain specific activities of the civil protection services inevitably conflict with these Regulations – eg the armed forces, the police, those engaged in civil protection services;

- mobile workers who are subject to the European Agreement on the organisation of working time of mobile workers.

  Mobile workers generally have only limited entitlements in respect of length of night work, daily rest, weekly rest and rest breaks. They are, however, entitled to 'adequate rest'.

c) Only the Regulations concerning rest breaks and annual leave apply to adults in domestic service.

d) Unmeasured working time

Only the Regulations concerning health assessments for night workers, allowing breaks where the work is monotonous or runs at a pre-determined speed and paid annual leave apply to adults in the following categories:

- managing executives and others with autonomous decision-taking powers;

- family workers; and

- workers officiating at religious ceremonies in churches and religious communities.

The Working Time Regulations 1999 provide that:

- where part of an adult worker's working time is pre-determined or measured,

- but the characteristics of the activity are such that, without being told by the employer to do so, he may also do work

  - of undetermined duration, or

  - which is determined by the worker himself,

then the Regulations concerning maximum working time, night work and health assessments in relation to night work apply only to that part of the worker's working time that is pre-determined or measured.

e) Other special cases

Subject to the requirement to provide compensatory rest (see h) below), the following requirements do not apply in relation to the categories of work and worker set out below.

The excluded requirements are:

- average length of night work;

- the set length of night work where the work involves special hazards of heavy physical or mental strain;

- provisions for breaks during the day, daily rest period and weekly rest periods.

The categories of worker are adults:

- whose place of work and residence, or different places of work, are distant from one another;

- engaged in security or surveillance where a permanent presence is required to protect property or persons – such as security guards or caretakers;

- in relation to whom there is a need for continuity of service or production, as may be the case in:

    - reception, treatment or care provided by hospitals or similar establishments, residential institutions and prisons;

    - work at docks or airports;

    - press, radio, television, cinema production, postal and telecommunications services, civil protection services;

    - gas, water and electricity production and distribution; household refuse collection and incineration;

    - industries in which work cannot be interrupted on technical grounds;

    - research and development activities;

    - agriculture;

- for whom there is a foreseeable surge of activity, as may be the case in relation to:

    - agriculture;

    - tourism; and

    - postal services;

- whose activities are affected by:

    - an occurrence due to unusual and unforeseeable circumstances, beyond the employer's control;

    - exceptional events, the consequence of which could not have been avoided despite the exercise of all due care by the employer; or

    - an accident or the imminent risk of an accident.

The Regulations are excluded in only two cases, in relation to young workers:

- Those whose employment is covered by the Merchant Shipping Act 1995 are covered by different Regulations;

- The requirements for rest breaks during the day and daily rest breaks do not apply where:

    - the employer requires a young worker to undertake work for which no adult is available;

    - the work is occasioned by:

- an occurrence due to unusual and unforeseeable circumstances, beyond the employer's control; or

- exceptional events, the consequence of which could not have been avoided despite the employer exercising all due care

- the work is of a temporary nature; and

- the work must be performed immediately.

In any such case the employer must allow the young worker an equivalent period of compensatory rest within the following three weeks.

f) Shift workers

Subject to the requirement to provide compensatory rest (see h) below),

- the requirement for a daily break and for a weekly break do not apply where the worker cannot take a break of the requisite length because of a change of shift;

- the requirement for a daily break and for a weekly break do not apply to workers on 'split shifts' – whose work is split up over the day – as might be the case with cleaners or restaurant staff.

g) Doctors in training

The activities of doctors in training which were originally excluded from the ambit of these Regulations. The 2003 amendment Regulation however brings them within the Regulations, but with modified effect:

The maximum hours of work in the reference period for doctors in training are:

- 58 hours from 1 August 2004 to 31 July 2007; and

- 56 hours from 1 August 2007 to 31 July 2009.

The reference period for doctors in training is 26 weeks.

h) Compensatory rest

In certain cases (set out in the text) where the Regulations are disapplied, a worker who is not provided with the breaks he would otherwise be entitled to should, wherever possible, be given an equivalent period of compensatory rest. If it is not possible to give compensatory rest for objective reasons, the employer must afford the worker such protection as may be appropriate to safeguard the worker's health and safety.

160.2 Workforce agreements and collective agreements

The concept of a 'workforce agreement' is one that is created by these Regulations.

A workforce agreement must:

- be in writing;

- last for a specified period not exceeding five years;

- apply:
  - to all the members of the workforce who do not have terms and conditions agreed under collective agreements; or
  - to all the members of the workforce of a particular group who do not have terms and conditions agreed under collective agreements;
- be signed by:
  - the duly elected representatives of the workforce or of the group; or
  - if the employer has not more than 20 workers, by the majority of workers instead;
- be given by the employer to all the workers who are to be covered by it before the commencement date together with any guidance which they may need to understand it.

There are certain rules set down concerning the election of representatives for the workforce:

- the employer must decide on the number of representatives to be elected;
- the candidates for election must be relevant members of the workforce or relevant members of the group in respect of whom they seek election;
- no relevant member of the workforce or group may unreasonably be excluded from standing for election;
- all relevant members of the workforce or group must be entitled to vote;
- all relevant members must be given the right to vote for as many candidates as there are representatives to be elected;
- the election must be by secret ballot; and
- the votes must be accurately counted.

There is no specific remedy set down by the Regulations for any failure in the election of representatives of the workforce. But if there is a failure in the election process, the representatives would not be properly elected and the workforce agreement would therefore be void, leaving workers to claim rights under the Regulations as if the workforce agreement was not in place.

A collective or workforce agreement can

- modify or exclude any of the following requirements:
  - average length of night work;
  - the set length of night work where the work involves special hazards of heavy physical or mental strain;
  - the reference period for night workers;
- modify or exclude the right to breaks during the day, daily breaks and weekly breaks, but where the worker is required to work at a time that would otherwise be a rest break he should, wherever possible, be given an equivalent period of compensatory rest (**see 160.1h above**).

160.3 Maximum weekly working time

a) General

Unless a worker has agreed in writing not to be subject to the maximum working time requirements, the worker must not work more than an average of 48 hours (inclusive of overtime) in each seven days of any reference period.

Subject to any different provisions in workforce or collective agreement, the reference period is either

- each consecutive 17-week period; or

- any period of 17 weeks in the course of the employee's employment.

  (The reference period for offshore work is 52 weeks.)

Until a worker has been employed for 17 weeks the reference period is the amount of time for which he has been employed.

In the case of workers in 'Other special cases' (**see 160.1e above**) the reference period is 26 weeks.

Where there is a collective agreement or workforce agreement in place, the reference period agreed can be from 17 weeks to a maximum of 52 weeks.

b) The average working time during each seven days of the reference period is calculated by using the following formula:

$$\frac{A + B}{C}$$

where

A is the worker's total working time during the reference period referable to that reference period;
B is the number of days worked in the following reference period to make up for any 'excluded days' (see c) below) in the current reference period; and
C is the number of weeks in the reference period.

c) 'Excluded days' are:

- days off taken by the worker due to:

  - annual leave entitlement under the Regulations;

  - sick leave;

  - maternity leave; or

- any days during the reference period when the worker had agreed not to be subject to the maximum working time requirements.

d) For an agreement to exclude a worker from the maximum working time requirements the employer must:

- obtain the worker's agreement in writing in advance to work more than the maximum number of hours provided for by the Regulations; and

- keep up-to-date records of those who have agreed to exclude the maximum working time.

e) Young workers' maximum hours

In the case of young workers their hours of work are not to exceed eight hours a day or 40 hours a week. If the worker is employed by more than one employer, the hours are to be aggregated and employers are required to 'take steps' to comply with these limits.

There are certain exclusions from the full force of these requirements: where

- the work is necessary to maintain continuity of service or production or to respond to a surge in demand;
- no adult is available to perform the work; and
- performing the work will not adversely affect the young worker's education or training.

These restrictions are also excluded where the work is in domestic service or the army.

160.4 Night work

a) The meaning of 'night time' and 'night worker'

(i) 'Night time' is:

- a period of at least seven hours which includes the period between midnight and 5 am.

The actual duration can be agreed by a contract of employment, workforce agreement or collective agreement.

In the absence of an agreement, 'night time' is taken to be 11 pm to 6 am.

(ii) A 'night worker':

- normally works at least three hours at night during at least half his working days; or
- is likely to work such a proportion of his time at night as may be specified by a workforce or collective agreement.

(iii) Night work by young workers:

Young workers must not be allowed to work during the 'restricted period'. This is either the period from 10 pm until 6 am or, if the worker works after 10 pm, it is from 11 pm until 7 am.

There are general exceptions to this for those in domestic service, in the armed forces.

There are limited exceptions where the young worker works in a hospital or similar establishment or in connection with artistic, sporting or advertising activities if:

- the work is necessary to maintain continuity of service or production or to respond to a surge in demand;
- no adult is available to perform the work; and
- performing the work will not adversely affect the young worker's education or training.

The restriction is limited to excluding working only between midnight and 4 am in agriculture, retail trading, postal or newspaper deliveries, catering, hotel, pub, restaurant, bar, bakery if:

- the work is necessary to maintain continuity of service or production or to respond to a surge in demand;

- no adult is available to perform the work; and

- performing the work will not adversely affect the young worker's education or training.

Where the restriction is either excluded or limited, the young worker must be given:

- such supervision as is necessary for the young worker's protection; and

- an equivalent period of compensatory rest.

b) Length of night work

A night worker's normal hours of work in any reference period must not exceed an average of eight hours in each 24 hours, and the employer must take all reasonable steps to ensure that this requirement is complied with.

If the night worker's work involves special hazards or heavy physical or mental strain, his hours of work, when on night work, must not exceed eight in any 24-hour period. The worker's work involves special hazards or heavy physical or mental strain if:

- it is identified as such in a workforce or collective agreement; or

- it is recognised in a risk assessment under the Management of Health and Safety at Work Regulations 1999 as involving a significant risk to workers.

The reference period for a night worker is either

- each consecutive 17-week period; or

- any period of 17 weeks in the course of the employee's employment.

    Until a worker has been employed for 17 weeks, the reference period is the amount of time for which he has been employed.

Average normal working hours during each 24 hours in the reference period are calculated by using the following formula:

$$\frac{A}{B-C}$$

where
A is the worker's total normal working hours during the reference period;
B is the number of days in the reference period; and
C is the total number of hours during the reference period spent on weekly breaks (see below) by the worker, divided by 24.

c) Health assessment of night workers

(i) General

Before assigning a worker to become a night worker the employer must ensure that the worker has the opportunity of a free health assessment, unless the worker has had one previously and the employer has no reason to believe that it is no longer valid.

Night workers must be given the opportunity of regular free health assessments.

(ii) Young workers

In the case of a young worker, the free assessments that are offered must include an assessment of the employee's capabilities.

The requirement for health checks applies to a young worker in respect of work during the period from 10 pm to 6 am (known as the 'restricted period'):

- ie it is not restricted to cases where the employee will become a night worker,
- but the provision does not apply if the work to which the young person is assigned is of an exceptional nature.

A health assessment cannot be disclosed to the employer unless

- the worker gives written consent to its being disclosed; or
- the disclosure is restricted to a statement that the worker is fit to take up, or continue, night work.

If a doctor advises an employer that a night worker is suffering from health problems associated with night work, the employer is obliged to transfer the worker to suitable work that is not 'night work', if it is available.

160.5 Records

a) The employer must keep records that are adequate to show:

- compliance with the working time limits in relation to:
    - the normal maximum average working week;
    - the maximum average nightly hours of night workers;
    - restrictions on work by young workers;
- which workers have opted out of the normal maximum average working week;
- that the requirements for both initial and regular health assessments have been met in relation to night workers and young people working during the restricted period.

b) These records must be kept for two years.

160.6 Rest breaks

a) Rest breaks

Where an adult worker's daily working time is more than six hours, he is entitled to a rest break of not less than 20 minutes. A different length of break can be agreed in a workforce or collective agreement.

Where a young person's daily working time is more than four and a half hours he is entitled to a rest break of not less than 30 minutes. (If a young person is employed by more than one employer on any day, his working time over the whole day must be added together for purposes of ascertaining whether or not he is entitled to a break.)

b) Patterns of work

Where the work that is being done by the worker is monotonous or the work rate is pre-determined, the worker must be given adequate breaks to ensure his health and safety.

c) Daily rest

An adult is entitled to at least 11 consecutive hours' rest in each 24.

A young worker is entitled to at least 12 consecutive hours' rest in each 24; however, this period may be interrupted if the work being done is split up over the day or is of short duration.

d) Weekly rest period

An adult worker is entitled to an uninterrupted rest period of:

- 24 hours in each seven-day period;

- two periods of 24 hours in each 14-day period; or

- 48 hours in each 14-day period.

This period is not to include the 11 hours' daily rest break that an adult is entitled to each day unless this is justified by

- objective reasons;

- technical reasons; or

- reasons concerning the organisation of work.

A young worker is entitled to an uninterrupted rest period of not less than 48 hours in every seven-day period but:

- this may be interrupted where the work involves periods of work which are:

    - split up over the day; or

    - of short duration;

- it may be reduced to no fewer than 36 consecutive hours where this is justified by organisational or technical reasons.

160.7 Entitlement to annual leave

a) General

An employee who has been continuously employed for at least 13 weeks is entitled to four weeks' paid leave in each leave year beginning on or after 23 November 1999.

If no leave year is agreed either in the worker's contract of employment or in a workforce or collective agreement, then the leave year starts on

- 1 October if the employee was employed on or before on 1 October 1998; or

- the date when the employee started in employment, if later.

If the employee is employed for only part of any leave year, the entitlement is pro rata with any part days' entitlement being rounded up to the nearest half day's leave.

b) Dates on which leave is taken

Leave may be taken in instalments, but it can be taken only in the leave year in respect of which it is due.

Where the worker wants to take any period of leave he must give the employer notice of at least twice the length of the period of leave that he wishes to take.

If the employer wants to

- prevent the worker from taking leave at any particular time, or

- make the worker take leave at a particular time,

the employer can effect this by giving the worker notice of it, so long as the amount of notice is at least the same length as the amount of leave in question.

The notice, in either case:

- may relate to all or only some of the worker's annual leave entitlement;

- must specify the days on which leave is or is not to be taken; and

- if the leave is for only part of the day, it must give the duration of that leave.

These notice provisions can be changed by the contract of employment, by specific agreement with the employee, or by a workforce or collective agreement.

c) Payment in respect of periods of leave

Where the worker is entitled to leave under these provisions, payment for the leave is calculated on the basis of the statutory 'week's pay'; the calculation date is the first day of the worker's leave.

(i)   Any contractual remuneration is set off against any payment that would otherwise be due under the Regulations.

(ii) Other than on termination of employment, no payment can be made in lieu of statutory annual leave entitlement.

(iii) On termination of employment the worker is entitled to be paid pro rata for any leave not taken.

(iv) Provision can be made in a contract of employment, by specific agreement with a worker, or by a workforce or collective agreement, to allow the employer to recoup payment or to have work done by the worker to compensate for any leave taken by the worker in excess of his entitlement, on termination.

160.8 Entitlement under Regulations and other provisions

Workers who have rights to rest periods, rest breaks or annual leave under the provisions of the Regulations *and* under a separate provision – for example their contracts – cannot exercise both rights separately but can 'pick and mix' the rights to obtain the best single composite rights.

160.9 Legal remedies to enforce the Regulations

a) Enforcement

Enforcement of the Regulations is by:

- the Health and Safety Executive;
- the local authority responsible for enforcing health and safety matters in relation to certain premises under the Health and Safety (Enforcing Authority) Regulations 1998 (SI 1998 No 494);
- the Civil Aviation Authority; and
- the Vehicle and Operator Services Agency.

Failure to comply with any of the provisions of the Regulations is a criminal offence.

The 2003 Regulations insert a new Schedule 3 into the Regulations which provides for the enforcement authorities to appoint inspectors to enforce the Regulations. The Schedule also sets out the powers of the inspectors.

b) Claim to an employment tribunal

An employee can complain to an employment tribunal where the employer has failed to

- provide proper rest breaks or daily or weekly rest periods;
- provide annual leave entitlement; or
- pay for annual leave entitlement.

A claim must be made within three months (or in the case of a complaint from members of the armed forces, within six months) of:

- the day or the first day of
    - any rest period, or
    - period of annual leave; or
- the day on which payment for any period of annual leave should have been made.

There is the usual provision for extension of time if it is not reasonably practicable for the worker to present the claim within the normal period.

c) The right not to suffer detriment or to be unfairly dismissed

Workers are entitled not to be unfairly dismissed for asserting a statutory right in relation to the Regulations for:

- having brought proceedings to enforce any right under the Regulations; or

- having alleged that the employer has infringed any such right.

Provided the allegation is made in good faith, it does not matter

- whether the worker has the right alleged to have been infringed; or
- whether it was infringed.

Workers are entitled not to suffer a detriment or to be unfairly dismissed because the worker:

- refused, or proposed to refuse:
    - to comply with any request that the employer wanted to impose in contravention of the Regulations;
    - to forgo any right given to him under the Regulations;
- failed to sign a workforce agreement or to enter into any other agreement allowed for by the Regulations;
- performed or proposed to perform any functions or activities as:
    - a representative of the workforce for purposes of a workforce agreement; or
    - a candidate for election as a workforce representative.

d) Restrictions on contracting out

The Regulations can be contracted out of only to the extent allowed for by the Regulations themselves.

The normal provisions apply allowing for compromise agreements and settlement via ACAS of any claims.

161 Working Time Regulations 1999 (SI 1999 No 3372)

Amend the Working Time Regulations 1998 – **see 160 above**.

162 Working Time (Amendment) Regulations 2001 (SI 2001 No 3256)

Amend the Working Time Regulations 1998 – **see 160 above**.

163 Working Time (Amendment) Regulations 2002 (SI 2002 No 3128)

Amend the Working Time Regulations 1998 – **see 160 above**.

164 Working Time (Amendment) Regulations 2003 (SI 2003 No 1684)

Amend the Working Time Regulations 1998 – **see 160 above**.

165 Workplace Health, Safety and Welfare Regulations (SI 1992 No 3004)

This is one of the 'six-pack' Regulations introduced in 1992 arising from European health and safety Directives. The Regulations amend the Offices, Shops and Railway Premises Act 1963 and the Factories Act 1961.

These Regulations are concerned with the premises provided for employees to work in and with the fixtures, fittings and services, such as heating, ventilation, sanitary facilities, etc, that are part of those premises. The requirements under these regulations include:

a) Ventilation

Adequate ventilation must be provided. Where adequate ventilation is maintained by a machine which, if it broke down, would create a health and safety risk, an audible or visible alarm must be fitted to the machine to signal any breakdown.

b) Temperature

The temperature in a workplace must be reasonable during working hours and an adequate number of thermometers must be provided to enable people to know what the temperature in the workplace is.

c) Lighting

The lighting in a workplace must be suitable and sufficient and, so far as is reasonably practicable, should be natural light. Where there would be special hazards in a workplace if the lighting were to fail, emergency lighting must be provided.

d) Cleanliness

The furniture and fittings in a workplace must be kept clean and waste must not be allowed to accumulate in the workplace (other than in suitable receptacles).

e) Working space

There should be approximately 11 cubic metres (eg approximately 2 metres x 2 metres x 2.75 metres) of room space per person, although this may have to be increased if furniture or other fittings take up a lot of space in the workplace.

f) Work station

(i) Every work station must be:

■ adequately protected from bad weather;

■ designed to ensure that the employee/s can leave quickly, or be assisted away in the case of an emergency;

■ designed to ensure that the person working there will not slip or fall.

(ii) Where work can or must be done sitting down, a suitable seat, and where necessary a suitable footrest, should be provided.

g) Floors and traffic routes

(i) Floors and traffic routes

- must be suitably constructed for the purpose for which they are used;

- must not have holes in them or be slippery or uneven.

(ii) The workplace must be organised so that pedestrians and vehicles can circulate in a safe manner.

(iii) Escalators and moving walkways must:

- function safely;

- be equipped with necessary safety devices;

- be fitted with an easily identifiable, easily accessible, emergency stop control.

h) Windows and doors

(i) Windows and other translucent materials in walls and doors must be made of safety material to prevent breakage and should be marked to ensure that people realise that the material is there.

(ii) Windows and skylights that can be opened must not be in a position such that opening them could give rise to a health and safety hazard.

(iii) All windows and skylights must be designed or constructed so that they can be cleaned safely.

(iv) Doors and gates must be suitably constructed and have any necessary safety devices – in particular:

- sliding doors must have a device to prevent them from coming off their tracks; and

- upward-opening doors must have a device to prevent them from falling down.

i) Falling, and falling material

There must be adequate protection against employees' falling or being struck by falling objects. Particular care must be taken to prevent employees from falling into or being struck by any dangerous substance (ie one that might burn or scald or which is poisonous, suffocating or corrosive, or which by its mere volume is likely to cause danger if it escapes). Adequate protection may include fencing or covering dangerous materials and making adequate safety provision where work is being carried out on ladders or scaffolds or where materials are stored high up. The protection envisaged by this Regulation is not the provision of personal protective equipment, training or information about the danger unless no other protection is possible.

j) Sanitary conveniences, washing facilities and changing facilities

(i) An adequate number of sanitary conveniences and washing facilities must be provided.

- Where the number of employees is less than five, only one WC and one washing facility must be provided

- A second WC and washing facility is required when the number reaches 25; and

- an extra WC and washing facility should be provided for each additional 25 employees thereafter.

(ii) Showers may also be required by the nature of the work.

(iii) Washing facilities must have hot and cold or warm water available.

(iv) Where employees change into different clothes for work, adequate facilities must be made available:

- to keep clothes secure;

- to separate work and personal clothes where this is necessary in health and safety terms; and

- to allow clothes to be dried where possible.

(v) Where employees have to change into different clothes for work, adequate changing facilities must be made available for them.

k) Facilities for rest, eating meals and drinking water

(i) Suitable and sufficient rest facilities must be provided:

- where necessary for health and safety;

- in which to eat food if:

  - food would otherwise become contaminated when eaten at work; or

  - where food is regularly eaten at the workplace.

  Rest areas must have suitable arrangements to protect non-smokers from tobacco smoke.

  Suitable rest facilities must be provided for pregnant women and nursing mothers.

(ii) There must be an adequate supply of drinking water, which is readily accessible to employees.

APPENDIX

Legislation due to commence on 1 October 2005

1 Employment Relations Act 2004

1 October 2005 brings into effect the provisions of the Act which change the information to be contained in notices given by unions in advance of industrial action ballots and subsequent industrial action.

2 Employment Tribunal (Constitution and Rules of Procedure) Regulations 2004

This statutory instrument introduces minor technical changes and corrections to regulations which came into effect on 1 October 2004.

3 Equal Treatment Directive amendments

These amendments update the SDA and Equal Pay Act 1970 to take account of case law and implement the amended Equal Treatment Directive.

4 Trade Union Recognition and Derecognition – Change of Union or Employer Identity

The statutory recognition and derecognition procedure is amended to deal with cases where a union which has been awarded recognition under the statutory regime subsequently merges with another union or the employer changes identity.

The DTI warns, however, that following further consultation commencement may be put back until 6 April 2006.

5 TUPE Regulations

This constitutes a revision of TUPE to allow for the EC Acquired Rights Directive to be implemented and to clarify the applicability of the Regulations in specified contracting-out situations.

INDEX

CIPD Policies and Procedures for People Managers

Sign Up for Your FREE 28-Day Trial Now and Save!

As a subscriber to *CIPD Employment Law for People Managers* you are entitled to an extra **10%** discount off the usual price of **CIPD Policies and Procedures for People Managers.**

Do you have time to create good practice policies compliant with the law?

Do you know what policies you ought to have in place?

Do you need resources to manage the HR function in your organisation?

Well, now help is at hand!

At the CIPD we are ideally placed to offer you example policies and procedures along with expert commentary.

In *Policies and Procedures for People Managers* you will find policies, procedures and documents covering every aspect of employment from recruitment to termination. Policies and procedures for every work scenario.

As part of your subscription all these documents are also *available free online* for you to download and adapt to your organisation's requirements.

What will I receive?

CIPD Policies and Procedures for People Managers is built around a loose-leaf volume including:

The manual – a comprehensive resource contained within an A4 binder

Updates – issued four times a year, these comprise the latest developments and legislative changes to keep the manual completely up to date, making sure you avoid problems in the future by ensuring that your policies and procedures are current now

Internet access – providing searchable unlimited access to the full service, including downloadable policies and procedures for you to adapt

Free book – a best-selling title from CIPD Publishing's portfolio, giving you further vital information.

To find out more, visit www.cipd.co.uk/ppfpm

CIPD Members	Non-members
Usual price £270	Usual price £300
You pay £245	You pay £270

Call 0870 442 1020 quoting media code EL1004 to get these special rates

Remember, you pay nothing for 28 days. If you are not entirely satisfied with *CIPD Policies and Procedures for People Managers*, you can return it with no further obligation.

Request your free 28-day trial of *CIPD Policies and Procedures for People Managers* today! Call 0870 442 1020 quoting media code EL1004

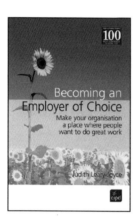

Membership has its rewards

Join us online today as an Affiliate member and get immediate access to our member services. As a member you'll also be entitled to special discounts on our range of courses, conferences, books and training resources.

To find out more, visit www.cipd.co.uk/affiliate or call us on 020 8612 6208.